SHROPSHIRE COUNTY LIBRARY SERVICE

www.shropshire-cc.gov.uk/library.nsf
Please return or renew before the last date stamped below.
You can renew in person, by telephone, or on the website,
unless it is required by another user.

Rooted in History

Studies in Garden Conservation

THE NATIONAL TRUST

First published in Great Britain in 2001
The National Trust Enterprises Ltd
36 Queen Anne's Gate
London SW1H 9AS
www.nationaltrust.org.uk/bookshop

ISBN 0 7078 0299 7

Cataloguing in Publication Data is available from the British
Library.

Designed by *Allen* Lebon

Printed and bound in Italy by G. Canale & C.s.p.A

Half-title: Trimming the hedge at Anglesey Abbey.
(NTPL/David Levenson)

Frontispiece: The Maze at Glendurgan Garden.
(NTPL/Stephen Robson)

Contents

Acknowledgements

Naturally a publication like this is only made possible by the ability to draw on many years' experience and activity. Indeed, it is due to the foresight of donor families and the commitment and efforts of generations of gardeners, staff, volunteers, committee members, Trust supporters and visitors alike that we have anything to talk about at all. In acknowledging all those who have been involved, thanks must go firstly to the authors. For many, contributing to this book has been a particularly challenging task in what was, by any standards, already a very busy year! I would also like to thank Lady Emma Tennant, Merlin Waterson, Graham Stuart Thomas, Alex Youel, Caroline Woodhill, Michael Hickson and John Sales for their constructive advice and comments on various aspects of the book.

Equally, without the constant encouragement and advice of Margaret Willes and James Parry in the Trust's Publishing Department, this book might still be an idea rather than a reality. I am also very grateful to all those who assisted with the picture research, particularly Ed Gibbons in the Trust's Photographic Library, and to colleagues in the Trust's Gardens Section, who helped get this book off the starting blocks and have contributed greatly to its formation. Katie Fretwell in particular deserves thanks for taking on so much of the planning and co-ordination, and also a great deal of the writing, on our behalf.

Finally, we would all like to thank the skilled and committed band of National Trust gardeners, both past and present, whom together deliver the standards for which the Trust is renowned worldwide. Without their constant dedication and unrivalled expertise, that world would be a poorer place.

Mike Calnan,
Head of Gardens,
The National Trust

Foreword

Few people can fail to enjoy the beauty of gardens. Unceasingly revelatory, inspirational and rewarding, they are one of our greatest national resources. The huge variety and quality of the gardens, landscape parks and plants in the care of the National Trust means that we have a particular responsibility to care for them in a sensitive and sustainable way. It is a duty we take very seriously, particularly in view of the fact that so many millions of visitors come to enjoy these special places every year.

Yet gardens are also places of work, and within their walls and hedges we are privileged to witness the continuation of a long tradition of skilled garden maintenance and development. The conservation of gardens is nothing new in this sense – gardeners have been doing it for years – but in recent decades the art and science of gardening have come together in a new professionalism. That the Trust is fortunate to have such a skilled and experienced cadre of conservation gardeners is beyond doubt; how best this team can work to secure the future of our garden heritage is always open to comment and analysis.

Rather surprisingly, this is the first publication in 50 years to focus primarily on the National Trust's work caring for its gardens. Many books and articles have been written about the design, history and contents of Trust gardens, but there has been very little published about how we actually manage our gardens and what our guiding philosophy is. This book helps set the record straight, and also goes some way towards explaining why we do the things we do and, perhaps more importantly, how we may need to change our approach in the future. It should be seen both as part of the wider debate on garden conservation and as a review of the Trust's record to date – one which, I hope, will inspire us to continue leading the way in the management of historic gardens through the rest of this century and beyond.

Fiona Reynolds,
Director General,
The National Trust

Rooted in History

1

Why Conserve?

Mike Calnan

'God Almightie first planted a garden. And indeed it is the purest of human pleasures. It is the greatest Refreshment to the Spirit of Man.' Francis Bacon wrote this in 1625, but the words still ring true. Gardens have always revived the spirits and bestowed a therapeutic benefit on us, and perhaps this accounts for why gardens and gardening have become so essential to many of us in the early twenty-first century.

The National Trust looks after gardens in England, Wales and Northern Ireland, so this book takes a very British view, even though many of the practices and considerations described can apply to gardens worldwide. As Bacon observed, gardens have long met human need, and clearly gardens, gardening and British culture are now somewhat inseparable. Although many households in the past had gardens, the tradition of garden-making, as opposed to the activity of gardening, was for a long time the passion of a minority of the rich and powerful, determined to give expression to their values and ambitions. Today, however, gardening has become Britain's most popular pastime, enthralling 27 million people, or almost the entire adult population. According to Lord Clark 'of *Civilisation*', gardens are Britain's greatest contribution to culture, along with parliamentary democracy.

For those bitten by the bug, gardening appeals on many levels. Perhaps most significantly, it brings us closer to nature and to the rhythm of the seasons, its scope and opportunity for continual creativity being encouraged by our favourable climate and generally equable British temperament. Caring for old gardens in particular offers participation in a living history that allows us to 'read' and appreciate examples of great aesthetic, cultural and artistic significance, and see how fashions have changed to reflect differences in our outlook on the world and, indeed, changes in the way we see ourselves. Like any

The gardens at Stowe are one of the jewels in the National Trust's crown. The Gothic Temple and the Chatham Urn, seen here from across the lake, are just two of over thirty individual structures and objects located throughout the designed landscape.
(NTPL/Andrew Butler)

The roofless shell of the late sixteenth-century Lyveden New Bield is surrounded by traces of one of the oldest surviving garden layouts in England. The National Trust has taken the decision to carefully conserve what remains, rather than restore the garden. (NTPL/Nick Meers)

heirloom, historic gardens remain as ghosts of the past and, without them, life would be a less rich experience. Given that our oldest gardens and parks reflect human activity going back over the last 500 years, and in many instances contain trees of immense antiquity, it is not therefore surprising that we are inextricably drawn to such places. Seeing, touching and experiencing the past satisfies a deep-rooted and fundamental need, and one that can be fulfilled repeatedly in historic gardens.

In the eighteenth century, gardening was considered to be one of the great arts, but subsequently it became the Cinderella, if recognised as an art at all. This attitude may explain why gardens generally have not, until relatively recently, been valued in the same way as the heritage of buildings. But this has changed, and thankfully gardens are now recognised for the contribution they make to society, culture and, through tourism, to our economy. This recognition has been matched by a growing desire to protect and 'keep alive' the very best gardens for public benefit. In effect, such gardens are viewed as historical artefacts, valued for their associations, botanical interest, historical significance, design or sheer beauty. Whilst many organisations and owners are now engaged directly or indirectly in the care of Britain's garden heritage, for the last half century it has been the mission of the

National Trust in particular to acquire gardens of international, national and local importance, for the benefit and enjoyment of present and future generations.

Given the Trust's unique mandate, sanctioned by Parliament, to hold property inalienably, these gardens are now in safe hands, forever. Put together, they would cover 60 square miles, or roughly three-quarters of the Isle of Wight, and currently include 69 landscape parks and over 200 gardens. They have been taken over by the National Trust in varying conditions, from completely derelict sites to those rarer examples in excellent order. They have also come in all shapes and sizes, from vast, 4,000-hectare (10,000-acre) designed landscapes, such as Stourhead and Stowe, to town gardens the size of a postage stamp, as at Carlyle's House in London.

Over 50 per cent of the Trust's gardens can be considered historically significant, and are listed by English Heritage as being of national importance. Some are survivors of the formal layouts that were fashionable in the seventeenth century, whilst others are examples of nineteenth-century eclectic taste, and yet more are thriving twentieth-century plantsman's gardens. Some are of international significance, such as the magnificent early eighteenth-century 'green landscape' garden at Studley Royal which, combined with the medieval ruins of the Cistercian Fountains Abbey, constitutes a World Heritage Site, a designation which puts it alongside such celebrated monuments as Stonehenge, the Great Pyramid complex at Giza, and the city of Venice.

The Moon Ponds and Temple of Piety at Studley Royal, one of the best surviving examples of a Georgian water garden and recognised as being of international importance.
(NTPL/Charlie Waite)

Each garden is unique, sometimes representing the passion of one person, as at Hidcote, the creation of Lawrence Johnston, or of a gardening partnership, as at Sissinghurst, the brainchild of Vita Sackville-West and her husband Harold Nicolson. Sometimes a garden owes its character to generations of the same family who, along with their head gardeners, worked and reworked their garden. Nymans, the Sussex garden created by the Messel family and their gardeners, is an excellent example of this particularly British tradition, as is Powis Castle (see case study on pp.14-17).

Recognising cultural milestones like these is one thing, but protecting them is something else entirely. In the museum world, protection is a relatively straightforward business. Institutions worldwide are now crammed with artefacts dating from the dawn of civilisation onwards. Monuments are ubiquitous across the globe: complete buildings, ruins and archaeological remains. The degree to which they are protected depends on the extent to which environmental controls and recognised curatorial procedures are applied. In these instances, protection is aimed at minimising the impact of change, natural or man-made. The ideal is no change at all, so that the artefact or building can survive, unaltered, for as long as possible. But caring for something composed of living things that change from day to day, is a very different matter. Gardens are in a constant state of flux, making the identification of their essential qualities, let alone any attempt to preserve them, rather like trying to hit a moving target. It is easy for whimsical decisions, or even well-intentioned actions, to lead to the loss of significant qualities, and ultimately a dilution of our garden heritage. How, then, can we preserve something which by its very nature is transient?

It is probably true to say that there are as many views on how to care for our garden heritage as there are those interested in the subject. The Trust's own philosophy, as set out in the pages of this book, has evolved slowly, based on growing experience across many types of gardens and sites, as John Sales demonstrates in Chapter Two. The National Trust regards its principal duty to be to care for our inheritance in a way that does not diminish its significance or value. In doing so, the Trust's sights are set far into the future, and it cannot allow itself to be blown off course by fashionable opinion. With ownership, however, comes an obligation to maintain the relevance of historic gardens to society as the latter evolves, otherwise there would be little point in owning them. By opening its gardens, the Trust provides not only public benefit, but also the financial means to support their maintenance.

Curiously, few controls exist to ensure the protection of Britain's historic parks and gardens, other than those that local planning authorities can exercise in considering planning applications that might affect registered sites. Whereas the management of wildlife sites can be enforced legally, no such protection exists to ensure that owners manage gardens appropriately. Therefore, like any other private owner, the Trust has considerable freedom in managing its gardens. However, holding these gardens on behalf of the nation places a moral obligation on the National Trust to look after them in the public's best long-term interest. But what constitutes 'best interest'? To those involved in the protection of gardens, this is understood to be the conservation of each garden's significant qualities, the combination of historical, aesthetic, botanical, archaeological, wildlife or local importance. It may also include the maintenance of standards, provision of access and interpretation of the garden's importance to visitors and to the public generally.

When assessing how best to conserve a garden, the Trust looks first to English Heritage and its 'Register of Historic Parks and Gardens of Special Interest in England', and in Wales to Cadw (there is no similar register in Northern Ireland). Gardens are graded I, II or II★ depending on historical importance, rarity value and the quality of landscaping. Grading also indicates whether grant aid is likely to be available for essential repairs, either from English Heritage or via other sources, such as the Countryside Stewardship scheme or the Lottery Commission. However, grading does not generally recognise the significance of a garden's plant collection, instead depending almost entirely on history and design criteria.

In the absence of any national grading for plant collections, the Trust works closely with plant conservation bodies, such as the National Council for the Conservation of Plants and Gardens (NCCPG) and Plant Net. Jointly, their aim is to promote the recording, analysis and conservation of species and cultivated plants growing in Britain. There are some 300,000 types of cultivated plants in circulation, including species collected from the wild and rare botanic or historic specimens. Within this context, the Trust has the largest collection in the world, simply because it owns so many gardens, and this holding brings with it serious responsibilities. Trust staff therefore maintain close links with a wide range of external bodies dedicated to the promotion, conservation and recording of gardens, the training of gardeners and the development of national standards. These bodies include the Garden History Society, County Gardens Trusts, the Royal Horticultural Society, the Henry Doubleday Research Association and ADAS. Links are also maintained with the Royal Botanic Gardens at Kew and Edinburgh, and with others worldwide. Especially important to the Trust is its long relationship with the National Gardens Scheme (see p.28).

Top: Head Gardener Barry Boden tending the aster border at Upton House. Upton contains the National Collection of asters, just one of 35 such collections in the care of the National Trust.
(NTPL/Stephen Robson)

Above: Mixed colchicums at Felbrigg Hall, home to the National Collection. They provide a very dramatic display of colour in autumn, a time when most gardens are winding down.
(NTPL/Stephen Robson)

For guidance on conservation practice and procedures, the National Trust can refer again to English Heritage and its publications and guidelines, and to the International Council of Monuments and Sites (ICOMOS), the body which represents and promotes worldwide conservation standards. Through its advisory staff, the Trust maintains regular contact with relevant organisations across the world, and views and experiences are exchanged via conferences, publications and other means. However, it is fair to say that for much of its history the Trust was 'out on its own' in the field of garden conservation, formulating policy and practice as much as emulating what had been established by others. This situation arose quite simply because there was not much else to follow in the early years, and because the range and quality of the Trust's gardens placed it in a unique position.

Although the chapters that follow will touch on individual case studies in more detail and explore the particular philosophical and ethical issues that arise with garden conservation, it should be noted at this early juncture that no garden has ever come to the National Trust with sufficient evidence for it to be restored to 'how it once was', or, to quote that overused and misleading term, 'to its former glory'. Despite recent developments in investigative techniques (especially garden archaeology), the success of every restoration is governed by the quality, quantity and availability of evidence. Even the massive archive for Stowe landscape garden, consisting of three-quarters of a million documents, provides only 5 per cent of the information needed to restore details beyond the overall layout. Stowe is exceptional, and the Trust's most ambitious restoration project to date. Other gardens rarely have anything like the same volume of available information. So, in the general absence of sufficient evidence, restorations are only able to go so far, principally in restoring the layout, before conjecture is called upon to fill the gaps, especially in the planting details. Perhaps, then, restorations at their best should be thought of as 'evocations'.

Despite the inherent limitations of restoration as an approach, it can still represent the most effective way of recreating a garden layout or example of period style. Equally, restoration can be an appropriate strategy for part of a garden, especially in cases where more of an earlier phase in the garden's development has survived, or is considered more historically significant than any other. However, we should not delude ourselves that a restored garden is an historically 'authentic' one. Authenticity in garden restoration is a quest, and one that is perennially elusive.

In gardens, history never repeats itself. Returning a garden to a particular period is effectively a reworking and reinterpretation of history. The term 'historic' may be applied to its built features; a planting effect

Rooted in History

such as an avenue, which might have been replaced many times over, can be considered historic, but the term cannot be applied strictly to the plants themselves unless they are the original plants or their off-spring, such as the descendant of that famous apple tree in Sir Isaac Newton's garden at Woolsthorpe Manor.

Where a period garden is deliberately created, when no such garden ever existed, we talk in terms of 're-creation'. In certain circumstances, this may be an acceptable way forward. This is particularly so when providing an historic house with an appropriate setting, as at Moseley Old Hall, where a garden has been created of the type Charles II might have seen when he hid there after the Battle of Worcester in 1651. At Washington Old Hall, the home of George Washington's family in Tyne and Wear, the Trust has established a 'period style' garden in a yard of the former farmhouse, even though a garden never existed there. This development was considered appropriate in providing an enhanced setting for the house, and additional benefit for visitors by interpreting the property and expanding the appeal of the site. The Trust has also created gardens of particular types in cases where few examples exist nationally; the Tudor-style herb garden at Buckland Abbey is a recent case. Restorations or re-creations are exciting activities, guaranteed to capture both our imagination and the interest of the media, but in reality they are often simply a new beginning for an old or derelict garden. Once a major restoration project nears completion, it moves on to another, equally important, stage, whereby the routine process of 'conservation' takes over.

Conservation is the process of managing change and negotiating the transfer of significance from the present to the future. It is not an exact science, nor is it purely an art. If anything, it is a blend of the two. Conservation can accommodate innovation at one end of the spectrum, or minimal intervention at the other, or indeed any combination of these on one site, as is described in Chapter Three. It becomes especially complex when applied to gardens with long histories, as Blickling Hall shows (pp.24–5). Over the centuries, this garden has changed to reflect the particular fashions of the day – formal, informal, and back to formal again. Through being repeatedly reworked and overlaid gardens such as this become rich and complex, and this is necessarily reflected in the way in which they are conserved. Few works of art can evolve in this way, by which they gain greater significance – rather than less – as more is added. With poetry, painting and sculpture, for example, additions may diminish or dilute the power of the artist's vision, if not destroy it entirely. This is not necessarily so with gardens, a fact that makes the task of conserving such sites infinitely more challenging and complex.

The gardens at Blickling Hall reflect the changing styles and tastes of previous centuries. The avenue leading to the Doric Temple is typical of the formal layout that was popular until the mid-eighteenth century (above). Closer to the house, the parterre reflects the later preference for colourful herbaceous borders and topiary (right).
(NTPL/Mike Williams and Nick Meers)

Rooted in History

The rich tapestry of an historic garden can incorporate many layers, some of which may date from man's earlier activities on the site. An Iron Age fort at Croft Castle and surviving Roman structures at The Weir are two examples of where archaeological remains have been incorporated into a designed landscape or garden. Equally, remains of medieval ridge and furrow field systems account for the undulating character of the area of garden known as Westonbirt at Hidcote Manor, whilst at the time of writing the relics of a medieval village are being unearthed in the park at Llanerchaeron. Evidence of past garden layouts may also lie as a thin layer below the surface. At Stowe, for instance, paths, building remains and fragments of statue bases were found below ground, having been 'lost' for more than a hundred years. Such evidence can assist the understanding of a garden's evolution, layout or content, and steer decisions on what to conserve and how to manage the whole conservation process.

Such layering is further enriched when wildlife interest is taken into account. Many of the Trust's oldest parks, such as Dinefwr, Dunham Massey, Knole and Petworth, contain ancient trees of more than four or five hundred years of age. Throughout their life they have provided homes for transient communities of wildlife, with rare lichens living on their bark, wood-rotting fungi thriving on their timber and generations of birds finding sanctuary in the slowly evolving architecture of their canopy. Their historical and biological significance is huge – for example, rare beetles inhabiting dead wood can provide evidence of a continuity of tree cover on site dating back to the last Ice Age, 10,000 years ago.

Yet another layer of complexity is introduced when gardens are opened to the public. The Trust's remit is to protect places of historic interest or natural beauty for the benefit of the nation. 'Benefit' has been interpreted traditionally as meaning physical access, and this is something that in recent years the Trust has worked hard both to extend and to manage appropriately. Seven out of the current top ten Trust visitor attractions are gardens, with over 200,000 people annually visiting each of Studley Royal, Wakehurst Place and Polesden Lacey. Welcoming increasing numbers of visitors to its properties has been one of the Trust's great successes in recent years, but access on such a scale does bring problems of its own. With these visitors come their feet, and various management tools are now required at the busier gardens to minimise the impact of visitors. For example, Hidcote and Sissinghurst each spend £3,000 annually on replacing worn-out turf, and an equal amount on protecting sensitive areas from further damage. At some gardens timed tickets are occasionally required to ensure that the garden is not overwhelmed by the number of people that wish to see it. As Susan Denyer explores in Chapter Eight, public access raises a whole range of delicate issues for the Trust.

Equally, the Trust needs to be constantly aware of the impact its own image and corporate presence can have on the conservation and presentation of its gardens. After all, these are not National Trust gardens, but gardens that the Trust happens to be looking after on behalf of the nation. In the final analysis, protecting and caring for their individuality counts above all else. Yet the National Trust is a large organisation, and strives to ensure that common standards of quality and presentation are maintained in terms of property signage, food in the tea-rooms and restaurants, goods sold in the shops, printed material such as leaflets and guidebooks, access provision for the less able, and so on. The Trust's success in developing its corporate image and 'brand' has increasingly raised the criticism that 'all Trust properties look the same'. Extended provision for visitors may well have led to this impression. Perhaps standardisation is the inevitable consequence of greater public access, and of the increased public expectation for on-site facilities of a certain standard, but it is important that the individuality of a garden is respected and that any uniformity is strictly avoided once the entrance gate has been passed.

Outside commentators often observe that standards throughout the Trust's collection of gardens are uniformly high. This is a flattering observation for, by historical standards, current staffing levels are low in most gardens. In the eighteenth century Stowe was maintained by 30 full-time gardeners, supplemented by 30 labourers and temporary help from estate families and farm workers after the summer harvest. The majority of the grounds today are maintained by four full-time gardeners, aided by up to five long-term volunteers and a number of part-time local volunteers. Such an achievement is partly the result of the use of labour-saving maintenance techniques, particularly in lawn care, weed control and planting. Resources are unlikely to permit a dramatic increase in gardening manpower in the future, so the Trust must look constantly at ways in which its gardens can be managed and conserved successfully within existing staffing levels.

Managing these various considerations, whilst not losing track of any significant aspect of a garden, is what conservation aims to achieve. Yet it is also the means of keeping alive the whole process of gardening. Gardening is a performing art, in which the performance, the influence of the individual 'performers' and the act of performing are inseparable. It is therefore inevitable that individual, small-scale interpretations, even innovations, will be part of this process. In some circumstances innovation may be an acceptable and desirable aspect of interpretation. Acorn Bank, home in the Middle Ages to the Knights Templar, today contains a comprehensive collection of medicinal and culinary herbs. The current gardener, Chris Braithwaite, has created in cobblestones a temporary 'snake in the grass' path through the orchard, now rebuilt as a permanent feature as its biblical connotations are entirely in keeping with the spirit of the property. At Antony, William Pye sculptures commissioned by Sir Richard and Lady Carew-Pole in the 1990s are an unashamedly modern addition within the eighteenth-century pleasure gardens (see case study on pp.120-3). As Sir Edmund Fairfax-Lucy of Charlecote Park has rightly said: 'When your family has such close associations with a property, each generation having left its own mark for posterity, you feel a deep yearning to do the same.'

Acknowledging this yearning and accepting the spirit of innovation, whilst ensuring the protection of a garden's historical significance, may be an acceptable conservation solution. This is certainly the position taken recently by English Heritage with its 'Contemporary Heritage Gardens' project, whereby leading designers have been asked to suggest new designs as a means of interpreting and making the past relevant in the context of gardens. The Trust is beginning to look at the appropriateness of such an approach and how it can be applied at its properties, as the case study on Dyrham Park in Chapter Ten outlines.

Finally, it is clear that gardens can have an effect on individuals, and that this effect plays as much a part in their significance as any physical quality. These subtle but significant ingredients are aptly summed up in the term 'spirit of the place', a quality arising from the combined effect of a garden's design, layout, aesthetics, history and special atmosphere. Some gardens have a more powerful effect than others. Stourhead undoubtedly has a special quality akin to visiting a great cathedral: it instils a sense of pilgrimage and reverence, and lifts the spirits. When Calke Abbey was acquired by the National Trust in the 1980s, the park and gardens were opened to the public for the first time in over a century. Many visitors commented on the transient beauty of decay felt so powerfully when visiting. Chastleton has a similar atmosphere and the Trust is working to retain something of the special quality that exists there due to decades of 'standing still' (see pp.18-19).

Of course, the objectives and standards of the Trust in managing its gardens could not be achieved without the gardeners themselves. It is they, after all, who are responsible for translating theory into practice, and it is upon their skills and expertise that the Trust relies. As Katie Fretwell relates in Chapter Nine, a number of them are renowned nationally, serving on committees, representing the Trust both at international events and as ambassadors when dealing with foreign visitors and dignitaries. They must, to an extent, be all-rounders, as equally skilled in caring for plants and understanding design as in the management of record-keeping, garden history and practical horticulture. They are a precious commodity and, sadly, there are not enough of them. With the endowment required for a single gardener post set at £1.7million (the figure required to ensure that the necessary recurrent income is available whilst the capital sum is retained in perpetuity), increasing the number of gardeners is a formidable task. However, creative and varied ways are being used to help fund gardening posts, through the use of income, investments and, potentially, sponsorship.

In the chapters that follow we hear from specialists in garden history, plant taxonomy and garden archaeology, and from craftsmen gardeners and conservators. These are very practical accounts of how gardens are run on a daily basis, and what goes into maintaining Trust standards. Finally, we address what the future might hold for historic gardens. How will society's changing attitudes and expectations impact on our fragile garden heritage? How can the Trust continue to ensure wide-ranging support, and therefore the income required to carry on its work? What may be the effect of our wider impact on the environment, particularly when the climatic conditions that gave birth to our

Richard Ayres, until his recent retirement as Head Gardener at Anglesey Abbey, was one of the Trust's 450 full-time gardeners. This total is a mere fraction of the number that would have been employed looking after the Trust's 200 gardens a century ago (when they were in private hands). (NTPL/Ray Hallett)

most important gardens are themselves becoming historical? How may our growing concerns for the environment find expression in the way we manage our gardens? And what other challenges may lie ahead?

By no means does the Trust feel it has all the answers. Indeed, this book leaves as many questions unresolved as answered. However, given its depth and breadth of experience and knowledge, and long history at the cutting edge of garden conservation, the Trust's approach must surely constitute a benchmark of standards in this field. As the new century unfolds, so too will the Trust's thinking continue to develop. The one constant will be the requirement to ensure that the gardens in its care remain protected forever, for everyone.

Case Study 1
Powis Castle

The British are not only a nation of gardeners, but also have a strong attachment to the past. How do these qualities express themselves in the way we have gardened, and how we look after our most cherished gardens? A classic example is provided by the garden at Powis Castle; even today it continues to influence the way we approach garden conservation.

Perched high on a narrow ridge and surrounded by ancient parkland, the castle commands breathtaking panoramic views across the Severn Valley towards England. Below its high red sandstone walls, lies a garden of 9.7 hectares (24 acres), with terraces, woodland walks, formal lawns, yew-hedged enclosures and a walled flower garden. Seventeenth-century formality is combined with eighteenth-, nineteenth- and twentieth-century modifications.

Although a great historic garden, Powis is not set in aspic and continues to develop. In the late seventeenth century, William Herbert, 1st Marquess of Powis, created a garden below the castle, dominated by three 500-foot-long terraces. Fruit trees, trained formally against the walls, provided a backdrop to ornamental and productive planting in the borders. Inspiration for the terraces came from continental Europe, and these vast, Italian-style, terraces remain central to the garden's significance. Like a horticultural catwalk, they have seen planting fashions come and go, and the tradition of change and evolution continues to play a key role in the Trust's management of the garden today.

Nathaniel Buck's bird's-eye view, published in 1742, shows the Baroque garden in its prime. But by 1771 much of the formal planting had been simplified in keeping with the contemporary taste for the picturesque. Whether it was love of the picturesque or the prodigalities of London that attracted the 2nd Earl, neglect set in and by 1794 a visitor was moved to note: 'Upon the terraces you cannot walk, as the balustrades are falling down; and should you slip you are lost.'

This parlous situation was reversed in the nineteenth century, when the terraces were repaired and replanted with the ornamental shrubs, trees and climbers fashionable at the time. In the early 1900s, Violet, wife of the 4th Earl, set out to make the garden 'one of the most beautiful, if not the most beautiful in England and Wales. I see velvet lawns and wide paths: rose gardens – fountains – clipped yews – marble seats – herbaceous borders.' Work first began in the decaying remains of the eighteenth-century kitchen garden, which she converted to fashionable Edwardian taste with herbaceous borders and hedged enclosures, ornamented with formally trained fruit.

Violet arguably succeeded in her objective for, a few years after her husband's bequest of Powis to the National Trust in 1952, the Trust's Gardens Adviser, Graham Stuart Thomas, remarked after a visit that 'the whole place was in extremely good order and has great beauty and attraction'. However, it was clear then that decisions needed to be taken on how to keep the garden looking its best.

How was the Trust to respond to the challenge of managing a garden in which the built structures had remained mostly unchanged but where the planting had been altered continuously over the previous four centuries? Clearly, restoration to an earlier date was inappropriate; few records existed of the historic planting schemes, and lack of resources precluded a large-scale project. To recreate only part of an earlier scheme by, for example, retraining the yews as seventeenth-century style topiary, would have been meaningless.

The Trust's first action was to remove some of the plantings that were considered inferior. For example, a bed of heathers by the entrance was replaced by lavender, rue, santolina, potentilla and hypericum, whilst beds on the Aviary terrace were grassed over. The herbaceous borders flanking the Orangery were cleared of weeds and replanted to a scheme by Graham Thomas and, to save labour, new plants were chosen that did not need staking. Instead of the traditional wall-trained fruit, climbers such as roses, clematis and honeysuckle were trained against the terrace walls. Plants were imported from other gardens, including irises from Hidcote, ceanothus from Polesden Lacey and carnations from Gunby Hall. In the Kitchen Garden, the tradition of annual bedding under the apples and pole-trained vines was abandoned in favour of ground cover plants. Ponticum was cleared in the Wilderness and replaced by species rhododendron, including varieties that provide visitors with additional colour after the first spring flush. Yew hedges were replanted. Seats were added for the convenience of visitors, and statuary moved to new locations.

In the 1970s, Powis entered a new phase of evolution, with much of the impetus coming from Head Gardener Jimmy Hancock, a great plantsman-gardener. In line with agreed policy and guided by John Sales, the Trust's Chief Gardens Adviser, Jimmy replaced various unsuccessful borders; for example, the Top Terrace was planted with exotics and semi-tropical plants, and sun-loving plants adapted to dry conditions were introduced to the Aviary Terrace. Jimmy's special talent was the planting of containers and urns with elaborate and imaginative bedding schemes, for which Powis is renowned. At this time Powis also became home to two National Plant Collections – for laburnum and *Aralia ssp.* – and the castle forecourt was redesigned to a 'quiet' scheme of evergreens around the reinstated central lead statue of Carpentière's *Fame Borne Aloft by Pegasus* (see p.104).

Jimmy Hancock retired in 1996 and was succeeded by Peter Hall, who has continued the tradition of experimentation and improvement

The gardens at Powis Castle date from the seventeenth century and are justly celebrated for their beauty. Italianate terraces, bedecked with statuary and clipped yews, lead down to the orangery below. (NTPL/Andrew Butler)

(see pp.184–6). The list of horticultural 'improvements' carried out at Powis during the 40 years of Trust ownership is indeed long, but every decision has been taken with the gardening style of Violet, the 4th Earl's wife, in mind. She was much inspired by Gertrude Jekyll, and the colour schemes of the main flower borders were selected purposefully to reflect this influence.

The way the Trust has approached the care of Powis very much parallels what a private owner might have done, had they had the means to improve the garden themselves. However, purists may condemn actions such as the removal of certain features as counter to the general aims of conservation. We might therefore ask whether we would allow ourselves the same freedom today? Probably not, as now the Trust would take the view that conservation requires a detailed

Rooted in History

archival and physical survey, including the cataloguing of all the plants in the garden, to ensure the conservation of whatever was thought significant.

Perhaps the recent development of a more rigorous approach to recording and surveying has fuelled the notion that a garden must be managed within equally strict conservation boundaries, or that it should be maintained precisely as the previous owner had left it. Yet no garden has managed to remain unaltered, no matter how recent its origin, and the older the garden, the more likely it is it to have gone through a great many changes. Such changes, reflecting the coming and going of gardening fashions, are as much a significant part of Powis's history as what survives and so continue to guide the garden's management.

Case Study 2
Chastleton House

Katie Fretwell

This tall, severe Cotswold stone house near Stow-on-the-Wold has remained remarkably unchanged, both inside and out, since its construction *c.*1612, and now constitutes a uniquely evocative 'time-capsule' of life in the early seventeenth century. The cause of its preservation lies in the fact that, as a previous owner was wont to point out, the family lost all its money 'in the War' (she was referring to the English Civil War, some 400 years earlier!), and had been forced to live in quiet obscurity ever since. Poverty ensured that Chastleton remained unchanged through the centuries.

The surrounding garden was claimed to be the same date as the house, and so potentially an even rarer survival. However, the archives show that it was at least partially replanted in 1828 by its antiquarian owners, the Whitmore-Joneses, in an early instance of garden restoration work. The garden was subsequently featured in *Country Life* in 1902 and in Inigo Triggs's *Formal Gardens in England and Wales* of 1904, both noting the formal circular topiary garden on the east front, known as the Best Garden, in its then guise as an 'Olde English' garden.

The Trust acquired Chastleton in all its crumbling glory in 1991. Surrounded by chronic damp and decay, the last owner, Mrs Clutton-Brock, had continued to live there with leaking roofs, patched windows and rampant wet and dry rot. The very future of the house and its contents was in doubt. Yet despite its structural problems, the place had immense appeal, with a strong sense of timelessness, of quiet, understated charm, and of remoteness. Similarly, the minimally managed garden, with old lawns surrounded by overgrown borders and orchards, had a romantic and idiosyncratic quality.

From the outset the Trust was determined to do as little as possible to both the house and garden, to repair rather than restore, and to attempt to preserve the fragile and subtle patina conferred by their long history. This approach had already been successful with a house, at Calke Abbey, but similar principles of minimal disturbance had not been applied to a garden before. It has therefore been something of a learning process for the Trust, both in terms of achieving the desired effect, and of convincing visitors that the apparently low level of gardening is intentional.

At first the minimal intervention policy was interpreted in the garden as a requirement for no more than basic, even unskilled, gardening. However, this did not achieve the desired effect of a garden that was run-down yet still cherished. Nor did it allow for any desirable changes, such as the replacement of trees that were being lost through old age. So a slightly more bullish policy has evolved, with decisions being taken to start afresh in certain areas — for instance, some lawns have been relaid and beds and borders replanted — and to then allow time to work

Rooted in History

its magic, softening the new and raw until they blend in with the old. Maintaining the sense of continuity is certainly helped by involving a member of the Clutton-Brock family in decision-making and helping to steer the garden's future course, while a local farmer continues to trim the topiary every summer, much as he has done for the last 40 years or so.

The whole Chastleton project is an exercise in restraint, of trying not to do too much, too slickly. National Trust ownership is central in this respect, as because the Trust holds Chastleton inalienably (and therefore 'forever'), it is able to take the long-term view and to experiment where appropriate, thereby allowing the house and garden to continue their alluring sense of slumbering peace. In this respect, Chastleton represents a rather different type of property from most other gardens in the Trust's care, being far from 'manicured', and yet this policy of contrived neglect actually requires as much planning and management as do other, more evidently maintained, gardens. As a conservation approach this has been well received by visitors, who seem to appreciate the different style of presentation of the house, in all its faded beauty, and accept the idea of the garden complementing this.

2

Learning by Experience

John Sales

Many of us can trace our enthusiasm for gardening to the time we first acquired a garden. An interest in gardens often develops from necessity. So it was with the National Trust, which did not set out to accumulate gardens although, according to Merlin Waterson in *The National Trust: the First Hundred Years*, the unhappy fate of the diarist John Evelyn's seventeenth-century garden at Sayes Court in Deptford, was a catalyst in the setting up of the organisation in 1895. In spite of the founders' interest, the Trust was in its fortieth year before it began seriously to acquire gardens and landscape parks and fifty before it developed sufficient enthusiasm to procure them in their own right.

Committed to the preservation in perpetuity of 'places of historic interest or natural beauty', the Trust's early emphasis understandably dwelt on the acquisition of threatened countryside and coast, together with small vernacular buildings, often semi-derelict, like the Clergy House at Alfriston and Muchelney Priest's House, where the gardens were insignificant or absent.

Similarly the Trust's first country house, Barrington Court, was a romantic sixteenth-century shell when acquired in 1907, uninhabited and used for agricultural storage. It was given an elaborate garden thanks to Colonel Lyle (of Tate & Lyle sugar fame), who took a long lease and employed the now legendary flower garden designer Gertrude Jekyll in the early 1920s. After three generations of development the sugar money dissolved and in 1991 the Trust resumed direct management of a 'model estate' incorporating a great garden created during its ownership; a useful pointer perhaps for the future.

The Trust's first important historic garden, in 1931, was Montacute, an Elizabethan house in mellow Ham stone with garden walls and buildings to match. This lovely place, including parkland and part of the

The Rose and Iris Garden at Barrington Court. The design follows suggestions made by Gertrude Jekyll, with old varieties of bearded iris interspersed with herbaceous plants.
(NTPL/Neil Campbell-Sharp)

village, brought with it some familiar challenges that the Trust has tried to come to terms with ever since. As well as having lost its family connection and its contents, the whole place was run down and in need of repair, with inadequate funds and little income. In the garden the intact Elizabethan layout had been retained but overlaid in the 1860s by Mrs Ellen Phelips and her gardener Mr Pridham, who reworked the garden according to the prevailing Italianate style. By the early 1930s it had been drastically simplified to save labour, a shadow of its former self.

With no prospect of finding sufficient resources or employing more than a small fraction of the number of skilled gardeners needed for restoration on any scale, the philosophical dilemma as to which period to favour did not arise. Nonetheless, in these straitened circumstances the Trust had to decide a strategy for the garden beyond tidying-up and repairing the fabric. Like houses without furniture, gardens stripped of plants and flowers can be sad places. How was the Trust to begin to give back to Montacute a garden appropriate to its past and one that also gives a measure of delight and satisfaction, the hallmark of any real garden?

Like everyone who takes on their first garden, the Trust was beginning to learn its gardening by practical experience. It was having to decide how, with small resources, to garden in someone else's name: to pick up the thread of the past, to retain and respect individuality and to work for the future of the place as well as satisfying current demands. There were no models to copy, no body of experience or established principles on which to rely.

The Trust's response to the challenge of Montacute's garden was to set up a committee of distinguished gardeners. Early efforts at renewal included asking Vita Sackville-West, already admired for her garden at Sissinghurst Castle, to redesign the borders around the East Court. Against the balustraded Ham stone walls, with their obelisks, pierced cupolas and delightful pavilions, her borders of pale, soft colouring were judged to be too weak and feeble. The borders were later replanted in a scheme of rich colours and strongly architectural foliage to a design by Phyllis Reiss of nearby Tintinhull, a theme that has been followed ever since to general approval. The Trust had made, and corrected, one elemental mistake – great gardeners, capable of producing inspiring results on their own ground, are not infallible in another garden with a different history, traditions and demands.

No wonder the Trust made mistakes. But it had, and retains, two huge advantages flowing from the foresight, opportunism and common sense of its founders. First, it decided to preserve by acquiring and managing property and in this way it has been both a direct force for conservation and a model for others. Second, and crucially, it was

Detail of one of the borders in the East Court at Montacute, showing the strong colour scheme advocated by Phyllis Reiss.
(NTPL/Neil Campbell-Sharp)

granted by Parliament the statutory authority to declare appropriate property inalienable in the ownership of the National Trust, a unique right giving it a rare degree of independence from government, local and national, as well as from commercial and social pressure. Once property is declared inalienable, the Trust cannot be dispossessed against its will, except by the express wish of Parliament.

For gardens and landscape parks, this power of inalienability has conveyed with it the crucial advantage of always being able to take the long view. The Trust has time on its side and many problems – human, social, horticultural, financial, political – can be solved by patience. Furthermore the conservation of gardens and parks is largely about continuity – of upkeep, management, skills, style, development, renewal – and clear, achievable objectives. While we should always seek to enjoy the present and work for the immediate future, it is vital that we should keep the long-term in mind because in gardens almost every job, however humble, has both an immediate and a lasting effect. Apart from garden buildings, the established architectural conservation principles of routine 'maintenance' and periodic 'repair' are inadequate in managing the complex interrelationships between a wide range of plants of all kinds growing together, interacting with site, buildings, climate, wildlife and people.

Not that the Trust in the 1930s had begun to explore the philosophy and practice of looking after gardens. The pressing conservation problem at the time was the plight of the country house with its contents, grounds and estate, the English country house being Britain's special contribution to European art and culture. Political, economic and social changes — war, death duties, taxation and steeply-rising maintenance costs — were threatening the continued existence of many of Britain's great country house estates and their way of life. Recognising their supreme importance historically, architecturally, artistically, aesthetically, and because of their various associations, the Trust launched the Country Houses Scheme in 1937. By a new act of Parliament, the Trust was able to acquire and hold land and invest-ments as endowments for the upkeep of a great house. In return for giving their property with an endowment to the Trust, donor families and their successors would be encouraged to continue living in part of the house, thereby retaining their historic link with the place. Free of any tax burden, the Trust would take on the role of the owner, meet-ing the ever-escalating cost of upkeep and repair. Each property would be self-supporting, a hope that in practice would rarely be fulfilled through endowment alone.

Gardens and landscape parks hardly got a mention, although their inclusion was assumed and inevitable. Even in 1946 when the Trust published *The National Trust: A Record of Fifty Years' Achievement*, James Lees-Milne was prepared to devote barely three pages to gardens and parks, and they were firmly absorbed in his chapter on 'The Country House'. Despite gardening and garden-making being Britain's great national talent and the eighteenth-century English landscape park being the country's sole original gift to international art, gardens were not yet taken seriously. At the time they were neither deeply studied for their 'historic interest or natural beauty' nor widely valued for their aesthetic, cultural, horticultural, social and wildlife qualities. They were seen as part of the culture of the country house and as settings for buildings rather than as works of art or subjects of historic importance in their own right.

The success of the Country Houses Scheme saw an influx of import-ant gardens and landscape parks, mostly during the Second World War when the future seemed ever more bleak. In the tradition of the Trust's early acquisitions, Little Moreton Hall's moated garden was largely derelict but Blickling Hall was the Trust's first garden where historical and horticultural continuity had remained unbroken for centuries. Significantly, it was bequeathed by Lord Lothian, who in promoting the Country Houses Scheme had referred to the ensemble of house, garden and park.

Here is a garden with a fascinating history of sequential development, adaptation and innovation stretching back to the building of the great Jacobean mansion early in the seventeenth century. As well as a seventeenth-century layout, eighteenth-century garden buildings and an English landscape park influenced by Humphry Repton, it has a mid-Victorian parterre, overlaid by an important 1930s flower garden by the under-rated Norah Lindsay, who was so influential at Hidcote and elsewhere between the World Wars. In the English tradition each generation has left its mark, reflecting the taste of the time and the fortunes of the family, whilst adding plants all the time and without entirely sweeping away what went before. This evidence of enrichment and retrenchment, and the fascinating palimpsest resulting from it, is both this garden's most precious quality and that of other British gardens like Powis Castle and Cliveden. Great works of gardening art, never designed as a whole but expressing their antiquity through a series of overlays and adaptations, are rare enough to be treasured. That Blickling can still be enjoyed with all these qualities intact, as well as for its undoubted sensual beauty, after more than half a century of National Trust ownership, is justification alone for the Trust's role in garden conservation.

The first ten years of the Country Houses Scheme saw the acquisition of several mansions of great importance – Cliveden, Coughton Court, Killerton, Knole, Lacock Abbey, Lyme Park, Petworth, Polesden Lacey, Speke Hall, Stourhead, Wallington Hall, West Wycombe Park – as well as places as diverse as Great Chalfield Manor, East Riddlesden Hall, Bateman's, Packwood House, Gunby Hall and Wightwick Manor. Most of these came with a garden of sorts, often a landscape park as well, some of outstanding importance. Whereas the house, its contents and the other historic buildings – follies, temples, chapels, summer houses etc. – would often have been documented and researched, there was never much information about the garden and rarely anything about its plants. At that time very little interest had been taken in garden history; this was long before the Garden History Society was founded.

However, gardens like Cliveden, Killerton, Wallington and above all Stourhead, and parks like West Wycombe and Petworth, were obviously of great significance. The qualities of many of the others would be revealed later. Already the Trust had assembled the greatest and certainly the most diverse collection of gardens ever owned by one private organisation, almost it seems without setting out to do so.

In Stourhead it had a seminal eighteenth-century pleasure ground, complete with house, park and, crucially, much of the estate. No garden acquisition of the Trust has surpassed Stourhead, not only because of its historic importance in shaping the eighteenth-century English landscape style, its distinguished buildings, the range and significance of its plant collection and its sheer beauty at any season, but also because, like Blickling, it had been continuously gardened, renewed, embellished and cherished by the same family for centuries. With Henry Hoare's great genius as a starting point, Stourhead is the product of a dynasty, the tastes of each generation so intimately embroidered that to disentangle one element, however it may offend or please one group or another, is liable to diminish the whole.

Change and development are inevitable in gardens and it is unreasonable to suppose that their owners could or should have attempted to treat them as museum pieces. Gardens restored precisely to a period following dereliction may well be interesting, educational, inspiring and even beautiful. But they are authentic only to the extent that they retain the precious thread of the past – the special qualities, traditions and style of upkeep and renewal of the place – as well as its historic abric and unique plant collection. The daunting challenge of a garden like Stourhead is to retain its fascinating complexity, while attempting to reveal its important qualities to visitors, without their being allowed to destroy those qualities in the process.

At that time the Trust's few staff were too busy with the technical, financial and administrative challenges of digesting ever larger and more complicated pieces of real estate to consider fully the problems of long-term upkeep, repair and renewal, let alone the impact of mass visiting,

The Pantheon seen from across the main lake at Stourhead, a classical 'pleasure ground' in the English landscape style (right). Approached from the house, the landscape is revealed gradually as a sequence of contrasting views and experiences. Stourhead's creator, Henry Hoare II, incorporated a variety of features into his design, including the estate parish church and a medieval market cross from Bristol (opposite). (NTPL/Nick Meers)

Rooted in History

which could hardly have been foreseen. The main aim was to save places for the nation and at that the Trust was immensely successful, despite sometimes striking deals with former owners for funding, management and access that would not be repeated today.

An important development of the Trust's acquisition policy occurred in 1947, when it decided for the first time to consider gardens for acquisition in their own right. The catalyst for this was Hidcote, created by Lawrence Johnston after 1907, following service in the Boer War. He had shown an interest in farming and his American mother, Mrs Winthrop, no doubt because of the arty, expatriate US population centred on Broadway, bought the manor house, farm and hamlet of Hidcote Bartrim. Although American by birth, Johnston grew up mostly in Europe and read English history at Cambridge. His gardening was entirely self-taught but he was influenced at the outset by Alfred Parsons, who lived in Broadway and later, after his mother died, by Norah Lindsay to whom he would have left the garden had she survived him.

Lawrence Johnston's garden is no less than the most imaginative, innovative and accomplished of its time. While developing an intriguing pattern of hedged spaces and vistas, he deployed a catholic plant collection with artistry and discipline to create the most influential flower garden of the twentieth century – ideal for the Trust as its first purposeful acquisition. That the outstanding qualities of this, at the time, comparatively unknown garden were recognised by the Trust is a remarkable tribute to the Trust's Historic Buildings Secretary James Lees-Milne and members of the Gardens Committee, not least Vita Sackville-West, who had written admiringly of the garden and whose own garden was influenced by Hidcote.

Moved by the post-war economic threat to so many great gardens, Hidcote's acquisition stimulated a joint National Trust/Royal Horticultural Society initiative to procure gardens of national import-ance for permanent preservation. A joint committee of eminent gardeners, led by Lord Aberconway, was set up to seek gardens and raise funds, partly by agreeing to co-operate with the development of the National Gardens Scheme ('the Yellow Book'), run by the Queen's Institute for District Nursing for the opening of private gardens for charity. A National Trust Gardens Fund was established to purchase and manage these great new gardens.

The energy and influence of the Gardens Committee resulted in the rapid accumulation of some of the most important gardens in Britain, indeed in the world. Claremont and Lord Aberconway's own Bodnant were followed by Tintinhull, Nymans, Sheffield Park, Mount Stewart, Trelissick, Rowallane and Winkworth Arboretum, in the 1950s; Trengwainton came in 1961, followed later by Glendurgan, Sissinghurst and Wakehurst Place. Meanwhile the Trust was continuing to take on gardens and landscape parks of great significance with the great houses and estates it was acquiring – Lanhydrock, Powis Castle, Hardwick Hall, Upton House, Waddesdon Manor, Tatton Park.

At Hidcote the special challenges of garden management and conser-vation began to manifest themselves. Norah Lindsay's daughter, Nancy, claimed an inherited right to manage Hidcote, which was unfortunate for the garden as it urgently needed firm direction and courageous renewal after marking time since the start of the Second World War. During the Nancy Lindsay interregnum the garden continued to decline and to this day the fate of Lawrence Johnston's papers, together with other personal effects and some garden ornaments, has never been clarified. The perils of devolving the direction and conservation of important gardens to individuals who may be answerable to no one but themselves were becoming only too apparent.

Furthermore, the Gardens Committee members, with their quite distinctive gardening talents, were unlikely to see eye-to-eye on any objective issue of restoration, renewal and style of upkeep. The National Trust was beginning to learn that gardening by committee was never going to be successful and that once gardens had lost their original owners they needed an effective alternative means of management and direction, both for their short-term appearance and their long-term conservation.

After the Trust's first Gardens Adviser, Ellen Field, died tragically in a car accident, Graham Stuart Thomas began his seventeen years as Gardens Adviser in 1955. Thomas's greatest contribution was to establish a rigorous system of regular garden visits at which all garden matters would be discussed and a programme of work agreed according to priority and resources. Detailed written reports were accurate and prompt and covered everything discussed, thereby establishing the Trust's tradition and reputation for attention to detail as well as long-term strategy. Written reports were a means of referring back at the next visit and, as a series, provide an important historical record. This system of day-to-day insight from head gardeners and others locally, plus financial and managerial control by regional staff, combined with the fresh eye and broader perspective of the Gardens Adviser, remains the strength of the Trust's system.

Graham Stuart Thomas in 1996, with the honeysuckle that was named after him. (NT)

As well as ensuring that everyone is committed to the programme, the discussion is highly educational for all concerned. By setting targets, resolving difficulties on the spot and focusing on steady improvement, sound practice is spread, standards are raised, awareness and understanding increased and morale developed.

Thomas worked largely intuitively, basing recommendations on his extensive experience and his perception of the gardening style and traditions of each place, guided by a general knowledge of its history. This was supplemented by discussion with former owners and others and by his own acute observation. The Trust's Historic Buildings Department, responsible for all historical research, was thinly stretched and garden history was unknown as an academic discipline.

The extent to which the Trust pioneered the conservation of historic gardens is remarkable. Stimulated by the work of the Trust, the Garden History Society was founded in 1965 but it was 1983 before English Heritage established its first register of historic gardens of outstanding national importance.

Although structural repair and renewal of the fabric were pursued as quickly as the strict financial limits of the time allowed, attention was focused on improving standards and enriching the horticultural quality of gardens. Economies were made by eliminating inessential features. While this led to a certain sameness of approach, considerable efforts were made to retain diversity. Gradually the Trust's gardens gained a reputation as places to visit, thereby increasing income and membership recruitment. As in the theatre, the first step is to attract the audience by putting on a good show. As visitors to gardens increased, interest in garden history and conservation burgeoned, together with the Trust's work generally.

Half a century later it is difficult to imagine the financial constraints and limited scope of the Trust in the 1950s and early 1960s, when membership was counted in tens rather than hundreds of thousands and before mass car ownership had made great houses and gardens so widely accessible. Few people anticipated the exponential growth of visiting, especially to gardens, or the opportunities and problems it would bring. Mistakes were made. Some properties were accepted on terms which allowed very limited opening. At others nobody foresaw the impact of so many visitors. Many were, and remain, seriously under-endowed. Understandable financial caution led to arrangements being made for houses and gardens to remain under donor families' control and for management agreements with local authorities. As a result standards of presentation, upkeep, conservation and management were very variable.

In this situation the job of Gardens Adviser has required great tact, persistence and long-term vision. As circumstances changed, donor families at such places as Nymans, Petworth, Glendurgan, Knightshayes, Scotney Castle and Sizergh Castle have relinquished the increasingly onerous task of management to the Trust's staff. Similarly the Trust has resumed direct management of most properties formerly run by local authorities, such as Speke Hall, Lyme Park, Osterley Park, Ham House, Clumber Park and Claremont. While this has made it possible in many cases to raise gardening standards and improve access, the Trust's approach is flexible and excellent results have been achieved with alternative arrangements – at Waddesdon, Bodnant, Tatton Park, Coughton Court and West Wycombe, for instance.

The Trust was also well ahead in the re-creation and restoration of historic gardens. Moseley Old Hall is a house of Elizabethan origin famous for having provided refuge for King Charles II after the Battle of Worcester in 1651. When it was acquired in 1962 the 0.4-hectare (1-acre) garden was totally derelict, having been used as a smallholding. There were no records, only the vestiges of a small Victorian front garden. To provide something appropriate and to enrich the visitors' experience, Graham Thomas and Christopher Wall, the Regional Historic Buildings Representative, recreated a seventeenth-century style garden. With a knot, tunnel arbour, nut walk, orchard and contemporary plants, it was complex enough to be interesting but simple enough to be capable of upkeep by a part-time contractor, which was all the Trust could afford. Its features and plants culled accurately from contemporary literature, this little scheme was the first of its kind since the war and at the time the most precise historicist re-creation ever undertaken in Britain. A garden on similar lines was laid out at Little Moreton Hall in the 1970s.

The knot garden at Moseley Old Hall, viewed from the upper windows of the house. The geometric design, using box trees shaped into balls set in a pattern of box-edged beds of gravel and cobbles, is based on a design of the 1640s by the Rev. Walter Stonehouse.
(NTPL)

Rooted in History

Westbury Court, situated on the edge of the flood plain of the River Severn west of Gloucester, was offered to the Trust following demolition of the house and an unsuccessful attempt by a property developer to secure planning consent for houses on the site of the water garden. Although one of the principal garden walls was demolished, the garden was saved thanks to the tall pavilion being a listed building and because of the far-sighted recognition in 1964 by the county council and local authority that here was something special. They offered the 2-hectare (5-acre) property to the Trust for restoration and with a grant from the Historic Buildings Council, money raised by an appeal and a generous anonymous donation, the Trust went ahead. It was a brave leap of faith.

The garden had been laid out alongside the house by Maynard Colchester between 1696 and 1705 (with mid-eighteenth-century additions) and is accurately described in the guidebook as 'a rare and beautiful survival … the earliest of its kind remaining in England'. Colchester created a formal, walled garden of Dutch inspiration, with canals, hedges, clipped greens, and a modest parterre, all overlooked by a tall pavilion. But his garden was useful as well as ornamental; abundant with vegetables and herbs and fruits on the walls.

Edwardian *Country Life* photographs show how, miraculously, the garden had been preserved more or less intact for 200 years but by the 1960s it was in a tragic state – buildings vandalised, yew hedges killed by flooding, canals silted up, brambles and nettles everywhere. Despite acute financial constraints, the Trust undertook a pioneering restoration beginning in 1967 (these things never finish), based on what could be seen and discovered on the ground, combined with two key documents: Kip's 1707 detailed bird's-eye view of Colchester's layout and his account books for 1696 to 1705 from the county record office.

The layout had to be adapted radically for upkeep by one gardener and the restoration involved compromises, including the spreading of the dredgings over an area of 0.8 hectares (2 acres), raising the level by nearly 1 metre (3 feet), where a section of the former parterre near the house was recreated. Nowadays the silt would be disposed of differently and a careful archaeological investigation would precede any work on the site.

With its collection of seventeenth-century plants and its quiet dignity, the restored garden gives interest, inspiration and enjoyment to thousands of visitors. All restored gardens are products of the values and understanding of those who restore them, as well as being a reflection of the past. Like Ham House garden and Claremont, which were restored in the 1970s, Westbury needs to be seen in the light of the date of its restoration, taking into account the resources and expertise then available.

The 1970s restoration of the garden at Erddig, which was totally derelict on acquisition, was another milestone. Instead of restoring to a specific date, as at Westbury Court, the Trust decided not only to renew as far as possible the eighteenth-century structure and planting but also to replace many of the family's additions made over two centuries of ownership. These subsequent alterations are judged to be as important as the original to the particular history and character of Erddig.

As membership increased and more was expected of the Trust, the period following my appointment as Chief Gardens Adviser (Head of Gardens) in 1973 saw a developing professionalism. The Trust had assumed a huge conservation role with insufficient technical expertise in the wide range of disciplines involved.

Neither quantitatively nor qualitatively did the Trust know exactly what it owned, particularly in gardens. Furthermore, for reasons of taste and fashion, there had been a tendency to undervalue some garden styles; Victorian and Edwardian schemes were especially misunderstood. Hence the garden at Ickworth, one of the earliest and most distinctive of nineteenth-century Italianate layouts, had been largely dismembered, partly in the interest of economy but mainly with the fallacious aim of making it more 'tasteful'. Since the mid-1970s Ickworth's garden has been restored according to the spirit of the original as far as this can be afforded and sustained. Again the Trust was ahead in leading a revival of interest in Victorian gardens – Belton, Biddulph Grange, Cragside, Dunham Massey, Hughenden, Lyme Park, Speke, Tatton Park and Waddesdon, for example.

In an attempt to measure and evaluate what it owned, the Trust pioneered physical surveys of parks and gardens combined with historical research to discover the full chronology and significance of each place. With the acquisition of Wimpole in 1976 a small sum was set aside and John Phibbs was appointed on a short-term contract to report on the complexities of a park and garden where Bridgeman, 'Capability' Brown, Repton and others had been employed. Simultaneously the Trust began at Osterley Park a series of surveys of parks and gardens using graduates on government unemployment relief schemes. Katie Fretwell, now the Trust's Gardens Historian, was recruited onto one of these. This new profession of parks and gardens historian was given a boost when the Royal Parks adopted the same procedure. It finally came into its own after the great storm of 1987, when English Heritage rightly made restoration grants conditional on a full survey and management plan.

The first long-term conservation and management plan for any major historic garden, for Stourhead, was completed in 1978, using author and historian Kenneth Woodbridge's exhaustive knowledge of the history and iconography of the place. It sought to identify and evaluate its special

When the National Trust undertook restoration of the formal garden at Erddig in the 1970s (left), use was made of early eighteenth-century drawings such as this illustration by Thomas Badeslade of 1740 (bottom).
(NTPL/Rupert Truman and NT)

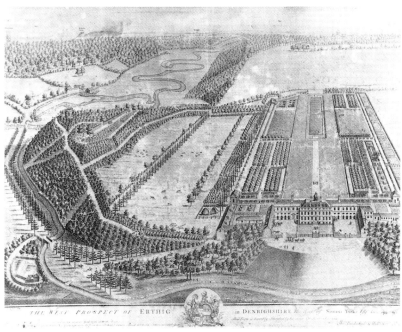

THE WEST PROSPECT OF ERTHIG in DENBIGHSHIRE

qualities, establish principles and set out proposals for conservation; also to guide the continuing development and renewal of the garden, taking into account the modern constraints of mass visiting and high costs. The plan endured and has been steadily followed, setting a standard for future conservation and management plans, as at Osterley, Dunham Massey Park, Biddulph Grange, Prior Park, Stowe and Studley Royal.

The remit of the gardens advisory staff had widened to embrace landscape parks and to include advice and guidance on technical, visitor management and managerial problems; also the vital matters of gardener recruitment and training. In achieving and sustaining high standards, it is the calibre, enthusiasm and expertise of gardeners that counts most and the Trust has taken a lead in initial training schemes and in-service training. The head gardeners' triennial conferences, held each time in a different location, are a particularly effective means of improving expertise and unifying the Trust's inevitably fragmented gardens staff.

The last two decades of the twentieth century saw the Trust acquiring 40 gardens, some like Studley Royal, Stowe, Biddulph Grange and Croome Park being icons of a period or style and requiring major restoration. Others, a fascinating assortment, came with houses of various dates and styles, sometimes containing gems of great historic value like the auricula theatre at Calke Abbey. The much-loved plantsman's paradise at Coleton Fishacre, and later Greenway, were acquired through Enterprise Neptune, the National Trust's initiative for acquiring coastline. Other acquisitions ranged from ancient places such as Canons Ashby and Baddesley Clinton to tiny gardens associated with humbler houses like Mr Straw's house in Worksop and Paul McCartney's house in Liverpool. The late-Victorian villa Sunnycroft is an interesting departure, having been acquired for the typicality of its house and garden rather than for its intrinsic quality.

While always depending on merit, acquisition policy has subtly changed over the years; judgement of quality depending at first on a committee of distinguished experts, now on more objective criteria covering rarity, national importance and historic interest, together with social, environmental and nature conservation values. Assessment of threat is important because the Trust should accept property only when it would be the most appropriate owner, (the Trust's huge membership being itself a threat in some circumstances!). The Trust has never had a 'shopping list' for gardens and has never sought to complete a representative 'set' of styles and designers. On the other hand it has intervened where important examples are in danger, gardens being so fragile. Cost is the deciding factor; the Trust is unable to accept gardens without a realistic prospect of their being able to break even, taking endowment and other income into account.

The view from the kitchen window at 20 Forthlin Road, childhood home of Paul McCartney in Liverpool. (NTPL/Dennis Gilbert)

Rooted in History

And of course it will all go on. While the need is there the Trust will continue to save gardens in peril. It will continue to learn about caring for gardens long term as well as restoring them. In the last analysis we are dealing not merely with an object but a process that has to be consistently and sensitively guided if the garden is to survive. To paraphrase a famous remark, there are three important principles in historic garden conservation: continuity, continuity and continuity.

The garden at Sunnycroft, a typical late nineteenth-century suburban villa on the outskirts of Wellington in Shropshire.
(NTPL/Clive Boursnell)

Case Study
A Guiding Eye: the Work of the Gardens Panel

Lady Emma Tennant

Members of the National Trust's Garden Panel amongst the British Worthies at Stowe. Left to right: Tony Lord, Lady Mary Keen, Richard Bisgrove, Paul Edwards (front), Lady Emma Tennant, Kim Wilkie and Anna Pavord. (NTPL/David Levenson)

I have sat on the National Trust's Gardens Panel for 20 years now, eighteen of those as chairman. At the beginning I felt somewhat overawed by the responsibilities involved, especially as – in the early days – my relative youth meant that on site visits I was frequently mistaken for an accompanying secretary, but my time with the Panel has proved to be infinitely rewarding. The Trust plays a leading role in garden conservation, and to be able to contribute to its work in such a stimulating way is an enduring pleasure and privilage.

What exactly is the Gardens Panel? There are currently nine of us, all variously qualified in the field of gardening and garden conservation. Present members include leading garden designers, professional horticulturists, dedicated plantsmen and garden historians, although by no means are we all professionals: the 'amateur' eye is often just as valuable. We meet three times a year, usually on site, and make as many flying visits as necessary through the year. We give advice, rather than orders, and work very closely with the gardens advisers and other members of the gardens team, reporting to the Trust's main Properties Committee and co-ordinating where necessary with the other advisory panels on nature conservation and architecture. Broadly speaking, our job is to assist the Trust's staff look after the gardens to the highest possible standard, thereby helping to establish and maintain core standards and practices. We are asked to look at a wide range of issues related to managing gardens, including their development, adaptation and renewal, and ranging from the training of gardeners to the establishment of 'Statements of Significance', by which the individual quality of each garden is defined and encapsulated into the property's conservation plan (see Chapter Three).

One aspect of the Panel's work which has, I think, been of particular value to the Trust, is the outside perspective we bring to bear. The talents and experience of the various Panel members serve both to promote the Trust and its gardens to a wider audience and help ensure that the Trust does not become too insular and subjective. The wide network of outside contacts that the Panel members collectively contribute can also be of real use when dealing with Trust issues.

A key area of activity for the Panel concerns prospective acquisitions. The scale and range of the Trust's collection of gardens and parks is discussed in detail elsewhere in this book, but it is worth saying here that the Trust has never set out to acquire a portfolio of properties as such (apart from coastline, looked after so well by Enterprise Neptune). It should, as the Trust's former Architectural Adviser Gervase Jackson-Stops famously said, 'gather the golden apples as they fall, but not go out and pick them off the tree'. The Trust is the last resort for properties that would otherwise be lost to the nation.

The Trust's criteria for accepting a new property are quite simple, but this does not mean that decisions are ever easy. The Panel has proved to be a valuable instrument in reaching such decisions, but how do we actually go about it? First, we need to assess the garden's merit. For the Trust to consider acquisition seriously, the garden must be of outstanding interest and quality. Opinions about merit are bound to be subjective, but several heads are – usually – better than one, and we generally come to a consensus. However, merit can be hard to recognise if the place in question is run-down or even derelict. In such instances the collective expertise and experience of the Panel can play a key role; the more knowledge the Panel members can muster of gardening and garden history, the better chance we have of recognising the quality of a Biddulph Grange or a Croome Park through the rampant undergrowth and silted-up lake. We are always learning of course, but I would like to think that our group knowledge and experience is such that little gets past us.

Second, the Trust's properties must provide 'benefit to the nation'. This is usually interpreted as ensuring a degree of public access, and so any potential acquisition must be looked at in terms of the practicalities of providing satisfactory levels of access and facilities for visitors. This is a growing part of our work, due to the huge increase in recent decades of interest in visiting gardens. Preserving the atmosphere of old and fragile places has become an art in itself.

I said earlier that acquisition by the Trust is the last resort. In some cases we feel that other options might be preferable. An interesting example came up fairly recently of a lovely manor house garden in the south of England, whose elderly owner was concerned that, as her children already had places of their own, this might be the time to offer the garden to the Trust. I went to visit, and although the garden was indeed a beauty, it was perhaps not quite in the top flight. The Panel agreed that, in any case, it was not in danger, and that acquisition by the Trust would be inappropriate. Now the old lady has died, and I imagine that a new family is happily setting up home there, which is as it should be. Even if a property is of the utmost merit we do not always recommend that the Trust takes it on. In 1979 the possibility was raised of the Trust acquiring the Chelsea Physic Garden, established by the Society of Apothecaries in 1676 and the second oldest physic garden in the UK. The quality and rarity of the place was beyond doubt, but for a variety of reasons the Panel felt that the Trust would not be the most appropriate owner, and I am glad to say that the garden is now managed very successfully by an independent charitable trust.

Finally, there is the question of money. The Trust undertakes to look after its properties forever, which means that they cannot be sold if they become a liability. In the early days, too many properties were taken on without an adequate financial endowment, and this has led to serious financial problems in some cases. Now we try to ensure that the figures add up before taking the decision to acquire. Money for acquisition (and subsequent conservation and maintenance) is raised in all sorts of ways. Legacies and donations remain our biggest source of income, but we also benefit from government grants and, increasingly, from lottery funds. In recent years the Trust has also run a series of highly successful appeals, such as at Biddulph Grange and Stowe, and public generosity has enabled us to take on properties that would otherwise not have been feasible.

One particularly rewarding area of the Panel's work is the allocation of the Trust's Gardens Fund, established in 1948. The principal source of income to the Fund is the annual donation from the National Gardens Scheme, taken from the gate money collected at over 3,000 mostly private gardens that open for charity. Over the years the Fund has made possible a variety of projects in Trust gardens, including the restoration of the peach house at Calke Abbey in 1992–4 and the reinstatement of eighteenth-century shrubberies at Farnborough Hall in 1994. More recently, the lion's share of the NGS donation has been directed towards Careership, the Trust's training scheme for gardeners, which has won a government award for the best modern apprenticeship programme.

Exciting new acquisitions and dramatic restorations attract the headlines, but the most important aspect of the Trust's work is the steady

Rooted in History

maintenance and improvement of its gardens. This depends on our skilled gardeners – the front-line troops – and the quality of the guidance they receive from the staff at Cirencester, a power-house of expertise. All of this work is enthusiastically supported by the Panel. We are also ready to take responsibility for difficult decisions. When, for instance, it was decided to fell the old cedars on the amphitheatre at Claremont, Lord Blakenham, the then chairman of the Panel, said that he was more than ready to defend the Trust on television.

The Trust's purpose, as defined by Act of Parliament, is to look after 'places of historic interest or natural beauty'. According to the Trust's policy paper on gardens and parks, this beauty is 'derived from natural processes, usually in pursuit of a version of Paradise'. Looking after paradise is a high calling if ever there was one, but I am sure that the Gardens Panel will continue to play a useful role in ensuring that future generations will be able to enjoy the Trust's unique corner of paradise.

3

Conservation in Action

Bill Malecki

'All restoration is a compromise between truth and the achievable.'
Christopher Taylor, *The Remains of Distant Time*, 1996

One of the fundamental differences between gardens and other visual works of art lies in the way they are created. An artist, architect, designer or sculptor will usually produce something that can be handed over as completed work. The process might take days, it might take years, but at the end there is a finished product. Job done. In the garden, however, the design and planting are never more than the start of the creative process.

The nature of working with living plants is that even the most experienced garden designer cannot hope to anticipate exactly how things will turn out. Virtually every garden has been developed, revised and refined by its creator in the light of experience. It is a point that television garden makeovers often miss. Just as much imagination, knowledge, skill and judgement (and fun!) go into nurturing and developing a garden as go into conceiving it in the first place.

This evolutionary creative process presents a couple of problems for those with the job of conserving historic gardens. First, it can be difficult, perhaps impossible, to define the moment when a garden has achieved its zenith. Woolly terms like 'former glory' point back vaguely in the direction of some past heyday, but in reality the place will have looked different from season to season, from year to year. Second, what happens to this process when those with the original vision are no longer around to steer its future development?

As John Sales has explained in Chapter Two, on acquiring its first handful of important gardens, the Trust's initial response was to set up a committee to oversee their care. The principle was fair enough: head

The box parterre at Westbury Court, with the tall pavilion in the background. When this garden came to the National Trust in 1967, it presented a scene of dismal dereliction.
(NTPL/Ian Shaw)

Leonard Messel inspecting a rhododendron in his garden at Nymans, with his Head Gardener, James Comber. This photograph was taken in 1947. (NT)

gardeners had never worked in complete isolation; they had worked in collaboration with their employer. But at some of these newly acquired properties like Hidcote, the owners had moved on. There was a void to be filled, and a committee that would support, guide and supervise the gardens seemed to be the answer. In practice, it soon became apparent that this was not the way forward. The chemistry was just wrong. The organisation recognised the value of seeking the views and advice of a wide range of people, but discovered that a garden actually run by committee is inclined to develop worrying personality disorders.

In an attempt to return to the principle that decisions should be taken by a small group of people, the Trust appointed a Gardens Adviser to visit the gardens to review plans and progress with the local team. As the number of gardens in the Trust's care increased, this system was extended with the appointment of additional advisers and specialist support staff. However, the key individual in the process remains the head gardener. The knowledge, skill and commitment of the person running the garden on a day-to-day basis is the biggest single factor determining the standard of conservation and artistry achieved.

Ask any head gardener and they will tell you that it is more than a job: it is a way of life. Most live on site. They see the garden at every time of the year, at every time of day; in all seasons and in all weathers. They know the nature of the soil: where it is deep and fertile, where it is thin and poor; where the damp spots are and where the ground is dry. They are familiar with the vagaries of the local climate: where and when the last spring frost is likely to strike; or which is the garden's warmest wall. The head gardener will have a close knowledge of the plant collection and will be able to tell you what thrives and what struggles on their site.

All sound horticultural practice has to be based on this kind of local knowledge; without it, any 'outside' advice will always be of very limited value. At the same time, however, familiarity can bring blind spots: parents might not notice how their children have grown until a visiting friend or relative points it out. A key aspect of the Gardens Adviser's role is to bring a 'fresh eye' to the picture; it can be surprisingly difficult to register creeping change in a garden when you see it every day. Trees and branches gradually eclipse vistas; shrubs stealthily advance over path and border; and, by tiny increments, hedges and topiary outgrow their allotted space. By noting and discussing these changes, the team has to decide when – and how far – to intervene. Similarly, borders can grow 'tired' and unbalanced and the cumulative effect of wear-and-tear on lawns can lead to a deterioration so gradual that it can be hard to spot where the change happens under your nose. Again, the garden meetings are an opportunity to review these sorts of matters.

At most of the Trust's gardens, there are generally two meetings per year and the key participants are the Head Gardener, the Property Manager, the Historic Buildings Representative and the Gardens Adviser. Typically, half the time will be spent looking at wider issues: major projects or developments; staffing matters; research; funding. The rest of the time is devoted to looking at garden work in more detail.

The Gardens Adviser's role in this process is to monitor standards, promote good practice and help in the planning process. As someone coming from 'outside' the garden, the adviser should be in a good position to be able to notice creeping change – whether improvement or deterioration. By working with a wide range of gardens, he or she should have a wider perspective and an understanding of garden history. For this reason, advisers are assigned to four or five regions (the Trust has a series of regional offices across England, Wales and Northern Ireland) in different parts of the country rather than confined to one geographical area. The experience of working with other gardens should also leave the adviser well placed to help disseminate examples of good practice. It is not the adviser's job to turn up and draw up a prescriptive list of instructions, but rather to act as a catalyst for discussion and a sounding block for ideas. After each meeting, a report is written giving a brief overview or commentary on progress and standards, followed by an itemised list of agreed work and, where appropriate, planting suggestions. When all is going smoothly and the garden is under the care of an experienced head gardener, the adviser's role is generally quite low key. More active involvement is called for at times of change when, for example, a big project is being planned or when a new head gardener is appointed.

The core team also includes the overall manager of the site. In some cases, the head gardener manages the day-to-day operation of all aspects of the property, including the running of the visitor facilities, shop, tea-room and so on. More commonly, the garden is part of a complex site under the direction of a property manager who has the challenge of ensuring that the place is run in a business-like way, welcoming visitors and making the best use of resources, without compromising standards of conservation.

Another key individual is the Historic Buildings Representative. The rather cumbersome job title is far from self-explanatory, but covers a role that touches virtually every aspect of the Trust's work. Their role is to advise on historical and curatorial matters, including practical conservation practices and the style and standard of presentation. Statuary, ornaments and garden buildings will be among their special concerns in a garden, but at the same time, the Historic Buildings Representative will be well informed about the wider history of the property and will help ensure that the policy for the garden sits comfortably within the philosophy for care of the property as a whole.

In addition to the staff team, representatives of the family that gave the property to the Trust sometimes remain involved in the process. Often, they have a unique insight into the personality, taste and aims of the people who created the place, and can play a vital role in ensuring continuity of purpose. Their input can also be valuable at times of change, helping to avoid safe, institutional solutions in situations where opportunities for appropriate new development arise. At Charlecote Park, for example, a bold new scheme devised by Sir Edmund Fairfax-Lucy is being planted up in the courtyard, where it might otherwise have been very tempting simply to accept the status quo. Additionally, the Trust's Gardens Panel, a committee of experts who give their time on a voluntary basis, helps steer the work by advising on general policy and – particularly at times of major change – by being invited to comment on progress and policy at individual properties (see case study in Chapter Two pp.36–9).

One thing that everyone concerned with the care of gardens soon learns is the fact that nothing stands still – not even the most fixed and formal garden. The scene might not appear to have changed much since the day an engraver's hand portrayed it a couple of hundred years ago, but the chances are that nearly every element in the picture has been replaced over the years. Much of the work that goes into conserving an historic garden is like invisible mending. The skill is to be able to perpetuate the character, proportions and vigour of the place despite the inevitability of growth and decay. As far as possible, this is achieved through routine, timely operations like pruning, thinning and replanting, ensuring that the rolling process of re-making a garden is hardly noticed. On the other hand, there are times when more drastic intervention is called for. Natural disasters like storms or devastating diseases like Dutch elm disease can rule out any possibility of a low-key approach. Sometimes, the only solution is to pull apart a whole section of the garden and start again.

It is the larger initiatives like recreating a lost parterre, restoring an abandoned walled garden, or felling and replanting an avenue that catch people's attention. Major projects like these are sometimes appropriate, often inevitable; but it is the routine work that really shapes a garden. The unrivalled precision of the hedges and topiary at Hinton Ampner, for example, is the product of years of skilful clipping and attention to detail. Well-planned regimes of turf care underpin the quality of fine lawns in gardens like Sissinghurst while, at the other end of the scale, careful judgements about the timing and height of mowing at Rowallane have ensured that the wild flower meadows have become

Above: Head Gardener Nick Brooks clipping one of the 30 Irish yews on the Long Walk at Hinton Ampner.
(NTPL/Stephen Robson)

Left: Bluebells at Rowallane. The mowing regime for these wild-flower meadows is carefully man-aged to enrich the floral interest and to provide habitats for wildlife.
(NTPL/Steven Wooster)

richer and richer each year. Equally, the success of the best herbaceous borders is generally the result of small adjustments, based on close observation, fine tuning the scheme and tweaking the combination of colours, textures and height. In each case, the routine work is just as important as the long-term planning in producing and maintaining the character of a garden.

There is, of course, a danger that with a diverse collection of gardens under the wing of one institutional owner they will, little by little, acquire a sameness or a corporate stamp. To guard against this, at the heart of the Trust's work is a commitment to try to understand the special features, character and qualities that are valued in each of the places in its care. The process needs to take account of the views of local people, visitors and the wider community, as well as Trust staff and volunteers. In recent years, the Trust has been writing 'Statements of Significance' for all its properties, whether they be a piece of coast and countryside, a grand mansion, an old workhouse, or an archaeological site. In each case, the aim is to define and describe what makes the place important and distinctive so that future policies and efforts can be directed to safeguarding its individuality and special qualities. But nowhere is this more important than in gardens, where the processes of change are more rapid and the character of the place is more inclined to evolve into something else when not carefully steered. The challenge is to steer that change in a way that strengthens the special qualities and character of the garden, rather than allowing its personality to drift. This is particularly important with plants. Losses inevitably occur and replacements are needed – so choices have to be made every year. If a garden is being cared for as an outstanding example of a period style, then these decisions are crucial. The cumulative effect of planting up, say, a Victorian garden such as Biddulph Grange with modern varieties would be a gradual but sure dilution of the Victorian 'feel'. In other gardens, like Nymans and Bodnant, where a long tradition of collecting and experimentation might be far more important, it would be wholly inappropriate to limit the palette to that of any one period. In each case, the key thing is that all decisions are based on an understanding of what is important about the garden and what qualities and aspects of its character we hope to be able to conserve and renew into the future.

On the whole, this has tended to be a fairly informal process with a small group of people working together, planning the care of the garden in the light of their knowledge of its history, significant features and problems. Increasingly, however, the Trust is recognising the value of underpinning this process with written conservation plans. These go into far greater detail than the broad-brush 'Statement of Significance', which tries to distil the essence of the place onto one page. There are many advantages to this approach: it can bring continuity, helping to avoid the frustration and expense of arbitrary changes in policy when personnel come and go; it can help enormously when planning the phasing and funding of future work; it can help identify and anticipate potential threats; it can help demonstrate to the public – whether individual visitors or statutory bodies – that we are working to a long-term plan; but, most critical of all, it says what is important about the place and sets out a vision for its future care. Of course, we cannot take away the right of future generations to take a different view of what is significant, but we nevertheless have a duty to put our efforts into ensuring that our care of the gardens is based on our best understanding of the gardens entrusted to us.

At properties where very little research has yet been done or where there are not the resources, time or personnel to embark immediately on a full-scale plan, a conservation statement is sometimes the answer. This is a short document, perhaps only a few pages long, sketching out the importance of the place, identifying the immediate conservation issues, and presenting a summary policy for its care. For a large, complex garden a conservation statement should be regarded as an interim document, whereas for smaller, more straightforward properties

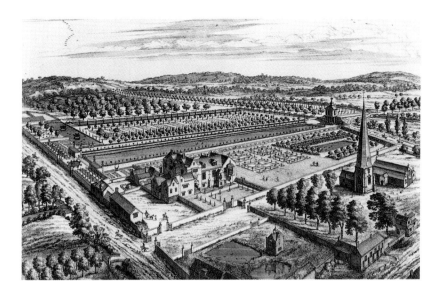

Johannes Kip's bird's-eye view of the house and formal Dutch style gardens at Westbury Court, 1707. (NT)

it may be all that is required to guide the garden's future care.

We have already noted that conservation plans can help avoid the 'corporate stamp' by sharpening the distinctiveness of each individual site. But it could be argued that, at the same time, these plans impose too many restraints and stifle any possibility of creativity. Well, yes – we have to acknowledge that in the business of conserving historic gardens, some constraints are indeed inevitable. A certain sense of humility and restraint is needed to be able to look after something that others have created without feeling the need to stamp your own personality on it. The degree to which the plan is prescriptive will vary greatly from site to site. There is a very strong case for conserving a rare, surviving example of a seventeenth-century formal garden like Westbury Court as a 'pure', faithful exemplar of a garden of its time. Here, the position and dimensions of its hedges, parterres and topiary can be quite tightly defined, and a 'cut-off' date designed to limit the planting to the range available before a particular period, helps ensure that the appropriate effect is achieved. Another garden might be equally important, but call for a quite different approach. At Trengwainton, much of the significance lies in the collection of rhododendrons and other exotics introduced from the wild, and the way that the planting has played to the possibilities offered by the exceptionally mild Cornish climate and the site itself. Here, conservation consists in perpetuating the richness of the botanical collection, keeping up the tradition of experimenting with lush, bold and informal effects, and maintaining key views.

The kind of conservation guidelines needed and the extent to which they should be 'tight' or 'loose' varies across the wide spectrum of gardens within the Trust's care. Although some gardens offer less scope for experimentation, their care demands no less skill. Even the most 'fixed' and formal gardens demand flair and technical skill if they are to be done well. The right approach to training, clipping and pruning of topiary and espaliers and an understanding of historic planting style are all essential. To dismiss the work that goes into the care of an historic garden as 'uncreative' is like suggesting that performing a string quartet written 200 years ago requires no creativity or imagination.

A typical garden conservation plan will start by setting the garden as a whole in its wider physical, cultural and historical context. The next stage is to consider in turn the various parts that make up the garden. One of the first steps in thinking about what makes a garden important is to look at its history, surveying what survives on the ground and researching any records, images or correspondence that might tell us more about how it was created and how it has subsequently developed. Katie Fretwell covers this subject in more detail in Chapter Four. A garden conservation plan needs to refer to the history of the garden and summarise its important phases of creation and development, but it is not the place for a detailed historical account. In virtually every case, a garden falls into a number of different areas, each with its own characteristics. After a brief summary of the history of each of these areas, a section on its character and special qualities follows. This is the key part of the plan, and attempts to capture in words and, perhaps, images, an enduring vision for the garden.

This 'character and special qualities' section will probably include historical elements: buildings and ornaments, the layout, associations with noted designers or public figures. It might include botanical significance: rare plants, original introductions, champion trees. It will certainly include aesthetic elements: colour schemes, views, compositions and contrasts; similarly, it will involve moods and effects: peace, drama, melancholy, excitement, spectacle, and it might also include symbolism: allusions to myth, classical ideals or other art forms. The character and special qualities might be associated with horticultural traditions and a certain style of upkeep, from relaxed, modest or informal, to manicured, detailed or ostentatious. The conservation plan must try to define the 'spirit of the place' in a way that will help guide our care of each garden, ensuring that, as far as possible, future generations will have the opportunity to enjoy those same special qualities in years to come.

Having attempted to describe a vision for the place, the next step is to consider the current state of the garden, along with constraints and threats that could limit what can be achieved. The constraints might include the obligations and pressures associated with opening a garden to the public: health and safety issues, access difficulties, wear-and-tear problems; or could be an inadequate availability of resources; and will possibly include changes in growing conditions, loss of shelter or the chronic decline of over-mature plants. Threats can range from local problems with pests or diseases to major concerns about inappropriate development on neighbouring land.

The final stage is to ask what all this means for the future. Given the constraints, what can we do to conserve and strengthen or restore the garden's character and special qualities? What steps do we need to be taking to avert any of the threats we have identified? Meetings with the Gardens Adviser are one of the main opportunities to discuss these matters and to plan future work and projects.

If I am giving the impression that this is a fairly cut-and-dried process, I should acknowledge that it is rarely possible to be absolutely definitive and conclusive. Almost always, there are dilemmas. Gardens like Westbury Court, Biddulph Grange or Sissinghurst, all relatively pure examples of a particular style, period or designer, are comparatively rare. More common are the places like Sheffield Park, Powis Castle or Kedleston Hall, where there are several layers of significance after succeeding generations have reworked the site, modifying, incorporating or erasing the efforts of their forebears. The relative value and condition of these different phases of work have to be assessed. In some cases, the various layers of design and planting sit comfortably together. Sheffield Park Garden is one of the Trust's most visited properties. There can be no doubt that one of the reasons it is so treasured is the wonderfully accomplished way that successive owners have added, boldly but sympathetically, to the work of their predecessors. To the lakes created by 'Capability' Brown in the eighteenth century, a further

The Top Lake at Sheffield Park. This photograph was taken in winter, after the full drama of the autumn colours was over, but the powerful structure provided by the trees and the lakes is still evident. (NTPL/Stephen Robson)

two lakes and rockwork were added in the nineteenth century and then, in the early twentieth century, Arthur Soames transformed this parkland scene with an extensive planting of trees and shrubs for spring and autumn colour. The value of the garden today lies in this harmonious evolution and there could be no question of erasing the contributions of the last two centuries to restore a pure 'Brownian' park.

The grounds of Kedleston Hall, on the other hand, presented more dilemmas. There, the changes over the last three centuries had been decisive reworkings of the site in response to changes in fashion. An early eighteenth-century formal garden laid out by the Royal Gardener, Charles Bridgeman, survived only 40 years before being swept away to make way for the informality of the English landscape setting for the mansion. In the late nineteenth and early twentieth centuries, some formality crept back into the pleasure grounds close to the house. When the Trust had to come up with a policy for the presentation of the grounds, the decision was taken to focus on the second half of the eighteenth century. First, the character of the property as a whole was overwhelmingly Georgian; secondly, the early formal garden had been completely erased whereas the landscape and pleasure grounds had survived. It was also decided that some of the later features should be removed where these detracted from the late eighteenth-century feel of the place. Generally, conservation policy will focus on one period only when the garden is a particularly good, complete or rare example of period, style or designer's work. Inevitably, the process of assessing the relative value of different elements and phases of development in a garden is to some extent subjective, but the important thing is that at least the issues are carefully researched, thought through and discussed.

Yet even in gardens where the long-term vision is relatively straightforward, dilemmas still arise. One of the most common relates to the older plants in a garden. On one hand, venerable old trees often make a huge contribution to a site: they convey a sense of the passage of time and are a living link with the past; they are often full of beauty and character in their own right; they might be an original introduction from the wild with their own story to tell; or they might have ecological value as a habitat for rare bats or beetles. On the other hand, they can be totally out of scale with their designed setting or blocking views; they might be depriving other plants of light and moisture; they could be declining and unsightly. Two things are sure: nothing lasts for ever, and decisions about trees almost always stir up strong emotions. Sooner or later, action will be inevitable. Visits by gardens advisers provide the opportunity to discuss such issues, but decisions are never taken in haste: often, the same plant will have been revisited over a period of several years before a verdict is reached. Hedges and topiary are frequently the subject of similar dilemmas. Despite their resemblance to 'frozen' architectural structures, they are living, growing features which fill out, almost imperceptibly, year on year. In many cases, this is not a problem; a little middle age spread is not always out of place. The great, rounded, clipped yews looming over the terrace at Powis Castle bear no resemblance to the neat, formal topiary pieces they were originally intended to be, but today they have become a distinctive and much-loved part of the personality of the place. There could be no question of chopping them back or replacing them in this garden, where the significance lies in each successive century's contribution, not with the work of one distinct period. In other situations, such as the set-piece Dutch Garden at Belton House where the overall balance and proportions of a formal scheme are more important than its component parts, cutting back may be necessary.

Generally, the business of re-stocking a garden should be another example of 'invisible mending'. A small percentage of the tree population is lost and replaced each year and the overall impact is minimal. But here again, the little-by-little approach is not always possible or appropriate. Take the example of a formal avenue. If symmetry, balance and uniformity are the effects the avenue is intended to create, then it is pointless trying to perpetuate the feature by patching up losses as they occur. In situations where the Trust has had to grasp the nettle and replace a decaying formal avenue, it has always been important to explain the plans and the reasons for them well in advance of any work. Generally, the heartache of the felling is soon forgotten as the young replacements are planted and growing away. In gardening, some tasks, like mowing, come around every week; others, like pruning the roses or replacing the bedding, are required once or twice a year; yet more, like replacing an avenue, might be necessary only once every two centuries.

There are some other situations where 'invisible mending' is no longer possible. Essential elements of a garden's character can be lost over the years through changes in ownership, natural disasters, lack of funding or general neglect. In these cases, restoration might be appropriate. Sometimes, the aim will be to reveal and repair an important design overgrown during years of inadequate care. The eighteenth-century landscape garden at Claremont is one of the most important historic gardens in the country, but it had fallen into decline with the fragmentation of the estate. It was overgrown with laurel, *ponticum* and self-seeded trees when the Trust acquired the site in 1949. Guided largely by early illustrations of the garden, the Trust set about restoring the site when funds became available for the project in 1975. In other cases, the aim of restoration might be to recover the completeness, richness or integrity of a garden. The formal garden at Erddig was a largely derelict, pared-down version of its former self. Here, the approach was to keep as much as possible of the original fabric, retaining but hard-pruning overgrown trees, topiary and hedges to recreate the sharpness and scale of the original design (see illustration on p.33). Alongside this work, key missing elements of the eighteenth-century gardens were reintroduced, restocking the walls with fruit trees, and replanting the pleached lime walks. Yet the Trust also restored significant later overlays, such as a Victorian flower garden and Edwardian parterre, a policy in keeping with the Erddig tradition of always assimilating, rather than discarding, its past.

The term 'restoration' implies that most of the original fabric of a place has survived and that, even after the necessary repairs and replacements, it is still essentially authentic. There are good historical and archaeological reasons for this approach, but the emotional argument is equally persuasive: we like to feel that the old yew we see today was planted there by an Elizabethan gardener; that the same path has been trod for centuries; that the Victorian vine has borne more than a hundred crops. As a general principle, the less of the original that survives, the harder it is to justify restoration. In some rare cases, however, whole gardens are recreated to restore the setting for a house or as an exemplar of a particular style. A large formal garden designed by George London at Hanbury Hall had been swept away in the late eighteenth century but has now been recreated by the National Trust on the basis of archaeological evidence, old maps, illustrations and contemporary accounts.

Another common dilemma relates to the degree of modification that is acceptable in an historic garden. If some visitors find an eighteenth-century shrubbery boring, to what extent – if any – should we change it to meet their expectations? If 'loud' Victorian bedding schemes are deeply unfashionable, should we tone down the punchy primary colours to avoid offending the modern eye? As far as possible, the answer is to stick to what is true to the spirit of each individual garden and, where necessary, put more effort into explaining why the garden is planted and presented as it is. Attempting to accommodate everyone's tastes and expectations can only lead to a dilution of character and style. Long may the subtle melancholy of an evergreen shrubbery walk at Stowe remain the polar opposite of the flamboyant impact of summer bedding at Calke Abbey and Lyme Park.

Some pressures for modification are generated within the garden or within the National Trust. Anyone involved in gardens has their own passions and aversions. As a result, there are countless examples of places where a head gardener's enthusiasm for a particular group of plants, or an historic buildings representative's or gardens adviser's interest in a particular period or style, has helped to move a garden on to new standards of achievement. Many of the Cornish gardens, for example, have been greatly and appropriately enriched through their head gardeners' knowledge of rhododendrons or half-hardy perennials. At the same time, there is always the danger that one individual's enthusiasm for his or her own speciality can move the garden away from the essential character of the place. To play around with a wide and modern range of plants, however tempting that might be, could be entirely inappropriate on another site. The understated dignity of places like Studley Royal or Rievaulx Terrace, for example, would be violated by an approach that might be the very essence of another garden. In every case, a garden conservation plan is a useful guide to the kind and degree of modification that might be appropriate on any one individual site.

The plan can also be an invaluable benchmark when it comes to considering other pressures for adaptation. There are health and safety guidelines to conform to and visitors' expectations to meet. Pragmatism and sensitivity are needed to ensure that, as far as is reasonably possible, these needs are satisfied without steadily eroding the character of the individual garden.

No matter how well thought out any conservation plan may be, it can never be a blueprint for all eventualities. The garden meetings remain the principal opportunity to evaluate how things are going and discuss future plans, but it is the day-to-day work of a skilful team under the guidance of a knowledgeable head gardener that is the real life-blood of a garden, ensuring that the gardens we treasure today can be enjoyed for the same qualities in the future.

Vivid colours provided by the Victorian-style bedding in the sunken parterre at Lyme Park. (NTPL/Geoff Morgan)

Case Study 1
Biddulph Grange

'China', looking at the temple over the pool from the Chinese bridge. (NTPL/Ian Shaw)

At Biddulph Grange, James Bateman, with the help of his wife Maria and the artist Edward Cooke, created a highly imaginative garden over the course of three decades, starting work in 1841. Bateman was influenced by the horticultural fashions of his day, and the garden has an unmistakably Victorian character. At the same time, he broke new ground by employing a variety of natural divisions to create an informal, asymmetric arrangement of separate gardens, each with its own distinct theme and character, and each designed to create a desired set of growing conditions. Among the gardens he packed into the 6-hectare (14.8 acres) site were 'China', based on the willow pattern plate, complete with temples, pool, bridge and rockwork. Others included 'Egypt', an audacious tableau of pyramid and obelisks sculpted in clipped yew; and a rocky 'Scottish Glen', linked to 'China' by a tunnel. He was also a passionate collector of plants, and many of the specimens in his wide-ranging collection were original introductions from the wild.

One of the very significant features of the garden is the fact that this remarkable creation survived with few major changes after the day when Bateman, having over-spent himself, moved away to a more modest house on the south coast. For 50 years, the garden was meticulously looked after by new private owners who modified very little (with the exception of some areas immediately around the house, which had to be remodelled after a fire destroyed the original building). In the 1920s, the site passed into the hands of various health authorities and it was early in this era that the garden suffered its only major modification. Although most of the garden was left unchanged, the formal gardens to the immediate south of the house were erased for ease of maintenance, and replaced with bank-terraced lawns.

When the National Trust acquired the site in 1988, Bateman's garden was over-mature and vandalised but, with the exception of the 'missing' formal gardens, remarkably complete. Its condition illustrated perfectly the fact that a garden cannot be simply maintained: although the place was loved and cared for by the health authority's staff, there were never the resources to undertake more than the day-to-day tasks like weeding, mowing and keeping on top of fallen leaves. Without a healthy rate of underlying replacement and renewal, a garden inevitably starts to decline.

The National Trust commissioned an extensive survey of the site and its plant collection, and research into its history. Biddulph Grange proved to be a particularly well-documented garden, with detailed contemporary descriptions of the place and its plants, together with many good photographs of the garden in early maturity. Archaeological excavation played a very important part. A series of systematic digs was able to provide information that old maps, texts and photographs could not. Supported by all this information, the Trust felt able to embark on a strategy that would combine both restoration and re-creation, and an appeal was launched for funding to rescue the place.

The missing formal parterres and the grand, sunken Dahlia Walk had been a small part of the garden in terms of area, but a very distinctive and integral part of Bateman's scheme. The combined evidence of the archaeology, maps, photographs and descriptions made it possible to recreate these vital missing elements. Certainly, their re-creation also meant a significant additional maintenance burden (the very reason why they had been destroyed in the 1920s), but otherwise the garden would have remained an impoverished version of the original.

Elsewhere in the garden, it was largely a case of restoration, rather than re-creation. Here, it was possible to set about repairing surviving areas and features to something like their intended state. In some ways, this ought to be more straightforward than having to start all over again, but in practice it is an approach that probably generates even more challenges and dilemmas. It is a process that has to happen on several time scales: it makes sense to get big, disruptive jobs out of

The Dahlia Walk at Biddulph, from a photograph taken by *Country Life* in 1905. When Biddulph became a hospital in the 1920s, the walk was filled in, so this image was used as reference when archaeological excavations were undertaken by the National Trust after acquiring the garden in 1988.
(*Country Life*)

the way at an early stage – especially the structural works, where the difficulties are usually of a technical, rather than philosophical, nature. A different challenge lies in dealing with the living elements in the informal parts of the garden. Unlike the formal areas with their built structures or hedges, there is no absolute benchmark to say what the shape, scale, character and composition of the various informal sections should be. Here, the conservation plan is vital in trying to define what the creator of the garden was trying to achieve in each area, and setting out an ideal to work towards. In the case of Biddulph, where the essence of Bateman's vision was to create a series of carefully composed scenes, a policy of favouring the whole picture over its individual components was agreed. This means that, occasionally, overgrown but otherwise healthy trees have had to be sacrificed for the sake of the overall effect. But the plan can only set down broad principles. In practice, individual cases have to be discussed – sometimes over a period of several years – and an assessment made of the relative merits of their value as mature specimens, their beauty or rarity against their condition, their impact on the overall composition and the need to create space for a new generation of plants.

After the initial period of great upheaval and disruption, the garden is gradually settling back down to a long-term, rolling programme of 'invisible mending' and, with the right rate of replacement and renewal,

Rooted in History

the need for a large-scale restoration project should never arise again. But, as we have noted, it is not always possible to tackle things in this way. A different approach was needed when it came to dealing with the Wellingtonia Avenue. It had been conceived as a grand, formal set-piece but, with the passage of time, was decaying into incomplete ranks of declining trees. The formality and symmetry of the avenue could never be regained by piecemeal 'gapping up'. Here, the only solution was to grow on new plants, remove what survived of the old, and start the whole cycle again. Once the decision had been taken, it was crucial to explain the plans and the reasoning to visitors and local people. Nobody likes to see trees being felled, but if you know that they are being removed as part of a long-term plan to recreate the avenue for future generations, then the bitter pill becomes much easier to swallow.

The recreated Walk, with dahlias similar to the nineteenth-century cultivars (now extinct) that were planted by James and Maria Bateman. The Shelter House at the end of the walk has been reconstructed from old photographs and archaeological evidence. (NT)

Case Study 2
Mount Stewart

The Italian Garden at Mount Stewart. Lady Londonderry initially devoted this area to roses, but later abandoned most of them in favour of a sophisticated scheme of plants better suited to Mount Stewart's damp conditions.
(NTPL/Stephen Robson)

If Biddulph Grange is a garden where a relatively 'tight' approach to conservation has been adopted, Mount Stewart is an example where a 'looser' approach is sometimes possible and appropriate. The two gardens are by no means at opposite ends of a scale, but they do serve to illustrate the need to tailor the approach to conservation according to the nature, character and history of each individual site.

The importance of Mount Stewart is defined by its setting, its scale, its design and symbolism, its plant collection and its association with a politically and socially influential family. The estate is situated on the Ards Peninsula on the banks of Strangford Lough in County Down, Northern Ireland. Before the twentieth century, the grounds were simply laid out with a lake, pleasure ground, walks and relatively little ornamental planting. That was to change dramatically when Edith, Lady Londonderry, began developing the gardens in the 1920s and 1930s. She created a series of grand formal spaces with a strong architectural framework and sophisticated colour schemes and, further away from the house, extensive informal gardens. The garden enjoys one of

the most favoured climates in these islands, allowing an unusually wide range of plants to be cultivated. Another distinctive feature of the place is the extensive use of statuary and topiary to convey symbolic references to myths, legends, family and friends. This is particularly evident on the Dodo Terrace, where an extraordinary collection of concrete creatures forms a quirky series of private jokes.

Apart from the fact that nearly a century separates the creation of the gardens at Biddulph Grange and Mount Stewart, another aspect of their history has had a decisive influence on the Trust's approach to their management. After an intensive period of creation, new development was almost completely suspended once the Batemans had left Biddulph Grange in 1871; at Mount Stewart, on the other hand, the tradition of experimentation and enrichment never really stopped. The degree to which it is appropriate to be innovative today differs from one part of the garden to another. In some areas like the Italian Garden, Spanish Garden or Sunk Garden, a decisive style and character was established by the end of Lady Londonderry's life. Here, the emphasis has been on faithfully perpetuating the schemes she created. Other areas like the Lily Wood or the slopes below Tír na nÓg remained in more of a state of flux. In these cases, the areas have been more or less continuously developed ever since.

It is often the case that a more prescriptive approach to conservation is needed in the more formal parts of a garden. They are generally composed of relatively fixed shapes and proportions, which interrelate in a preconceived way. Informal gardens, on the other hand, are more inclined to be the result of a process of experimentation and evolution. The relationship between the various elements of the scheme is almost always more fluid and it can be more difficult to define the creator's intentions.

Let us first take the example of the Sunk Garden. This area was laid out between 1920 and 1922 on the basis of a scheme by Gertrude Jekyll, creating a formal, terraced garden framed by a pergola walk and enclosed by hedges. Set into the corners of the lower level, four beds edged by dwarf hedges are set around a scallop-edged lawn. Structurally, the area has changed little since it was laid out, but the planting evolved over the years as Lady Londonderry experimented with various colour combinations, settling – by the end of her life – on a bold scheme of blazing orange, vermilion and gold along with strong blues and purple. The Trust's approach here is to respect both the structural framework of the area and its distinctive colour scheme. There is, however, no slavish adherence to a planting plan. A few key stalwarts will probably always find a place in the scheme, but the emphasis is on working in line with Mount Stewart's great tradition of artistic plantsmanship, using whatever combination of plants best creates the desired effect. Although Lady Londonderry assembled a remarkable range of plants at Mount Stewart, she never amassed them simply for the sake of collecting: she was interested in them for their beauty, colour, form or scent, and for the way they enriched her painter's pallette.

On the slopes of Tír na nÓg, below the family burial ground, another of Mount Stewart's traditions has been pursued. Here, a willingness to play to the strengths and possibilities of the site, its soil and climate has led the garden into new territory. The rhododendrons that had been planted here never really thrived on the hot, dry bank and were replaced, little by little, with other plants better suited to the conditions. Among the replacements, plants from the Southern Hemisphere seemed to do particularly well, becoming in time a strong and distinctive new theme. It is a good example of a situation where a pragmatic and innovative approach, entirely within the spirit of the garden's traditions, has enriched the place where faithful adherence to precedent would have merely repeated old mistakes.

There are, no doubt, other properties where even greater innovation can be accommodated without overwriting their historically important qualities. Equally, there are those masterpieces and rarities which we have a responsibility to conserve with a relatively inflexible rigour. The essential point is that gardens cannot be run like branches of a chain store: to apply a standard formula to the management of each place in the Trust's care would be disastrous. Plans for the long-term conservation of historic gardens need to be based on a thorough knowledge of each site, and an insight into the aims, interests and tastes of those who created them.

The Dodo Terrace, with its array of creatures, both mythical and real. These relate to Lady Londonderry's Ark Club, founded during the First World War.
(NTPL/Steven Wooster)

4

Digging for History

Katie Fretwell

'Because gardens are constantly developing and changing, they can be fascinating documents of the past, if you know how to read them.'
John Sales, *Gardens of the National Trust*, 1996

All conservation involves first knowing what you have. At the most basic level a museum will have a catalogue listing each object, its history, cabinet number and condition. But how to go about cataloguing an historic garden, where every feature is closely interwoven through design: buildings are framed by shrubs and backed by trees, reflected in pools and set on grand vistas; and borders are comprised of carefully planned colour, texture and scent effects? How do you document the constantly changing scene, both through the seasons and over years as plants grow and die? And how do you record the complex histories of gardens, which may well consist of layer upon layer of different, often contradictory, designs? The best answer we have come up with so far, and one that seems to work, is to produce a detailed survey recording the fabric of the garden and its individual elements, along with the history of each and an analysis of the design.

Only when we fully understand a garden, its past history and present state, and how each part relates to the whole, can we begin to evaluate its significance and make recommendations for its conservation. Because gardens are always in a state of flux, they risk drifting on the tides of fashion, weather and the whim of the gardener. A survey can be like a chart, plotting both where a garden has come from and its current position. The conservation plan is then the captain, using the information to set confidently the best future course. In other words, detailed information and thorough analysis enable sound decisions to be made on conservation policy. Survey information also provides a

The east front of Lodge Park, built by John 'Crump' Dutton *c*.1635. The turfed area between the lodge and the main gates formed part of the deer course.
(NTPL/Nick Meers)

View of Lodge Park, painted by George Lambert, 1749. The deer course lies in front of the house, with the backdrop formed by the landscape designed by Charles Bridgeman.
(NTPL/John Hammond)

valuable fixed reference point against which to measure future change, and can also be used for interpretation. And so a full historical and field survey is a vital tool of the garden conservator, to be compiled as soon as possible in the conservation process.

The Trust was a pioneer of park and garden surveys some 20 years ago, and nowadays such surveys are a standard requirement of garden conservation schemes. As Gardens Historian, my remit is both to carry out and commission surveys, working closely with plant surveyors, gardens advisers, archaeologists and other conservators. Survey work is time-consuming, specialist and expensive, so any help from skilled volunteers is greatly appreciated, as is grant aid, such as the Ministry of Agriculture's scheme Countryside Stewardship (Historic Parks Option). Fortunately, garden history is a growing field and, when we have the funds to employ them, there are now more experts to call on, with different ranges of skills and expertise.

The costs of survey work can be frightening. In 1995 £30,000 was earmarked for the initial survey of Croome Park as part of the acquisition budget. This was soon swallowed up and a further £30,000 has been spent since on further, more detailed and wider-ranging work. To date, Stowe has required some £400,000 of survey work.

The Trust aims to produce surveys of all its parks and gardens, and about 75 per cent have been fully surveyed to date. Ideally, surveys are carried out at the time of acquisition, as at Croome, and although they were initially regarded as 'one-offs', it has become clear that in order to maintain their relevance and value they must be updated periodically. Meanwhile, surveying and recording standards have risen and remits broadened, so although more and more time and energy are spent on surveys we seem destined never to attain a higher percentage of completed coverage! Kitchen gardens, for example, were unfortunately often omitted from earlier surveys (as they were from English Heritage gardens register entries), but are now rightly recognised as important features in their own right, whilst archaeology has become a far more significant – and valuable – part of garden survey work.

Whilst concentrating initially on the most important gardens, the Trust gradually realised that surveys are worthwhile for even small or seemingly insignificant places. For instance, Little Clarendon is a modest Wiltshire garden, previously the home of George Engleheart, a dedicated daffodil breeder. Recent research showed that he had maintained extensive trial beds beyond the garden, and this discovery has resulted in some of his own raised cultivars being returned to the property. Equally, survey work at the ostensibly unimportant Lodge Park on the Sherborne estate uncovered a rare intact Charles Bridgeman design from the early eighteenth century, and highlighted the uniquely well-preserved deer course. As a result, English Heritage have upgraded the site from a modest Grade II to Grade I.

Besides needing more detailed, more accurate, more up-to-date and wider-ranging survey information, we also want it to be more accessible. So we digitise plans and reports for easier updating, reproduction and transmission, and compile interim ongoing reports. There is also growing demand for other types of survey information – on subjects as diverse as drainage and soils, visitors and environmental and presentation audits. The 'Red Queen effect' – you have to do all the running you can just to stay in the same place – is rife, making for an interesting, if demanding, job.

There are three main interlinked aspects to garden survey work: historical research to elucidate the past history; field work to record the present layout and features, which may also contain clues to the past; and analysis of findings and assessment.

A crucial part of each survey is the brief; it must be closely tailored to the individual requirements of the garden. It must also establish both the area to be covered and the scope of the work; a survey for restoration purposes will of course require a far more detailed level of work than an initial survey. Surveys should aim to be holistic, both in physical terms – considering the garden in its widest possible setting, including its relationship with the house and with the 'borrowed landscape' beyond; and also in terms of disciplines – integrating the results of plant, biological and archaeological surveys. In fact, one of the great strengths of the Trust is that it brings together specialists in all these varied disciplines. However, choreographing the diverse elements for surveys of large, complex landscape parks, such as Osterley and Stowe, with all the complications of different owners, tenants and staff, can be an awesome task in itself.

Looking for Clues – Historical Research

This has to be the most exciting part of garden conservation – who knows what treasures lie waiting to be discovered, mouldering away in some dusty cupboard? It can also be the most tedious – spending many hours in the same dusty cupboard and finding nothing of note, but still having dutifully to record the negative results.

As with all detective work, there must be an overall plan of work and a dependable filing system. Initial steps include identifying and reviewing existing material and setting up files for the copious notes, letters, contact names and photocopies that will be generated. This will provide direction as to the main areas for research and the main questions to be answered.

Although there have been attempts at establishing a standard methodology for garden research, to some extent each researcher has their own preferred method. It is useful at this initial stage to compile a chronology, identifying in particular successive owners of the site, and a list of potential sources of evidence – local records offices, county gardens trusts, past gardeners, etc. This is also the time to begin to get to know the site, starting with its boundaries, topography and its salient features.

In Britain there is generally a wealth of manuscript archives to be found on the gardens of the great country houses, each of which had their own muniments room, where nothing was ever thrown away. The Stowe archive, now held at the Huntington Library in California, probably holds the record, with some three-quarters of a million documents. At the other extreme, humble working cottage gardens were rarely, if ever, recorded, and so their conservation is generally dependent on non-site-specific information. With small sites it may be possible to hold all the archival information on a simple card system or word-processor. But for larger properties, such as Waddesdon, with a full archive and extensive documentation, a database (the 'Collection') is almost a necessity, enabling quick and easy sorting and searching of records.

On large country estates it was vital that close account was kept of all expenditure and income. The Croome Park estate ledgers include every

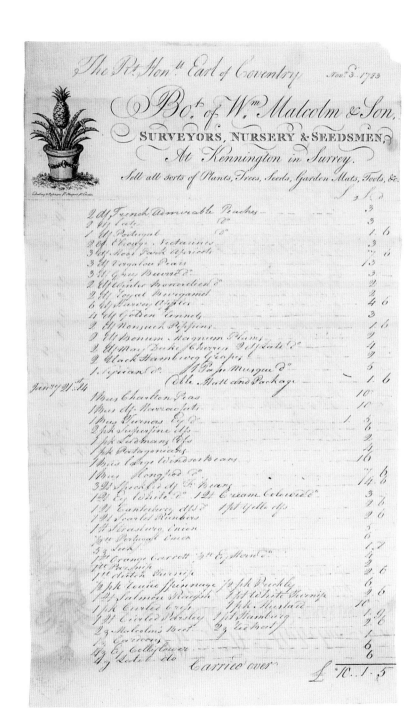

A nurseryman's bill of 1783 from the extensive archives kept by the Earls of Coventry at Croome Park. (Trustees of the Croome Estate/ Robert Anderson)

single plant bill from 1750 to 1816 – some 600 in total – with details of every plant acquired. Primary sources like these are extremely valuable, not least because they are usually reliable, although a degree of interpretation is always required – place names may have changed, whilst plant names almost certainly will have done so. Inventories are another dependable source – a 1742 inventory of Dyrham Park lists all the plants in the orangery ('31 oranges, 30 bays and 6 aloes, all in tubs') as well as the fittings ('15 Chairs, 2 Tables, 89 Mapps and prints, a sundial, 6 Chairs, a table and 12 prints'). This document came into its own in 1997, when the Victorian climbers and modern tea bar were removed and the layout of 'beautiful and fragrant walks', as Stephen Switzer had described in 1718, was recreated on the basis of the inventory.

Although some estate archives remain in their original muniments room, many have been handed over to county records offices for safe storage, conservation and cataloguing. Catalogues vary greatly, but all have their quirks. For example, access to the archive records of Coughton Court is according to their previous location in the house, by entering such requests as 'drawer three in the chest in the hall'! Fortunately for the modern researcher, the National Register of Archives (NRA) holds a database of catalogues that can now be searched via the NRA website. Increasingly, the Internet enables rapid access to collections and catalogues, especially those held by the important American institutions.

Personal records such as letters and diaries may contain literal information on park and garden developments, but, almost more importantly, they often also provide insight into the thought-processes and preoccupations of their creators. Peregrine Langton Massingberd's diary accounts of his tree planting at Gunby Hall are horribly pious and self-congratulatory, but clearly convey his aims. He obviously loved trees, and planned for the long term. In 1810 he planted 16 acres east of the Hall with acorns, 'which will be to my Grandson a noble & striking effect from the house & a means of procuring a very considerable additional share of comfort & luxury within the house'. Unfortunately, Algernon, the said grandson, in 1851 'proceeded to go "pussies Road to ruin" as hard as he could gallop', letting the house and leaving for South America, never to be seen again. The estate remained in Chancery until he was presumed to have died on his voyage up the Amazon. It was Peregrine who started the Gunby Tree Book, an invaluable list of plantings containing an early tree survey, to which later generations added their notes on planting and other family developments (including the loss of the ill-fated Algernon).

And so we see that, although research must primarily detail the physical development of a garden, it should also seek to record and

understand the aspirations, ideas, background and social milieux of the people who created them. By understanding the people we understand the *raison d'être* of the garden.

Back at Gunby, Margaret, a later, more sympathetic Massingberd, made the decisive moves in the creation of the present garden around 1900. The Tree Book records her planting, but it is her 1903 portrait by Arthur Hughes which most eloquently expresses her ethos. She appears as a romantic, almost Pre-Raphaelite, figure in white, embowered with pink, red and white roses and surrounded by other symbolic, old-fashioned flowers – white Madonna lilies for purity, red poppies and white dianthus, whilst carrying a basket of roses and with her flock of white doves flying overhead (all made more poignant by knowing of her death a mere three years later). For me, this painting demonstrates the power of an image to illustrate the character of a place far more simply and expressively than several essays, and I would always advocate searching for the definitive picture to guide and inspire a garden's future development and conservation. The garden today carries on Margaret's romantic, old-fashioned, flowery concept under the aegis of another talented lady gardener, Mrs Wrisdale, tenant for the last 30 years.

A page from the Gunby Tree Book, kept by the Massingberd family and containing records of the park and woodland planting dating back to the seventeenth century.
(*Country Life*)

Somehow, historic gardens seem to spring to life when we come to know and understand their creators. The formal garden of parterres, canals and fountains laid out at Dyrham in the first years of the eighteenth century makes so much more sense when we appreciate that William Blathwayt, its creator, lived and worked in Holland, where he had an apartment overlooking the fine Baroque garden at King William III's palace of Het Loo. And it virtually lives and breathes when we find him as Governor of Plantations accepting gifts of plants

William Blathwayt, the builder of Dyrham Park (above). As Secretary of State to King William III, he spent some of his time at the Dutch palace of Het Loo, and would have been familiar with the formal layout of its gardens (right). This provided inspiration when he came to design his own, very elaborate layouts at Dyrham, as can be seen in Johannes Kip's bird's-eye view of 1710 (below). (NT and Paleis Het Loo/ E.Boeijinga)

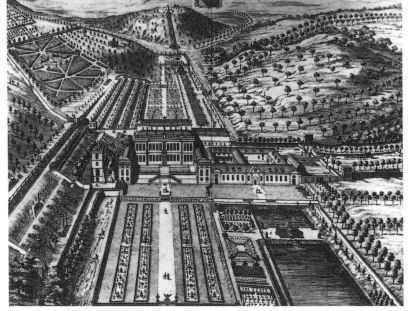

from the colony of Virginia – plants which at that time were unknown in this country, except to the top botanists and the King himself.

By understanding the people, we come closer to understanding the design. At Stowe the vast landscape was laid out according to a complex iconography stemming in part from a pun on the Temple family name (*Templa Quam Dilecta* 'how beautiful are thy temples'). Each ornamental building, inscription and statue, and even the planting, articulated classical and contemporary political themes, forming a sort of intellectual guessing game for eighteenth-century fashionables, steeped in the classics. However, such allusions are, of course, very obscure to most present-day visitors.

Tourist accounts are another valuable source of primary evidence. Since at least the seventeenth, and more especially in the late eighteenth and early nineteenth centuries, country houses were definitely on the visitor route, and tourists dutifully recorded their varied impressions. Celia Fiennes gives breathless accounts of many houses in the 1690s, including Stowe, with its gardens 'one below the other with low breast walls and taress walkes, replenished with all the curiosityes or requisites for ornament pleasure and use'. Stowe's later reincarnation as an informal landscape proved so popular with tourists that an inn was built at the park gate expressly to accommodate them, and in 1744 it became the first garden to have its own published guidebook.

Understanding the handwriting of historical documents, especially phonetic spellings of plants, can take considerable time and effort, while Latin may be required to translate emparkment orders. Earlier sources such as the Domesday Book can help in tracing the previous history of sites. Published sources such as county histories are more accessible, and become especially useful in Victorian times with the rise of the garden journal. John Claudius Loudon's *Gardeners' Magazine* included detailed reports on kitchen gardens, while his *Arboretum et Fruticetum* of 1838 took on the massive task of recording trees across the country.

Maps are of course a great source of historical information. Early types include county maps (John Rocque's of around 1720–40 are very accurate and detailed), estate maps and tithe maps, with their useful schedules of field names. The best are probably the first edition of the 1:2500 Ordnance Survey of *c*.1880, primarily for their accuracy and detail, which go down to individual park trees and make this edition so much more rewarding than the modern revisions. Design plans are always interesting, but require careful interpretation. John Davenport's design plan for Coughton Park enlarges the scale wondrously, and was never implemented (but does, incidentally, show his debt to 'Capability' Brown, for whom he had probably worked previously).

Maps may also illustrate the expansion and contraction of park boundaries through history, according to the vagaries of finance and fashion, in much the same way as the length of women's skirts varied.

Wealthy owners liked to adorn their walls with illustrations of their houses and gardens, and the late seventeenth-century fashion for detailed bird's-eye views provides much information for the garden historian. Johannes Kip's bird's-eye of Dyrham shows the lost formal garden of *c*.1700, where archaeology has since confirmed a statement of 1791 that it was 'drawn with more than his usual fidelity'. Humphry Repton specialised in producing his now famous Red Books, with pretty watercolours showing 'before' and 'after' views. However, caution is required here, as the 'after' scene may never have been realised. Generally speaking, later impressionistic views are less informative, but growing interest in historic gardens at the turn of the nineteenth century led the architects Reginald Blomfield and Inigo Triggs to publish careful records of 'olde-worlde' gardens.

Inigo Triggs's drawings of the garden at Montacute, from *Formal Gardens of England and Scotland*, published in 1902.

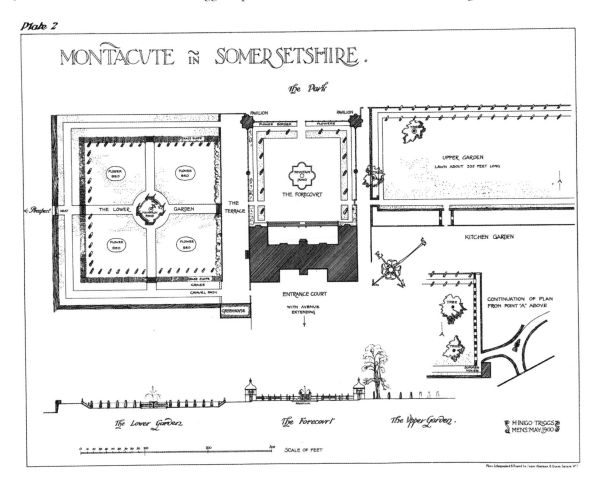

Rooted in History

We know the camera does not lie – but unfortunately early photographs all tend to show the same view of the front of the house (boring!), and almost never the garden (exciting!). This is slightly ironic, given that William Henry Fox Talbot of Lacock Abbey, a keen botanist and gardener, actually invented the ground-breaking calotype process as a means of recording plants. *Country Life* photos, which may date from as early as 1895, are especially useful for gardens (and many more were taken than were ever actually published). Aerial photographs may be useful, especially the complete national coverage undertaken by the RAF in 1949–50.

Surprisingly, more modern gardens often have poor records, perhaps because we tend not to value the recent past. Garden records are in any case particularly vulnerable to loss and decay, with planting books stored in damp workrooms and working plans dirtied and damaged in use or when hung on the back of the potting shed door. Survey work provides a good opportunity to make back-up copies of archives, to catalogue them and arrange for their future protection.

It can be fascinating, and very entertaining, to talk to people about the recent history of a garden or, more rarely, its creation. Was Mr Hicks of Greenway, the Trust's most recently acquired garden in Devon, being entirely serious when he told us his aim had been to maintain the garden 'so that it looks as though it's on the verge of going wild, and has just been saved by the skin of its teeth'? And does he realise quite how much of a conservation challenge that is?

After all, history does not stop at any one defined point. Events such as Dutch elm disease in the 1970s and the storms of 1987 and 1990 all impacted heavily on our gardens and should be recorded as part of their story. And the social history of gardens and parks – of the owners, garden staff and others connected with the place – is almost always intriguing, furnishing especially tangible links with the past.

While bills and such like often tell us what was planted, they very rarely record where, or to what pattern, or how the plantings were subsequently managed. For this type of information we must resort to contemporary gardening treatises, such as London and Wise's *The Retir'd Gardener* of 1706. More recent theme studies may also be helpful. For instance, much is known about 'Capability' Brown and his design tricks, such as 'losing' the end of a lake in dark woodland to make it appear larger. But garden history is still a relatively new subject, with scope for striking discoveries, as was recently demonstrated by Mark Laird in *The Flowering of the English Landscape Garden* when he revealed that English landscape gardens, far from consisting simply of temples, trees, water and turf, as previously thought, also contained flower-packed shrubberies.

Detail of the sunken parterre at
Hanbury Hall. The original layout
was probably designed by George
London, *c.*1700, but was swept
away some 70 years later when this
kind of formality was out of
fashion. The National Trust has
recently restored the planting.
(NTPL/Stephen Robson)

Overall, garden research work requires much painstaking labour, and
the odd imaginative leap. It is always worth trying out any new
theories on knowledgeable fellows in the garden history world. And
at the end of the day, we must accept that we shall never know
everything about the past; there is no such thing as the perfect intact
archive, and that is perhaps a good thing, as it leaves scope for
individual imaginations to play.

Casing the Joint – Recording the Present Garden

Field survey, involving the recording of each element of the present
landscape, should run alongside historical research. The results will
suggest priorities for management and act as a permanent record.
And, as each site is itself essentially a record of its past, they may also
tell us something of the history of the place. Trees, for instance, form a
living record of past planting schemes and management practices (in
the case of graffiti, quite literal records), while stumps remain to mark
the sites of lost trees.

Rooted in History

Mapping by theodolite or its modern equivalent, Electronic Distance Measurement (EDM), can create an incredibly useful base map, on which information on trees, archaeology, features, services, etc. can be built up. Unfortunately it is also expensive, especially for large or dense sites, and so tends to be reserved for the more important properties.

The less tangible aspects of a site – views, design and character – should also be recorded. A visual survey should identify main views and any blocked or lost historical vistas, as well as eyesores. Assessing the character of a place is rather open to individual interpretation, but it can be helpful to note, for instance, whether the present character accords with the past. It is also useful to note how the historical design was effected, how intact it is, and whether it is, or was, successful. All three aspects are likely to be closely interlinked; at Saltram, for instance, the garden has become more inward-looking in recent years because the historical views, designed to overlook the picturesque sailing ships and fortifications of Plymouth, now look onto the modern monstrosities that have sprung up since.

At some point current land-use, visitor use and access routes should be recorded. This is also a convenient moment to note other landscape designations such as conservation areas, tree preservation orders and public footpaths, along with other uses, threats and opportunities, all of which will have implications for future management.

Looking for Clues – Archaeology

Nowadays archaeology is an essential tool in the investigation of the past history of landscapes. It is still something of a new science, and the study of gardens is an even more recent addition to the archaeologist's repertoire. In the Trust the use of archaeology in gardens has really only taken off in the last fifteen years or so, but it is now seen as a vital element of garden conservation and restoration, and many of the Trust's in-house archaeologists are also knowledgeable garden historians.

There are several progressive layers to archaeological survey, with the most well-known technique, excavation, actually something of a last resort. The first step must always be a field survey to identify and record earthworks and standing remains, as well as buildings and other features, so that a Sites and Monuments Record (SMR) can be created. This can reveal much information, and also has the merit of being inexpensive, especially compared with excavation.

At Dyrham the field survey has involved recording the earthwork remains of William Blathwayt's early eighteenth-century formal garden, still clearly discernible despite later re-landscaping. Some early gardens exist only as earthworks – Sir Thomas Tresham's Elizabethan garden at Lyveden New Bield was never finished and was abandoned around 1605. These earthwork gardens can be particularly informative because they were never modernised, and so tell us more about the style of gardens of that period than do surviving examples.

When working in the relatively new and specialised area of garden archaeology, archaeologists may need some 'tuning in' to the features, qualities and design styles. At Croome the very subtle earthworks that characterise 'Capability' Brown's work were highlighted for the Trust by John Phibbs, something of a maverick expert on both Brown and garden field survey. Earthworks here also provide negative information, such as where the presence of ridge and furrow indicates an area not smoothed out by Brown. Such earthworks may show up well in aerial photographs, as may parchmarks, which appear in hot, dry summers and can indicate the location of buried foundations of features now lost.

Volunteers helping with archaeological excavations at the site of the Regency rose arbour at Tatton Park.
(NT)

Parks, because they were rarely ploughed, tend to be rich in all sorts of earthworks, not just ornamental, designed features, but also the fossilised remains of earlier landscapes. For instance, the parks at Wimpole, Gunby and Croft all contain the 'tofts and crofts', holloways, boundary banks and plough headlands of lost medieval villages, all of which need to be recorded and safely preserved.

It is especially important that any features vulnerable to loss or removal, whether intentional or through decay or accident, are fully recorded. These include earthworks, buildings and trees. We know only

Rooted in History

too well how difficult it is to find out more about the odd glasshouse or two that were 'tidied away' in the past.

At each level of survey the archaeologist will assess the present condition of features and make recommendations for their safe future care. Sometimes this creates management quandaries. Many archaeological sites were historically planted with trees, but now the importance of the underlying remains may dictate against replanting. For instance, the well-preserved prehistoric long barrow at Lodge Park was marked in the eighteenth century with a tree clump, but this cannot be restored as the tree roots could cause damage to the underlying fabric.

After field survey, the next level may be a resistivity survey, which plots the differing electrical resistance of buried materials in the ground to locate accurately, and non-destructively, below-ground remains. At Dyrham the resistivity survey produced an incredibly sharp plot, indicating that the foundations of the walls of the formal garden survive just below the present ground surface. Generally, however, results are not this conclusive, and garden remains, such as plants and beds, tend to be elusive and difficult to distinguish.

Excavation, although exciting and newsworthy, should always be regarded as a method of last resort. It results in the destruction of the evidence – once excavated, a site can never be excavated effectively again – and is hugely expensive. The Trust could never hope to match the figure of over £200,000 spent by Historic Royal Palaces on the excavation alone of the entire late seventeenth-century Privy Garden at Hampton Court Palace in 1993. We should be extremely circumspect in our justification of any excavation. With good archive records, for instance, excavation may well prove unrewarding. We must also consider closely how we excavate – much can be achieved with small 'key-hole' excavations, which are cheaper and less destructive. Garden excavation results are in any case notoriously difficult to interpret, with overlays and drains, etc. clouding the evidence. Sometimes very little is revealed; when the site of the early eighteenth-century parterre was excavated at Hanbury Hall, it was found that most of the historic layers had been obliterated by later landscaping. Christopher Taylor, the eminent landscape historian, cautions us in *The Remains of Distant Time* (published in 1996) that excavation is 'an extremely clumsy and crude method of trying to understand the past which should be used with great care'.

Although it may seem tempting simply to dig in the trowel and see what remains beneath, this should be resisted unless absolutely necessary. Parchmarks of the cascade at Dyrham are very clear, implying that substantial remains survive below the ground, but, as the site is not under threat, nor about to be restored, there is little point in excavating.

So for now we will leave it safely alone, and perhaps in the future new technology will allow us to record buried features without disturbing them at all. In the meantime, we need to do more to explain to visitors how earthworks can be read to tell the history of a garden.

Where excavation is appropriate, it can reveal a lot about a site. At Croome Park the excavation of the grotto revealed several stages in its development, relating to changes in the garden design. As excavation techniques have improved, so it has proved possible to identify even flowerbeds by slight changes in soil colour, while analysis of organic material from historic layers may give clues to past planting; for instance, apple seeds were recovered at Hanbury, along with ubiquitous weed seeds. Watching briefs, when groundworks such as drainage are being carried out, are another opportunity to glean information. Occasionally even biological surveys can tell us about the history of a site, generally through the identification of indicator species, such as herb paris, the presence of which suggests a wood has ancient origins. So it is important that we continue to improve the integration of all disciplines in survey work.

Sifting the Evidence – the Report, Analysis and Assessment

Without the technology simply to download the survey results direct from the brain to the computer, they must be laboriously tapped out into a written report. But this is a good discipline in itself, enabling one to mull over and organise things. And as it would be sad for the results of all this hard work to sit gathering dust on shelves, it does help to make the report concise, readable and well illustrated.

The main narrative of each report should tell the story of the landscape, setting out its key periods, styles, features, characters and influences, and interpreting any ambiguous episodes through possible alternative scenarios. The report should analyse the present landscape in terms of its past – what remains, what has been lost – as well as highlighting new discoveries, assessing the archive and setting out future research and survey priorities. Other important components are a gazetteer of areas and features, both extant and lost, and a series of historical maps as overlays at the same scale, if possible. All of this needs to be closely referenced, so that any information can be tracked to its source. And as gardening, and garden conservation by extension, is a creative process, the report, although largely consisting of detailed, factual material, should ideally also aim to inspire.

Finally, the report should evaluate as far as possible the relative significance and the main priorities for the future management of each element, and attempt a definition of the overall significance of the site. It should highlight which areas should, by virtue of their interest, be considered sacrosanct, and note others where more leeway might be permissible. Any recommendations must be realistic and based on sound knowledge of the aims of the Trust – although a few contentious ideas always help to stimulate healthy debate.

Significance will depend on many aspects of the site – the quality of the plants, buildings and archive, links with famous designers or owners, the intactness of each aspect, and the integrity of the whole. It will also depend on the site's context – its rarity, its typicality and its degree of influence, as reflected in its English Heritage Gardens Register grading, as well as its contemporary value for recreation and public access. Sometimes it is difficult to estimate significance simply because the contextual information does not exist. In order to establish the significance of the deer course at Lodge Park, for example, we had first to make a basic stab at researching the history of such courses and at identifying other sites; so little was known about them at that point that we had no guide as to how typical or rare this one was.

Once the report has been handed over, it is worth thinking about publishing new or significant findings, both as a means of enabling critical appraisal of one's work, and of placing the information in the public realm. Publication may also lead to other rewards, perhaps bringing new information to light, or stimulating useful further research and discussion.

Although the Trust has published some articles on the history of individual gardens in the past, survey reports have generally only been made available to serious researchers. We are now conscious that we need to find more and better ways of making the behind-the-scenes stories of these gardens accessible to all, at different levels, so that everyone is enabled to understand and appreciate our gardens in the same way that Trust staff feel privileged to do. This might mean producing more books, articles and CDs, developing the Trust's website further or expanding on-site interpretation and access to archives, or – more likely – a combination of all three.

The following case studies help demonstrate how information is collected and used to guide decision-making.

Case Study 1
Hidcote Manor
Garden Survey

Hidcote was the very first garden to be taken on by the National Trust as a garden in its own right. It was saved in 1948 in the nick of time as its creator, Lawrence Johnston, descended into senility. An impressive campaign was run to raise the necessary finance (as there was no endowment).

Today it is widely recognised that Hidcote, with its series of exquisite garden rooms strung along a strong architectural framework and decorated with an overflowing abundance of choice plants, is the quintessential garden of the twentieth century. Thanks to far-sighted, dedicated staff and committee members, the garden was saved, but perhaps the extreme thinness with which staff were spread at the time accounts for the unfortunate, almost complete loss of the garden archive. Eyewitnesses recount seeing Nancy Lindsay, Johnston's friend and self-appointed guardian of Hidcote (but 'that witch' according to James Lees-Milne, Historic Buildings Secretary), set light to a pile of papers in the courtyard, probably in a fit of pique. Johnston was fairly meticulous, and we can only assume that his papers included garden plans, photographs, plant lists, etc. Sadly, the losses did not stop there; the departure of Johnston's head gardener around 1957 coincided with the disappearance of the garden planting book.

So it was quite a research challenge when I began the task of adding more flesh to the bones of the Hidcote story in 1999. The lack of a body of archives made it potentially a very time-consuming project, with many slender clues to be followed up and many dead-ends to be eliminated. Thankfully, two very dedicated researchers at the sharp end of the garden were able to help. David Owen and Pete Dennis, both long-standing gardeners at Hidcote, had independently begun to trace Johnston's family background in the United States, and to build links with his other garden, Serre de la Madonne, in the south of France.

Working together, we sought to understand Johnston himself. An expatriate American, cultured, artistic and reserved, he had created the garden on the blank canvas of the Gloucestershire countryside presented to him in 1907, when his wealthy, domineering mother purchased the property. He became increasingly enthralled by its possibilities, extending the garden, scouring nurseries for new choice and rare plants, and later even hunting for plants himself in the mountainous regions of the world. One exciting find was Johnston's only known article, describing his 1928 expedition to Mount Kilimanjaro, where he sadly admitted his failure to find many garden-worthy plants.

Another new discovery was a letter from George Forrest, the famous plant-hunter, dating from their 1929 joint expedition to western China and Tibet. The two did not get on. 'Had I raked GB with a small tooth comb', stormed Forrest, 'I couldn't have found a worse companion.'

Lawrence Johnston's book-plate, showing some of his interests. The dachshunds invariably make an appearance in the very few photographs that survive of him.

Later Johnston fell seriously ill and retired, but somehow still managed to bring back choice plants, including *Jasminum polyanthum*, the tender scented climber.

Another find was a set of colour photographs of *c*.1915, produced by the recently invented autochrome process. These show Johnston's keen awareness of colour, and how he aimed right from the start for an aged, soft-edged appearance, using old-fashioned, 'off-the-shelf' topiary shapes to punctuate the formal shapes and confer instant maturity. They also show that he was not content just to look to the past – his planting broke all the rules, promiscuously mixing alpines with shrubs, scattering plants to emulate natural seeding and threading tall plants through to the front of borders to brush the shoulders of passers-by, thereby creating the 'jungly look' for which Hidcote became renowned. Johnston's close friend, Norah Lindsay (Nancy's mother), the plantswoman and garden designer, was probably a great influence on his planting, but we could discover little concrete evidence of her involvement at Hidcote. Even Johnston's great friend, Edith Wharton, the novelist, only noted 'garden radiant' in her diary on her annual visit to Hidcote in 1925.

Although most of the garden had been faithfully conserved by the Trust down the years, particularly the great set pieces – the Red Borders, the Old Garden – a number of features were lost in the early years of Trust ownership, when the garden ran at a loss, and regrettable

A *Country Life* photograph taken in 1930, showing the plant-house built by Johnston to protect tender exotics and which converted to a pergola in summer. The Trust hopes to reinstate this feature in the future. (*Country Life*)

Digging for History

cuts were made. Johnston's large, impressive, but flimsily-built plant-house, shown in *Country Life* photographs of the 1930s, was demolished and his collections of antique pots and tender plants scattered. In other areas labour-intensive alpines were replaced with low maintenance ground-cover. Jack Percival, a former gardener, now aged 83, has helped to detail some of the original plants.

The Hidcote project culminated in a dense 200-page report, essentially a full statement of our knowledge at the time (2000), detailing the development of both Johnston and his garden, and backed up with compendious appendices. This is now complemented by a comprehensive 'copy archive' which will be added to as more material is found; nowadays research does not stop when the ink on the report is dry.

Altogether, the project shed more light on Johnston's dedication to plants and highlighted some later erosion of the plantsmanship element at Hidcote. Happily, the Trust has since taken on the long-term challenge of restoring the garden closer to its 1930s heyday, when the garden was, as Dame Sylvia Crowe put it, 'a gardener's workshop for experiments of many kinds'. As yet, however, nobody seems to have seriously considered bringing back the flamingos and ostriches which once ornamented the wilder parts of the garden!

Case Study 2 Wimpole Parterre

Head Gardener Philip Whaites had always been conscious of the lost formal garden at Wimpole Hall. A series of irregular bumps and ridges made mowing the north lawn tricky, and he dreamed of one day recreating the underlying parterre. Gradually, as he brought the rest of the garden under control, the re-creation of the lost parterre began to seem feasible, and valid as a means of bringing back colour and interest.

Research revealed several stages in the history of the parterre. An engraving by Johannes Kip of 1707 showed a complex design which was swept away later in the century by the landscape designers Robert Greening and 'Capability' Brown. In the early nineteenth century a more modest parterre was recreated, perhaps influenced by the earlier design and by Humphry Repton's unexecuted proposals. This parterre was later simplified and, as with so many other examples, was turfed over early in the twentieth century. However, the lawn was never relaid, so the earthworks remained as a ghostly vision, clearly visible in aerial photoraphs. Such a complicated sequence of layers is far more typical of most British gardens than the single layer of Hidcote and makes for more complicated decision-making as to which layers should be restored or highlighted.

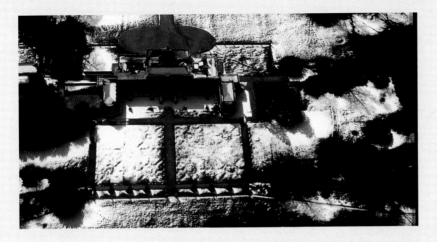

Aerial photograph taken by the Cambridge University Archaeological Survey, showing the garden at Wimpole. The snow has shown up the marks of the early eighteenth-century formal parterre. (University of Cambridge Collection of Air Photos)

In 1992 the Trust decided to investigate the parterre further, with a view towards restoration. An archaeological dig was carried out by the Trust's Archaeologist for East Anglia, Angus Wainwright, with help from Cambridge volunteers. As the garden plan was symmetrical, with fairly minimal excavation they were able to establish from soil profiles the precise location and form of the beds and paths. Armed with this information, a plan was drawn up for the re-creation, with 36 beds in four 'Union Jack' patterns on each of the two symmetrical lawns. A planting scheme was devised, and in 1997 the parterre was finally recut and planted by Phil and his team, with the help of a substantial donation from the National Gardens Scheme.

Today the stunning parterre, resplendent with 12,000 bedding plants (usually geraniums, ageratum and *Verbena venosa*, replanted annually) and two-thirds of a mile of edging and box hedging, forms a fine tribute to the hard work and vision of Phil and his volunteers, with visitors appreciating the bold area of colour which now adds zest to the north front of Wimpole.

The restored parterre, with the long north front of Wimpole Hall. (NTPL/Nick Meers)

5

The Plants

Melissa Simpson

Plant Introductions

The story of how plants were acquired for gardens is a fascinating one, inextricably linked with the history of the development of trade and exploration. But plant introductions are nothing new; the flora of these islands has been enriched by new arrivals since well before recorded history. Imagine a barren wilderness, the tundra, all that survives after the retreat of the massive glaciers of the last Ice Age some 10,000 years ago. The temperature has risen just enough to allow wind-blown seeds from the warmer lands to the south to germinate. Self-sown birches and willows start to clothe the land and to change the shape of the landscape over the centuries that follow. As the first plants take hold, they begin to build up soil and create shelter, so enabling other species to colonise. These natural waves of introduction and succession resulted in the 1,500 or so plants that are now thought to be true natives of this country. Only later was this collection augmented by human activity.

The precise history of man's earliest plant introductions is unclear, but the migrating peoples who first populated Britain from continental Europe quite probably brought their familiar and useful plants with them. We know rather more about the plants carried to these shores by the Romans, who brought not only their well-loved pot herbs, such as fennel and dill, but also fruit-bearing trees such as sweet chestnut and walnut. The garden weed, ground-elder, was probably a Roman introduction which has long outstayed its welcome, although many of their other introductions probably died out soon after the collapse of the empire. Some of their plants are grown today in a small Roman-style garden at Chedworth Roman Villa.

The auricula theatre at Calke Abbey. The Huguenots were responsible for the introduction of auriculas into England during the sixteenth and seventeenth centuries. The plants were highly prized, and considered worthy of display in purpose-built structures, designed to provide shelter from sun and showers.
(NTPL/Stephen Robson)

Through the long Dark Ages, the vital skills of growing and using medicinal plants were harboured by the religious orders, with cloister gardens for their cherished herbs. This knowledge survived, to be passed on in the form of the first texts and books on plants in medieval times, and inspired the publication of the first herbals in succeeding centuries. One such is Henry Lyte's *A Niewe Herball* of 1578, largely a translation of Dodoen's *Herball*, with his own annotations, including a note of *Hyacinthoides nonscripta* (bluebell) which grew well 'not far from my poore house at Lytescarie', now a National Trust property.

By the sixteenth century England's increased prosperity and influence fuelled a growing thirst for overseas exploration. This took Britons increasingly further from their native shores, on often perilous expeditions to Africa, the East, and ultimately to the New World. They brought yet more – and increasingly exotic – species of plants back to Britain, although the discovery of such plants was rarely the primary motive for an expedition. More often, they were gathered as a peripheral or coincidental activity and so must rank as 'fortunate' introductions. For example, the potato first came to notice in Britain in Sir Walter Raleigh's account of Virginia.

The growing interest in the fauna and flora of these new-found lands was based, at least in part, on their potential use and commercial value. This economic interest led to increasing numbers of 'scientists' being

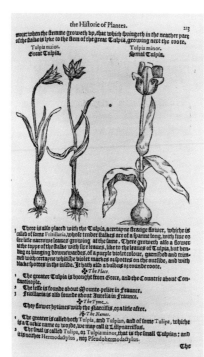
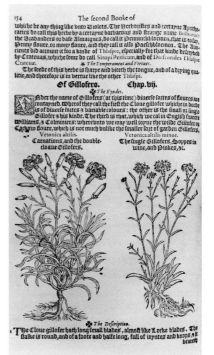

Henry Lyte's *A Niewe Herball* includes details of plants that grew near his home at Lytes Cary Manor, now in the care of the Trust.
(British Library)

Rooted in History

This recreated seventeenth-century border at Ham House shows how relatively plain flower gardens were at that time. Only with later, more exotic, introductions did it become possible to create the colourful displays with which we are now familiar.
(NT)

included on overseas voyages, their task being to collect and attempt to catalogue the huge variety of living material they encountered. Foremost among these early naturalists and botanists were John Tradescant and his son, also John, who travelled extensively in the Mediterranean and later to Virginia, collecting plants, becoming royal gardeners and establishing England's first physic garden at Lambeth in London. The Tradescants are credited with the introduction to Britain of the lilac, acacia and occidental plane, as well as influencing many other aspects of horticulture.

The early introductions by the Tradescants and others were also greatly valued by gardeners. Until now British gardens had of necessity been rather muted places, relying on the largely deciduous, small-flowered palette of native plants, with their relatively short season of interest. The enthusiasm lay in discovering new evergreens, bigger and brighter flowers, and 'curiously striped' leaves, to add to the potential of gardens. The Trust's examples of early gardens – Westbury Court, Little Moreton Hall, Ham House and Moseley Old Hall – demonstrate the limitations of the native flora, and show how plants which we now regard as commonplace, tulips, double daffodils, etc., would have been a showy revelation to early gardeners.

The polite arts, including gardening, were interrupted by the upheaval of the Civil War, but foreign influences were apparent during the Commonwealth, and especially at the Restoration, bringing a wealth of plants. At Claydon Sir Ralph Verney imported vines and fig trees on his return from exile in France in 1653, as well as 'Persian tulips' from Holland.

The Plants

The invention of the Wardian case revolutionised plant hunting. For the first time, it was possible to create and maintain the micro-climate under which a plant had at least a chance of surviving transportation home.

As British colonies became established in the New World, so the trickle of plants became a flood. Thanks to his post as Auditor General for the Colonies, William Blathwayt of Dyrham was one of the first to acquire the latest plant introductions. In 1695 he received a consignment of plant material from Virginia, including seed of *Magnolia virginiana*, yucca and persimmon. Unfortunately, we do not know how many of the plants were actually grown, but the improved cultivation facilities, which included his splendid new-fangled orangery for the tenderer plants, must have helped.

By 1801 Arthur Young could note that Croome's 'pleasure grounds … are embellished with … a profusion of the choicest productions from the East and West Indies, from the Cape, and from Botany and … with other kings of trees from America and other parts of the world'. His account is corroborated by the archives, which record 'papers' of seed arriving from Maryland, Carolina, Florida, Canada, Jamaica and even the Falkland Islands. A letter from the nurseryman, John Bush, in 1771 demonstrates the perilous nature of plant-hunting. Newly arrived in St Petersburg, where he had been well received by the Empress, he had already sent off one box of plants, but there would be no more collecting until the spring as 'it is dangerous in these woods to collect plants, there being large wolves and bears'.

Plant-hunting was always a dangerous occupation, but Nathaniel Ward's invention of the Wardian case in 1833 at least raised the odds of the plants surviving the long, salt-ridden sea journey home. One of the first golden larches (*Pseudolarix amabilis*) was brought back from China by Robert Fortune in this way, to be planted in the area of garden known as 'China' at Biddulph Grange, where it still survives. Gradually, plant-hunting became a specialist career, requiring an encyclopaedic knowledge of plants and a detailed knowledge of a particular geograph-ical area, as well as courage and endurance. The great plant-hunters of the nineteenth and twentieth centuries – Robert Fortune, David Douglas, Ernest Wilson, Frank Kingdon-Ward and George Forrest – were generally attached to individual botanic gardens and were sponsored by wealthy clients with particular requirements. The search was on, for example, for ever hardier rhododendrons, to be found high in the unexplored wildernesses of China. Ernest Wilson was attached first to Veitch's nurseries in London, and later to the Arnold Arboretum in Massachusetts. Henry Morris Upcher of Sheringham was one sponsor of Wilson's 1920s expeditions to the Himalayan foothills, receiving in return seed of at least twelve species of rhododendron.

Unfortunately, there was one unwelcome side-effect, in that certain of the new introductions, including *Rhododendron ponticum* and Japanese knotweed, responded rather too well to the equable British climate, eventually escaping from gardens and becoming notorious weeds of the wider environment. *Ponticum* is now a particular pest at Sheringham, and subject to intensive, and expensive, clearance campaigns, both here and elsewhere.

Meanwhile, back at home, dedicated plantsmen continued to increase the diversity and number of plants by hybridising the newly arrived plants, producing new cultivars with improved qualities, such as larger flowers and a longer season of interest. At Nymans, Leonard Messel's plant collection included the latest new material from the expeditions of Wilson, Forrest and Kingdon-Ward, as well of those of Harold, the son of his Head Gardener, James Comber. Messel's experiments and trial gardens resulted in important new hybrids, including the magnificent *Eucryphia x nymansensis* 'Nymansay', with its exceptionally abundant trusses of large white flowers which now grace many gardens.

Plant-collecting expeditions continue today, but with rather different intentions, and subject to very stringent controls. The objective now is not to plunder the world's natural habitats of their most beautiful and intriguing plants, but to help ensure that the wealth of plant diversity survives, through projects such as the Millennium Seed Bank established by Kew at Wakehurst Place. Material from more recent plant-hunting expeditions also continues to enrich gardens; material from Keith Rushforth's 1994 expedition to Bhutan has found a home from home in the steamy valley garden at Glendurgan.

Today, of an estimated 380,000 known plant species in the world, perhaps some two-thirds can be grown in Britain's temperate climate. It is impossible to estimate how many cultivars exist globally, but the number must run into millions – for instance, with 1,200 known species of rhododendron, some 50,000 cultivars have been produced.

This, then, is the vast palette from which the gardens of the National Trust are stocked. The collection of gardens covers almost every type of natural British climate, from the warm, wet west of Northern Ireland to the wild coasts of Northumberland, as well as including artificial microclimates in the form of glasshouses. The variety of plants is correspondingly wide, ranging from British natives to temperate zone spermatophytes (ferns), woody trees and shrubs, many thousands of herbaceous plants, bulbs, annuals, biennials and perennials through to tender exotics from the tropics. The total number of different species and cultivars currently grown in Trust gardens is thought to be around 2 million, in perhaps some 120,000 different taxa. As a conservation organisation, the Trust has a responsibility to ensure the continued survival and integrity of the plant collections within its gardens. To do this, we need first to record, and secondly to assess the significance of each collection.

Trust gardens have a long pedigree of involvement in plant collecting and horticultural experimentation. At Nymans the results of this process include the dramatic *Eucryphia x nymansensis* 'Nymansay'. (NT)

Plant Recording

The tagging of plants, as here at Sheffield Park, is an integral part of work on the Woody Plant Catalogue, which is updated annually.
(NT)

The Trust's main concern has been to establish exactly what we have in our care; a daunting prospect, given the sheer scale and diversity of the collection. The process started in a limited way in 1976 when Michael Zander, an American botanist, recorded conifers only in 52 National Trust gardens, with considerable help and co-operation from the Royal Botanic Gardens, Kew.

Following on from this initial survey, the decision was taken to begin to make complete records of plants in selected gardens, starting with Nymans. In 1980 Michael Lear took over responsibility for what was then known as the Woody Plant Catalogue, or WPC. By 1984 the WPC covered eighteen of the most important tree and shrub collections within the National Trust, with some 25,000 plants tagged and recorded and their details entered on a computer system, again with help from Kew. A report on each garden outlined the history of the plant collection and its main strengths, and set out a policy for its continuing development. The records for each garden were updated annually, and an additional garden was added to the system each year. At first sketch maps were used to show the location of plants within gardens, but gradually teams employed through the Manpower Services Commission were able to create proper, accurately surveyed plans of each garden.

The records included notes on each plant, including its species and cultivar, if known, its size, and perhaps also shape, as well as anything known about its past history, including provenance, ie the nursery from which it was purchased, or occasionally even the plant-hunting expedition during which the seed was gathered. Bills, planting diaries, even labels, can all help to trace the history of individual plants, although the many changes of names can make establishing this pedigree very time-consuming.

The felling of dead or damaged trees provides an opportunity to count the trunk rings and establish the precise age of each specimen.
(NT)

When the great storm struck in October 1987, and vast numbers of trees were destroyed, including many rare, unusual and champion trees, the system was really put to the test. Using the WPC data, an emergency propagation list was drawn up, and skilled propagators were sent out to collect cutting material from the rarest fallen, but still just alive, trees. Despite the unsuitable time of year, about 95 per cent of the material took, to our delight, and we were able to send replacement stock back to the gardens. The system had proved itself with flying colours. A second campaign followed the 1990 storm. In a similar vein, in 1992 an overall priority propagation list was drawn up from the WPC data, highlighting the rarest and most notable plants across the Trust. And in 1994 plant recording within the Trust was given proper long-term backing, with the creation of the new permanent post of Horticultural Taxonomist.

Rooted in History

The Woody Plant Catalogue

WPC gardens	Year first surveyed	No. of plants listed 1994
Biddulph Grange	1989	636
Bodnant	1978–80	2,879
Coleton Fishacre	1986	1,105
Cotehele	1984	584
Cragside	1988	139
Emmetts	1988	457
Glendurgan	1984	616
Killerton	1978–80	937
Knightshayes Court	1978–80	1,385
Lanhydrock	1984	1,048
Mount Stewart	1984	3 675
Nymans	1978	1,757
Osterley Park	1990	385
Penrhyn Castle	1984	408
Plas Newydd	1984	605
Powis Castle	1984	1,099
Rowallane	1984	2,360
Sheffield Park	1984	1,421
Stourhead	1984	866
Tatton Park	1984	977
Trelissick	1984	717
Trengwainton	1984	1,365
Winkworth Arboretum	1984	1,345
Total		26,766

Since 1994 the recording system has been broadened, working towards the aim of eventually recording the main plants in all of our gardens, that is, herbaceous plants as well as woodies. At the same time, a new database has been established within the Trust to hold the many thousands of records, including those previously held by Kew. Another major development has been the transfer of most of the garden plans onto a digital mapping system, making updating and archiving far easier. Further technological developments should continue to aid the standardisation of the system, as well as making the data more accessible to others.

Gardeners have always been encouraged to keep planting books for their garden, with the information then being picked up during the annual updating of the Woody Plant Catalogue. A basic six-field recording standard for the layout of the planting books helps to ensure consistency of data and easy transfer to the database (the fields are accession number, plant name, location, source, date of planting and reason for planting). But nowadays more and more of our gardeners are taking on direct responsibility for the whole plant recording system for their garden, inputting new records and updating directly onto a computer themselves. Although this constitutes yet another drain on precious gardening time, it does make a lot of sense – the records are accessible to, and answerable to, those with most need for them. In many cases, trainee gardeners or volunteers are able to take on responsibility for plant recording, as part of their learning process.

A second stage in the process of recording is to ensure the correct identification or 'verification' of any individually significant plants. Without verification the scientific and historical significance of a collection is limited. Verification is carried out through reference to a range of supporting material, including written descriptions, botanical illustrations and herbarium specimens. Here the Trust's small, but growing, library of key reference publications is very useful, while access to a herbarium is becoming increasingly important. Herbarium specimens, ie preserved specimens of the actual plant, are an essential reference tool, but unfortunately most British herbaria concentrate on wild plant species, and only two hold collections of cultivated plants: the Ulster Museum in Belfast collects material from some Trust gardens, and the Royal Horticultural Society at Wisley in Surrey collects new cultivars and plants from trials both there and elsewhere, including Trust gardens. Specialists in particular types of plants may also advise on identification and verification. A rhododendron expert helping with identification at Emmetts in 1998 was completely overwhelmed when he discovered by chance a cultivar of Ghent azalea thought to have been lost to cultivation!

Other ongoing work includes commissioning more detailed surveys of gardens, usually at a scale of 500:1, but on a smaller scale for more intricate areas such as borders. These plans, besides acting as records, can help us understand the significance of collections by showing the different layers of planting, or the location of older plants in relation to new ones or to lost or dead plants.

Increasingly it is seen to be important to carry out detailed plant survey work as soon as a new property is acquired, before it has been changed by the Trust, either intentionally or inadvertently. This is also the time to establish what is at risk and arrest any potential loss. When

Ongoing survey work can throw up all sorts of exciting discoveries. This Ghent azalea cultivar, believed extinct, was found quite by chance during a survey at Emmetts. (NT)

Croome Park was acquired in 1995 a small but significant proportion of the once magnificent plant collection survived. Here it was possible to strip away the more recent layers like old wallpaper, first the scrub layer that had invaded during the years of neglect, and then the two overlays of forestry planting, to leave just the mature, original fabric, which was to be the subject of careful recording.

The Trust's gardens database now contains some 2 million records. Although this represents a huge achievement, we still have a long way to go, having covered perhaps as little as 5 per cent of our overall holding, although with very good coverage for some individual properties.

Assessment

The importance of plant collections can be assessed under three main headings; aesthetic value, historic value and scientific value, although all three need to be considered in an integrated approach.

The plants in the Trust's care quite obviously contribute greatly to the beauty of the gardens in which they grow. For hundreds of years people have been collecting, breeding and selecting the most attractive forms, and the vagaries of changing fashions are reflected in the Trust's gardens. Our gardens may act as a refuge for currently unfashionable types of plants, such as the gaudy, labour-intensive and short-lived displays of dahlias in the Dahlia Walk at Biddulph Grange.

The scientific value of our collections has, perhaps, traditionally played second fiddle to aesthetic and historical concerns. Yet it is becoming of increasing importance as we become more aware of the impacts of climate change and environmental degradation. Many of the plants in our gardens were originally collected from the wild, and as their natural habitats have become seriously degraded or threatened, the cultivated plants are becoming increasingly valued for their potentially unique genetic material, in much the same way as some zoos are valued for their contribution towards the survival of endangered species of mammal or bird. In future, plant material from Trust gardens could be used to help repopulate the wild or to ensure the continued survival of a species which otherwise would be lost forever.

Evaluating the importance of a collection is necessarily subjective, and we have been trialling the use of the Radcliffe Criteria to give a structured framework to the assessment. The system involves measuring each item or collection against a range of criteria. It was originally developed for natural habitats, in particular woodland, but, with a few changes, can be applied equally well to cultivated plants. The criteria include fragility (eg susceptibility to factors such as disease); rarity (measured against various published lists, commercial availability, etc.); quantity (one snow-drop is not as valuable as a whole drift!); diversity; potential economic value; importance of position (eg prominence, context); typicality; recorded history (the more comprehensive a plant's recorded history, the greater its significance, much as antiques with proven provenance are more valuable); originality; and finally, intrinsic appeal (although that is, of course, highly subjective). Following this method it is even possible to rate different collections against each other.

Each garden is individual, and only by objectively assessing and under-standing its plants are we able to keep alive that individual character through the next step of devising planting policies to feed into the conservation plan. The planting policy should include an individual propagation list, as well as a desiderata list of 'wants' for the garden, to guide future planting. At Hidcote, for instance, the plant survey high-lighted the plantsmanship of Lawrence Johnston, and the conservation plan recommended propagating plants that are particularly associated with Johnston, such as *Camellia pittardii*, which he introduced.

Propagation

The lime nursery at Dunham Massey supplies clones propagated from eighteenth-century specimens of *Tilia x europaea* for the replanting of avenues at Trust gardens and parks across the country, including here at Cliveden.
(NT)

Generally, the Trust's responsibility is to replace, like for like, individual plants that have been or might be lost in gardens, whether through old age or other factors. This may seem straightforward enough, given the excellent nursery trade in Britain and the existence of the Royal Horticultural Society's *Plantfinder*, which lists the current suppliers of over 70,000 plants. However, this huge number of commercially

Extensive work is continuing into the propagation of cedars of Lebanon, using grafted material from existing specimens in Trust gardens.
(NTPL/Stephen Robson).

available plants comprises only the fashionable or new ones, and sourcing out-of-fashion plants can be difficult. For these reasons, the Trust established its own specialist nursery facility at Knightshaycs Court to propagate rare and unfashionable plants (see case study on pp. 98–9). In addition, a special lime nursery was set up at Dunham Massey in 1994. Many of our splendid formal eighteenth-century lime avenues are now coming to the end of their life, and tend to be made up of historical clones with very distinctive shapes. As these are not available commercially, the nursery has 'stool beds' which provide replacement stock to be grown on before being sent out for planting.

Another species valued for its shape is the magnificent cedar of Lebanon, which graces many Trust gardens. However, more recently planted cedars do not seem to attain the same monumental scale and sculptural shape as their forebears. The original seed probably came from high altitude wild stands of cedars, but these have all now been destroyed or are inaccessible. In an attempt to replicate the original stately form, the Trust has embarked on a project with Reading University, which will involve collecting and propagating vegetatively from our best specimens of cedar.

In some cases the historical types of plants have been completely lost. In the tulipomania of the seventeenth century, prized streaked tulips were grown by fanatical collectors, with individual bulbs changing hands for immense sums of money. However, the streaking was caused by a virus, and so the varieties were inherently unstable. Today all the old varieties have completely died out, and in order to recreate a historical garden like Westbury Court, we must make recourse to the nearest in looks, and the few older types available.

At other properties a different ethos applies. At a place like Nymans, where the garden's creators were constantly trialling new plants, we seek to preserve the spirit of that tradition, rather than any one set of 'original' plants. Here we rely on dedicated nurserymen, botanical gardens and independent plant specialists to supply us with the latest new and unusual plants, and on our Knightshayes nursery to search out and propagate them.

Types of Plant Collection

The Trust's plant collections cover a huge range of different types. Collections of certain types of plant have been built up in gardens where they are deemed appropriate; for instance, Graham Stuart Thomas's important collection of old roses was found a permanent home in the redesigned kitchen garden at Mottisfont Abbey. This collection is also a registered NCCPG collection, ie it is recognised by the National Council for the Conservation of Plants and Gardens, and

National Trust gardens contain many examples of champion trees. This huge holm oak at Westbury Court was probably planted *c.*1600, making it one of the oldest in the country. (NTPL/Christopher Gallagher)

Rooted in History

conforms to their standards. Currently there are some 33 NCCPG collections in Trust gardens, including hemerocallis at Antony and large-flowered *Scabiosa caucasica* at Hardwick Hall. Similar, but different again, is the collection of Herefordshire varieties of apple planted in association with the local NCCPG group in the old kitchen garden at Berrington Hall, where displays and tastings are held each Apple Day in October.

Another collection, and a different link with another organisation, occurs at Calke Abbey, where historic vegetables are grown in the kitchen garden in association with the Henry Doubleday Research Association (HDRA) Heritage Vegetable Scheme, and visitors are encouraged to buy and taste the old varieties. Trust gardens also include collections of champion trees, which are the UK's tallest or fattest specimens. An immense oak discovered during survey work in a quarry at Croft Castle is probably the largest in the country, while a better known example is the venerable holm oak in the garden at Westbury Court. The 'collections' of ancient, generally native, trees in several parks are greatly valued as a wildlife habitat, supporting rare deadwood invertebrates and unusual lichens, as well as the more usual birdlife and animal life (see Chapter Seven).

There are also collections of plants associated with different individuals. Biddulph has a fine collection of plants collected by Robert Fortune, the plant-hunter, while Barrington Court is home to a collection of 1920s irises, of the types recommended by Gertrude Jekyll for the Rose and Iris Garden she designed (see p.20). At Hidcote, the plant collection revolves around Lawrence Johnston, who collected and trialled many plants, introducing many excellent garden plants such as lavender 'Hidcote', while rose 'Lawrence Johnston' was named after him. Winkworth Arboretum houses a collection of trees with good autumn colour, while Knightshayes specialises in spring plants. Several gardens have collections connected with particular geographical areas, such as Glendurgan's link with Bhutan.

Each garden has such a different personality, so many stories to tell. Every time I venture into a Trust garden I am on a journey of discovery, filled with excitement at the possibility of finding a 'lost' plant, a new cultivar or a potential champion. I can be struck with awe at being able to touch one of my hero Frank Kingdon-Ward's original introductions, or even tasting the nectar of one of his rhododendrons in an attempt to identify it. Conveying this deep sense of excitement and interest to our visitors is a future challenge for the Trust.

Case Study
Plant
Conservation
Programme,
Knightshayes
Court

The Plant Conservation Programme (PCP) at Knightshayes was established during the mid-1980s by Head Gardener Michael Hickson and the then Chief Gardens Adviser, John Sales. Given the range and importance of the National Trust's plant collection as a whole, it was recognised that the different gardens would require plants that were particular to individual sites, or at times no longer fashionable and thus not available within an ever-diminishing nursery industry. The then modern propagating facilities at Knightshayes included greenhouses, tunnels and a frame-yard, and so were able to accept seed from plant expeditions as well as surplus plants from botanical gardens and horticultural organisations from around the world.

The propagation department at Knightshayes was soon to prove its worth when, in October 1987, the first of the two great storms in three years wreaked havoc across the southern and south-eastern counties of England, destroying many trees and gardens with hurricane force winds. Helped by British Rail, which waived delivery charges, propagation material was sent in rapid succession over many a night from the various devastated gardens to Knightshayes. With the expert help of Peter Catt, an experienced propagator and nurseryman who volunteered to help during the crisis, careful records were kept of the many unique plants received from the affected gardens. This joint enterprise saved 77 per cent of the plants felled in that storm, of which at least one plant of each type has been returned to its original garden. Surplus plants are distributed to other gardens for future conservation of these important genetic lines. Similar conservation work was undertaken after the second storm in 1990, when the gardens of south-western Britain were likewise ravaged.

In the past ten years, the role of the programme has developed to encompass propagation of additional plant materials: wild source stock from plant-hunting expeditions; unusual and exceptional forms; endangered and threatened species; champion trees – the tallest, stoutest, etc.; groups of plants to maintain genetic diversity within gardens; and historically significant plants related to a person or property.

The PCP has recently rescued and propagated a large collection of old juglans (walnut) cultivars from a private orchard in Worcestershire. These now form part of the National Collection of juglans being held at Wimpole Hall. A collection of unnamed perry pears, discovered in the park at Dyrham and thought to be original seventeenth-century plantings, have been budded and are now growing well on two different understocks. The original varieties are unknown, so by experimenting with these understocks, and then waiting for fruit to develop, it is hoped to determine their identity. The imposing cedar of Lebanon (*Cedrus libani*) has for the past 200 years proved to be an eye-catcher in many a great garden and park. As it is now down to just twelve remaining stands in its native habitat in the Middle East, it has become impossible to obtain dependable seeds from which to grow the true Lebanon cedar. Through grafting, PCP staff are currently propagating material from known provenance stock within the National Trust's estates with a view to replacing specimens that will inevitably be lost through age.

Knightshayes has probably the largest Turkey oak (*Quercus cerris*) in England, measuring some 7.3m (24ft) in girth, and with a spread of 41m (135ft). Seedlings from this giant specimen tree are also being grown so that they to can be used in other Trust parkland planting schemes where large trees are required in the next millennium.

Approximately 2,500 containerised plants are held for the PCP at any one time at Knightshayes, and over the last five years some 10,000 plants have been sent to other Trust gardens, with their respective 'pedigree passports'. These passports contain all the relevant information on each specimen; if the plant is from a natural source, such details ideally include the collector's name and the date harvested. Data such as longitude, latitude, altitude, aspect soil types, tree and other plant association in the wild are all helpful to the gardener when it is time to set out the plant in their garden.

Knightshayes has good relationships with botanic gardens both in Britain and in temperate zones throughout the world. In particular the staff work closely alongside the Royal Botanic Gardens of Kew and Edinburgh, not only to develop the skills of plant conservation but also to exchange ideas in growing methods. The use of environmentally green composts that do not require the additives of peat or coir are being tried and tested on a variety of plants. To help reduce the amount of plastic sent to landfill sites, the PCP is conducting trials with pots that are either made of papier mâché or of other semi-permanent materials that are also biodegradable. Interestingly, those pots made from grass bonded with pine resins appear to be the most successful to date. By planting this type of pot directly into the soil, it helps add more fibrous matter, reduces the workload and also benefits the plant by avoiding root disturbance.

The present propagator at Knightshayes, Christopher Trimmer, attends the Propagators' Forum, which meets twice a year to formulate and debate new growing methods and ideas. Members of this forum come from botanical, commercial and conservation sectors of the horticultural industry. One of the areas being developed is a greater understanding of mycorrhizal activity in the soil and its interactivity with plant root growth, thus making possible a reduction in the use of fertilisers and soil sterilisation.

Michael Hickson at the potting bench at Knightshayes. The Plant Conservation Programme plays a central role in the conservation and development of the Trust's horticultural resource. (NTPL/Stephen Robson).

6

Temples in Trust: the Garden Buildings of the National Trust

Tim Knox

From the landscape garden at Stowe, which boasts over thirty ornamental temples, to the prosaic concrete shed in the pocket handkerchief
of turf behind No. 20 Forthlin Road in Liverpool, the gardens of the
National Trust contain an astonishing array of garden buildings, together
with other features, both useful and ornamental, such as statues, vases,
paving and ironwork. Diverse though this assemblage is, the National
Trust has never set out to form a representative collection of garden
features. Many of our most interesting garden buildings were acquired
by accident, as adjuncts to country houses acquired for their great art
treasures, or with estates accepted because of their natural beauty. It is
all the more remarkable, therefore, that – if more by chance than design
– the Trust now preserves an unparalleled succession of historic garden
structures, with remarkably few periods, styles and building types
unrepresented.

The earliest strictly ornamental garden buildings cared for by the
National Trust date from the Tudor era and take the form of belvederes
or viewing pavilions. The octagonal gabled Pavilion in the garden at
Melford Hall is such a vantage point, but it was probably built as much
for security as for pleasure, for it commands a strategic view over the
main road to Bury St Edmunds. At Lacock Abbey the belvedere takes
the form of a three-storey tower attached to the house. Built by Sir
William Sharington in about 1550, the tower contains two vaulted
octagonal banqueting rooms, one above the other, each equipped with
a grotesquely carved stone table. As well as being used for viewing the

The Temple and Parlour of Venus at
West Wycombe, built by Sir Francis
Dashwood, 2nd Baronet, in 1748,
and reconstructed by his descendant,
the 11th Baronet, in 1982.
(NTPL/Vera Collingwood)

The Octagon Pavilion in the garden at Melford Hall, built in the 1570s by Sir William Cordell as a look-out tower and banqueting house.
(NTPL/Rupert Truman)

formal gardens that surrounded the house and for the enjoyment of cool breezes in the summer, the banqueting rooms were used for a specific purpose; guests repaired here after dinner to partake of a dessert of sweetmeats, fruit and wine. There is another roof-top banqueting house at Hardwick Hall, built in the 1590s by Bess of Hardwick, Countess of Shrewsbury. Indeed, there were once four such banqueting rooms at Hardwick, two in the garden, one in a ground-floor loggia and one on the leads of the house. In the 1580s, at Lyme Park,

Rooted in History

pavilions for banqueting and watching the hunt were built far from the house, out in the extensive deer park. One of them still survives and contains the remains of an elaborate plaster overmantel – suggesting it was once a place of some comfort and sophistication.

Perhaps the most ambitious garden layout of the period owned by the Trust is at Montacute. Here, in the 1590s, Sir Edward Phelips encompassed his house with series of courts and gardens. Before the east front lay 'a large Tarris walke paved with Freestone and Rayles and Ballasters with very large high Pillers of Freestone and Piramids betweene, all of Freestone', at the end of which stood a 'faire Banqueting house'. The banqueting house has gone, but the terraces, garnished with balustrades bearing obelisks and circular *tempietti*, still survive, together with a pair of domed 'lodging Chambers'. A columned loggia or arcade was another characteristic feature of English Renaissance gardens – one at Knole was decorated within with elaborate illusionistic paintings – but many of the structures in Elizabethan and Jacobean gardens were ephemeral; mazes or parterres of cut yew or box, pergolas of brightly painted wood, or tunnels of trained hornbeam. Of these nothing survives, but at Lyveden New Bield there are the remains of an extensive water garden of the late 1590s (see p.2). Described by its creator, Sir Thomas Tresham, as 'my moated orchard', it comprises a system of canals overlooked by no fewer than four mounts – two pyramidal and two spiral – which were doubtless once surmounted by ornamental seats and summer houses. Gardens of the

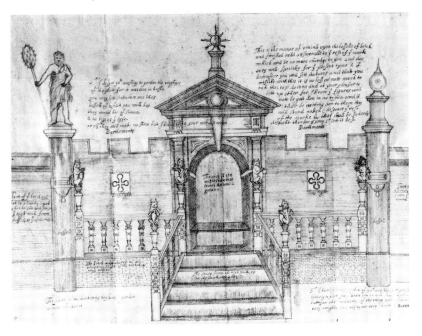

Robert Lyminge's design for a banqueting house for the garden at Blicking Hall, *c.*1620. It takes the form of a toy fort, with castellations and arrow slits, defended by a balustrade garrisoned with heraldic beasts.
(NT)

period frequently embodied the highly allusive imagery popular at the time, and those at Lyveden may have continued the elaborate crypto-Catholic programme found in the architecture of the house – itself intended as a 'garden lodge' to Tresham's principal seat at Rushton.

The sophisticated culture of the court of Charles I is evoked by the summer house at The Vyne, built in about 1635. It is a complex domed structure, circular in plan with four full-height protruding porticoes, like some Renaissance centrally-planned church – suggesting the influence of Inigo Jones through his pupil John Webb. Built of red brick, it was originally rendered, and was one of a pair of such structures that perhaps once flanked a terrace or bowling green. Another rare survival is Lodge Park, an expensive stone grandstand erected by John Dutton of Sherborne Park in 1634, and which combines advanced classical ideas with old-fashioned Jacobean motifs. Banquets and other entertainments were held in the Great Room on the first floor while spectators crowded on the balcony and roof to watch deer pursued by dogs along the mile-long ride or course which lies before it (see pp.62 and 64). Much mutilated and converted into a private house, Lodge Park has recently been restored to its original form and is now open to the public.

The most complete seventeenth-century garden layout owned by the National Trust is that at Ham House, near Richmond, where, between 1672 and 1675, the Duke and Duchess of Lauderdale recast the gardens according to the newly fashionable Dutch taste. The present planting and layout is a re-creation, restored by the Victoria and Albert Museum and the National Trust since 1975 to accord as closely as possible with the surviving documentary and physical evidence. But the bones of the Lauderdales' garden – the lofty brick walls which surround it, pierced with iron grilles, or *clairvoyées,* giving views out into the surrounding country – are largely original. In recent years efforts have been made to return to the gardens, in the form of replicas, some of the statues, seats and pedestals, with which it was originally decorated.

The desire to survey landscape from a height was a popular preoccupation of the era – as is attested by the contemporary bird's-eye views of gardens and parks engraved by Kip, or painted by Siberechts, Knyff or Harris. The dramatic series of terraces below Powis Castle were laid out by the architect and military engineer William Winde in the late 1690s, assisted by the Frenchman, Adrian Duval. The terraces were decorated with lead vases and statuary, some of which still survive, and an orangery and aviaries were housed behind arcades on the different levels. At the foot of the terraces were extensive water gardens, with fountains and more statuary. The great lead group depicting Fame borne aloft by the winged horse Pegasus, now in the Castle forecourt, originally formed the centrepiece of a fountain in this Baroque water

Borne Aloft by Pegasus, by ˌdries Carpentière, *c.*1705, now iɪ the forecourt of Powis Castle. (NTPL/Andrew Butler)

Rooted in History

garden. At Dunham Massey, which lacked the dramatic topography of Powis, a steep motte, said to be the remains of an ancient castle, was pressed into service as a spectacular mount, encircled by rings of clipped hedges and surmounted by a gazebo. The mount survives, though reduced in size and shorn of these embellishments. The deep vale in which Dyrham Park lies proved to be both an advantage and a hindrance to William Blathwayt when he came to lay an elaborate Dutch-style garden out around his newly rebuilt house between 1692 and 1704, advised by the Royal Gardener, George London. While the natural contours and abundant water supply favoured the construction of a grand cascade of 224 steps, crowned by a water-jet 20 feet high – 'the finest in England except the Duke of Devonshire's' – the earth-moving that was required to make the associated terraces and walks on the steep hillsides caused Blathwayt to exclaim in a letter of 1698, 'when will this levelling be at an end?'. The cascade at Dyrham was directly on axis with the orangery, a monumental classical structure designed by William Talman in 1701. Here 'all manner of fine Greens, as Oranges, Lemons, Mirtles &c. set in the most beautiful order' were wintered, the potted trees being brought outside to decorate the walks and parterres in good weather. Blathwayt's orangery was additionally 'hung round with the most entertaining Maps, Sculptures &c. And fur-nish'd with fine Chairs of Cane for the Summer'.

Apart from a lonely figure of Neptune, which still surveys their site, the cascade and most of the formal gardens at Dyrham were swept away by the late eighteenth century, but the lost formal gardens of Hanbury Hall, laid out by George London from c.1700, have been restored by the National Trust from the evidence of Joseph Dougharty's bird's-eye view of 1732, which has been confirmed by archaeological investigation. To date, a sunken parterre, fruit garden, wilderness, juniper grove and bowling green have all been reinstated, along with two pairs of pavilions (recreated in timber rather than the original brick and stone), two pairs of stone piers and a wrought iron *clairvoyée*, set at the end of the central walk that leads through the parterre and fruit garden.

Another garden of the period restored by the Trust is the rare Dutch-style water garden of Westbury Court. Here, the road and the country-side beyond can be glimpsed through an iron *clairvoyée* at the end of the canal, flanked by lofty stone piers bearing pineapple finials. The use of imposing ornamental gate-piers to frame views is a device also employed in the gardens at Canons Ashby, laid out between 1708 and 1717. But the garden of this romantic Northamptonshire manor house is perhaps more important for its wooden garden seats and gates, near-miraculous survivals of early eighteenth-century outdoor joinery.

Rooted in History

Relics of one of the great 'formalised' landscape gardens created under the direction of Charles Bridgeman in the early eighteenth-century survive at Claremont. From 1714, Thomas Pelham-Holles, later 1st Duke of Newcastle, cut a series of rides or *allées* through Chargate Woods, one of them terminated by Bridgeman's amphitheatre of 1722, a stiff semi-circle of concentric turf terraces modelled on the amphitheatres of classical antiquity, which overlooked a pond known as the Round Bason. Another grassy ride led to the belvedere, a white-washed Gothic observatory. Later, from about 1729, the influential designer William Kent began to irregularise Bridgeman's axial layout, transforming his round pond into an informal lake with an island on which he built a rusticated tea-house. A triple-arched artificial grotto was established on the shore in 1750, 'compos'd of Spars, fossils, &c', while the network of straight rides was gradually softened with additional planting. By 1766 the amphitheatre was entirely submerged by dense shrubbery, from which it only emerged during the Trust's restoration of the gardens in 1975. Claremont exemplifies perfectly how the taste for naturalism transformed formal gardens during the eighteenth century.

This process of evolution can be traced on a still more grandiose scale at Stowe where, from about 1711, Richard Temple, 1st Viscount Cobham, created what was to become the most ambitious and cele-brated landscape garden of all. Indeed, in its sophistication, scale and complexity, Stowe is the glass through which all other eighteenth-century landscape gardens are reflected. Cobham first employed Charles Bridgeman to lay out an axial garden, which by 1724 encom-passed some 28 acres and contained ten ornamental buildings. Its perimeter was defined by avenues, punctuated by bastions on which buildings afforded glimpses out over the park, and the whole was enclosed by a ha-ha or stockade ditch. This was one of the first of its kind to be built in England and was perhaps inspired by the fortifica-tions Cobham had seen during his military campaigns in Flanders. Vanbrugh designed most of the buildings in the Western Garden at Stowe – a temple to Bacchus (1718), a cave dedicated to Dido (*c.*1720), a classical Rotondo containing a gilded statue of the Venus de' Medici (1720–1), and a 60-foot Pyramid (1724), all of which – through the medium of statues, paintings and inscriptions – enlarged upon a theme of love, particularly its hopeless and unrequited aspects. After Vanbrugh's death in 1726, Cobham consulted James Gibbs and then William Kent, who built for him in 1731 the Temple of Venus on the southern bastion of Bridgeman's ha-ha. The Temple took up the venereal motif of the Western Garden, and its charming concave front was adorned with antique marble busts of famous debauchees and adulteresses, whilst

Lead statue of a shepherd boy with flute and dog, framed by the gates to the Green Court at Canons Ashby.
(NTPL/Andrew Butler)

inside were paintings representing orgies. The decidedly *risqué* symbolism of the buildings at Stowe was to inspire one of its neighbours, Sir Francis Dashwood, the libertine 2nd Baronet, to build his own erotic garden in the late 1740s at West Wycombe Park. Venus's Parlour at West Wycombe is perhaps the most outrageous garden building of the eighteenth century; an exedra which takes the form of the spread-open legs of a woman, its cave-like entrance representing the vagina. To ensure visitors could not mistake the meaning of this brazen *mons veneris*, it was originally accompanied by a tall flintwork phallus. Not surprisingly, neither monument survived the Victorian era, but the 11th Baronet, a direct descendant of its creator, rebuilt the Parlour in 1982, so it once again shocks visitors to this most idiosyncratic eighteenth-century landscape garden.

Elsewhere at Stowe, Kent went on to build a series of evocative monuments along the slopes of the Elysian Fields, the serpentine valley he created on the eastern side of the garden. Its construction coincided with Cobham's fall from political grace in 1733 and the temples and statues in the new garden served to illustrate a complex moral allegory, enshrining Cobham's trenchant views on corruption in contemporary political life. Thus the Temple of British Worthies, which contained a gallery of busts of great historical figures whom Cobham admired (see p.146), looked across the Worthies River to a domed rotunda, dubbed the Temple of Ancient Virtue, harbouring statues of their classical counterparts. Nearby stood a squalid, overgrown ruin, the Temple of Modern Virtue, presided over by a mutilated statue, said to represent Sir

Anthony Walker's 1758 coloured engraving of the gardens of Studley Royal, which exploited the ruins of Fountains Abbey as a picturesque eye-catcher.
(NTPL)

Rooted in History

Robert Walpole, the Prime Minister of the day and Cobham's great enemy. Cobham's 'garden of exile' has affinities with gardens created for solace by other outcasts, notably Studley Royal, laid out by the disgraced financier, John Aislabie, between 1720 and 1742. Although the water gardens at Studley have none of the bitter political agenda of Cobham's Stowe, Aislabie's smooth lawns and chain of mirror-like pools (see p.134), littered with classical structures and copies after antique statuary, were created as a refuge from public opprobrium following the bursting of the South Sea Bubble.

At Studley, the romantic ruins of Fountains Abbey were deliberately exploited as a picturesque feature, just as at nearby Rievaulx, where two richly furnished temples enable the 'horrid graces' of the Gothic to be viewed in comfort and safety. At Stowe, which lacked genuine medieval relics, Lord Cobham was forced to create his own Gothic Temple on the Hawkwell Field above Kent's Elysian incursion. Designed by Gibbs in 1741, it was only completed by Sanderson Miller in 1748, but is important as an early monument of the Gothic Revival. Dedicated to ancient Saxon or 'British' liberty, its ochre-coloured stonework was intended to contrast with the pallid 'Roman' structures elsewhere in the garden, and the primitive character of the building was further emphasised by a set of statues of Saxon Deities, which dwelt in a near-by glade of yews.

Many of Lord Cobham's buildings at Stowe were pioneering structures: the Chinese House, put up by 1738, was probably the earliest garden building in England in the Chinese style (see case study on pp.118–20), while the Rotondo and Vanbrugh's vanished Pyramid inspired a host of imitations in other gardens. Of course, not all the buildings at Stowe were deemed worthy of emulation and visitors frequently censured their flimsy construction and crude decoration. The domed Shell Pavilion was 'cover'd with the Shells of large Tortoises', while the Witch House had a nightmarish interior, 'daub'd over with Scenes … by a Domestick'. Neither of these structures survive, but one building at Stowe which elicited almost universal admiration was Lord Cobham's last building project, a huge temple which he erected in a valley in the north-eastern extremity of the garden. The Grecian Temple, as it was first known, was begun in 1747 and roofed within months of Lord Cobham's death in 1749. It was intended to be an exact reconstruction of an ancient Greek temple and, although it more closely resembles a Roman structure, it may be said to be the first building of Grecian intention to be built in England. After Cobham's death, his heir and nephew, Earl Temple, altered and embellished the Temple to make it more archaeologically correct. He rechristened the building the Temple of Concord and Victory, dedicating it to the British victories over the

The Temple of Concord and Victory at Stowe, Lord Cobham's last building venture, begun in 1747.
(NTPL/Andrew Butler)

French during the Seven Years' War – continuing the tradition of political gardening at Stowe that had been started by his uncle.

The Grecian Temple at Stowe was designed to preside over a great artificial valley, formed to resemble an Arcadian landscape, called the Grecian Valley. This vast earth-moving operation was entrusted to Lancelot 'Capability' Brown, who had come to Stowe in 1741 and immediately set about naturalising Bridgeman's formal landscape, sweeping away the great parterre, irregularising and extending the lakes. Lord Temple continued this purification of the gardens in the 1760s, altering the Rotondo and the Palladian Bridge, and demolishing several of his uncle's flimsier follies altogether. Other structures – like Vanbrugh's Lake Pavilions – were bodily moved to more convenient locations, although the difficulties encountered caused Lord Temple to complain in a letter in 1764, 'Why cant we move Buildings with as much ease as we do Pictures'. New features were also built, such as the imposing Corinthian Arch which closed the main southern vista in 1764–5.

On his death in 1779, Temple left Stowe 'a work to wonder at' and the National Trust's restoration of the gardens attempts to return it to its late eighteenth-century heyday, when Lord Cobham's plantations had matured and most of the ornamental features we see today were in place. However, such was the restless activity of Stowe that conservation decisions can become complex. Few buildings remained completely unaltered throughout their history, and the character of individual garden areas was often transformed out of recognition by successive proprietors. The cost of this work is immense, but in recent years generous

Rooted in History

grants from the Heritage Lottery Fund have enabled the Trust to buy back the Home Farm estate, separated from the gardens since 1921, and make improvements to the park and its outer eye-catchers. Each year more garden areas and buildings are restored, and this same heartening cycle is now occurring in the main house – which remains in the occupation of Stowe School – through the newly formed Stowe House Preservation Trust. Indeed, it is increasingly evident that complex landscapes on the scale of Stowe can only be revived through a spirit of co-operation, and the example of Stowe has inspired similar partnerships, notably at Gibside, and at Croome. The Trust is also currently working with English Heritage and local bodies towards the revival of Cobham Park, particularly the rescue of the great Darnley Mausoleum, hitherto one of the most intractable heritage *causes célèbres* in Britain. The mausoleum, one of the most dramatic in Britain, is located in a remote wooded location and had been allowed to fall into a scandalous state of disrepair by a succession of unsympathetic owners. Repeatedly vandalised, it was at real risk of being lost entirely, but a collaborative effort is now in hand to repair it and secure its long-term future.

Croome was the first of a series of influential landscapes created by 'Capability' Brown after he left Stowe in 1750. The National Trust acquired the derelict gardens in 1996 and is gradually restoring the series of intimate temples, seats and other ornaments which populate the pleasure grounds around the lake, including the greenhouse, designed by Robert Adam in 1760 and which was once home to a celebrated collection of exotics. Adam also designed a series of garden structures for Kedleston Hall, his masterpiece in Derbyshire, notably the luxuriously appointed Fishing Room of 1770–2, which the Trust has recently restored, and a stupendous three-arched bridge and cascade. But perhaps the most famous of these temple-strewn landscapes is the garden laid out at Stourhead by two generations of the Hoare family between 1744 and 1838. Here most of the classical buildings that fringe the lake – the Temple of Flora, the Grotto and River God's Cave, the Pantheon with its statue of Hercules, and the Temple of Apollo – follow an itinerary loosely based on *The Aeneid* and their form seems directly inspired by the Claudian landscapes that hang in the picture gallery in the house. There were also Gothic incursions in the form of a medieval market cross from Bristol, a rustic convent, and a triangular tower, 160 feet high, dedicated to King Alfred and British Liberty.

A gilded personification of Liberty – a recurrent motif in English garden buildings – surmounts the giant column erected in 1757 by George Bowes in the park at Gibside. The column is answered at the other end of a grand avenue by a domed funerary chapel, designed by

James Paine in 1760–4. Egyptian sepulchral practices were recalled in the pyramidal Buckinghamshire Mausoleum at Blickling of 1794, but a more useful memorial is the Mussenden Temple at Downhill, a domed classical rotunda perched on a rocky promontory overlooking the sea. Built by the eccentric Earl-Bishop of Derry in 1785 and dedicated to his cousin, Mrs Mussenden, this was not a tomb but a library – a comfortable clifftop eyrie where the Bishop could consult Lucretius high above the raging Atlantic Ocean.

The work of the influential landscape gardener and polemicist Humphry Repton can be found at Tatton Park, Attingham and Sheringham, for which 'Red Books' of proposals were supplied in 1791, 1798 and 1812. Repton disliked the 'useless and unmeaning' novelties found in eighteenth-century landscapes, and sought to convey the impression of limitless ownership, discreetly patrolled by elegant classical lodges and picturesque estate cottages. When William Sawrey Gilpin, another contemporary arbiter of garden taste, advised on the gardens around the new house at Scotney Castle in 1835, he piously preserved the ruins of the Old Castle, which, festooned with ivy and surrounded by its moat, became a picturesque garden ornament. The enduring Regency fashion for rustic garden features is exemplified by the Heather House at Florence Court, Co. Fermanagh, of *c*.1830, or its descendants, the brace of twiggy Edwardian summer houses that lurk in the gardens of Peckover House, Wisbech.

The Old Castle at Scotney. In 1835, when William Sawrey Gilpin was laying out the gardens at Scotney for Edward Hussey, they decided to retain the old fortified manor house as a picturesque ruin. (NTPL/Stephen Robson)

Rooted in History

More substantial and expensive was the great orangery designed by Lewis Wyatt for the Egertons of Tatton in 1818. The building made use of the newly available cast-iron and sheet-glass, and was flanked by aviaries and trellis seats. Sadly, however, the Victorian passion for grandiose winter-gardens is poorly represented in the National Trust's estate – only the foundations survive of H.E. Kendall's spectacular Jacobean-style conservatory at Wimpole. Built in 1842, it extended from the Library nearly 100 feet in an uninterrupted enfilade of ferns and palms, until its demolition after the Second World War. But the fernery at Tatton Park survives. It dates from 1859 and was built, probably by Sir Joseph Paxton, to house a collection of New Zealand tree ferns, although, more recently, it was also home to the late Lord Egerton's pet snakes. The gardens at Tatton, with their diverse amenities and exotic features – which after 1910 included a large Japanese Garden, laid out by workmen brought over specially for the purpose, as well as an African Hut – came almost to resemble one of the great international exhibitions of the period.

Some sense of the profusion of grand Victorian gardens is evoked at Biddulph Grange, where the series of atmospheric, but also instructive, gardens created by James Bateman between 1842 and 1868, is being

The Fernery at Tatton, designed in 1859, probably by Sir Joseph Paxton.
(NTPL/Derek Harris)

The *Fountain of Love* by Thomas
Waldo Story, set up in 1897 by
William Waldorf Astor on the
grand avenue at Cliveden.
(NTPL/Colin Clarke)

restored. A passion for outlandish plunder is recalled by the huge pink
granite obelisk at Kingston Lacy, a genuine Egyptian antiquity which
stands on the south lawn. It originally had its own wooden cover to
protect it from frost in winter. Other exotic interlopers in National
Trust gardens include the Maori Hut at Clandon Park, rescued by the
4th Earl of Onslow while Governor of New Zealand in 1892, and the
great balustrade from the Villa Borghese in Rome, which adorns the
gardens at Cliveden. The latter feature was acquired by William Waldorf
Astor and installed in 1896, together with other valuable garden
ornaments – including nine superb antique sarcophagi and Thomas
Waldo Story's astonishing *Fountain of Love*, a monster marble clam shell
manned by squirming nymphs – making Cliveden the most important
collection of garden statuary in the Trust's care. All these treasures incur
a grave responsibility; not only does the Trust have to protect them
from the ravages of the British climate, but also that more sinister
phenomenon, the threat of theft and vandalism. In recent years the
National Trust has pioneered the development of physical and
electronic protection for its garden statuary and ornaments.

Expressions of bold self-confidence like Cliveden have been rarer in
the twentieth century, and the most celebrated gardens of our own era,

Rooted in History

The Well Court at Snowshill
Manor, with a shrine to the Virgin
Mary on the roof of a former cow
byre.
(NTPL/Nick Meers)

places like Hidcote and Sissinghurst, have relied as much on the effects
of planting as on traditional ornamental features like pavilions and
statues. A characteristic of these gardens is their sense of enclosure,
with compartments bounded by clipped yew or walls of mellow brick.
At Snowshill Manor Charles Wade incorporated adjacent farm buildings
into the garden he laid out around his decrepit Cotswold manor house,
charmingly embellishing them with gables and statues, all the joinery
being painted in his preferred shade of peacock blue. The traditional
pergola was memorably revived at Bodnant, with its spectacular laburnum arch, and at Sissinghurst mundane objects like old well-heads and
worn-out copper boilers were deployed alongside priceless bronze
vases that had once graced the gardens of the Bagatelle. New buildings,
when they were needed, were often made to look like old ones, like
Philip Webb's 1910 summer house on the Upper Terrace at Standen.
However, caprice on an almost Victorian scale can be found on the
Dodo Terrace at Mount Stewart, infested with absurd home-made
cement statues of animals, from pteradactyls to iguanas, representing
members of the 1920s political club, the 'Ark' (see p.61).

After the Second World War, country houses, which had long been in crisis, were being abandoned, broken up and demolished at an alarming rate. The National Trust's Country Houses Scheme, which had been inaugurated in 1937, ensured that some of the most notable ensembles were preserved intact, but for many parks and gardens the post-war era spelt ruin. The mansion at Gibside was stripped of its roof and Forestry Commission plantations engulfed its park and monuments, while Stowe, which had gone to the breakers in 1921, survived as a school, its temples turned into tuckshops, boathouses and classrooms. This wholesale destruction gave unprecedented opportunities to the few who had the means and vision to embark upon the creation of new gardens, philanthropists like the 2nd Lord Aberconway, who rescued the ruined Pin Mill from Frampton Court and re-erected it at Bodnant in 1939, or the 1st Lord Fairhaven, who until his death in 1966 filled his gardens at Anglesey Abbey with salvaged trophies, including statues from Stowe and columns from Chesterfield House. Another beneficiary was Buscot with its famous water garden designed in the 1920s by Harold Peto for the 1st Lord Faringdon, which his grandson, the 2nd Baron, extended and embellished with an eclectic collection of garden ornaments between 1934 and 1978. As yet, the Trust has little in its estate to represent the Modern Movement and its relationship to landscape, although Henry Moore's *Three Piece Reclining Figure* stands in the garden at Scotney, and the terraces at The Homewood, Patrick Gwynne's 1938 house, attest to the era's devotion to sun worship.

The National Trust now rarely builds new follies in its gardens. Today, its efforts are usually rightly concentrated on the restoration of existing features, or on the improvement of visitor facilities. In its great restoration projects – at Stourhead from 1946, Westbury Court from 1967, Claremont from 1974, Stowe from 1990 (building on the work of the school and the Historic Buildings Council), and still more recently at Biddulph, Gibside and Prior Park – the Trust's work has generally been limited to returning the parks and gardens to their 'former glory'. The Trust's heroic rescue of structures like the Temple of Concord and Victory at Stowe, or the shoring-up of the cliffs below the Mussenden Temple, were immensely costly undertakings, demonstrating the high regard in which these 'follies' are held as cultural monuments. However, in the past the Trust has sometimes been less concerned with ensuring the survival of the more utilitarian structures in our gardens – walled gardens, ranges of glasshouses, humble bothies and sheds. These have often been left to decay or, in some cases, were actually swept away by the Trust as uninteresting eyesores. Recent projects, like the revival of the walled gardens at Tatton and Wimpole, provide a welcome opportunity to redress this neglect.

The eighteenth-century Pin Mill, transported from Gloucestershire by the 2nd Lord Aberconway in the 1930s, and erected in his great garden at Bodnant.
(NTPL/Ian Shaw)

Rooted in History

As well as restoring surviving features, sometimes the National Trust returns lost elements to a garden, so as to restore its meaning or artistic integrity. At Stowe, sixteen of the giant columns that support the peristyle of the Temple of Concord and Victory are replicas, carved to replace those removed in 1927, while five of the seven Saxon Deities have already returned to the gardens in the form of copies; the originals are now in museums or private collections, and are too valuable and fragile to stand outdoors. However, whenever it can the Trust tries to keep actual historic features in their original settings. Indeed, perhaps the rarest and most fragile of all garden buildings, the Chinese House at Stowe, has returned to the garden after an absence of nearly 250 years (see case study pp.118–20).

But the Trust does occasionally build anew: the triumphal Entrance Arch at Polesden Lacey was built in 1958 to a design by Hugh Casson, in fulfilment of wishes of the donor, Mrs Greville, and at West Green House, a private initiative by a Trust tenant, Lord McAlpine, led to the erection in 1976 of a column dedicated to Margaret Thatcher. But usually the Trust has been reluctant to clutter its gardens with alien introductions, and there is a strict policy forbidding memorial inscriptions and municipal park benches, which could make historic landscapes like Stourhead or Stowe look like Forest Lawn Cemetery. In exceptional circumstances, contemporary sculpture has been introduced into Trust gardens as a permanent feature, such as William Pye's water sculpture, *Torpoint*, at Antony House (see case study pp.120–123) or *Patagon*, a giant Portland-stone foot by the sculptor Vincent Woropay, in the Wilderness at Powis. The latter is a thought-provoking survivor of a temporary outdoor sculpture exhibition held in the gardens in 1988. These have become popular attractions in National Trust gardens in recent years, none more so than the one held at Blickling in the year 2000, which provoked enthusiasm and outrage in equal measure. Such shows encourage new visitors to come to our properties, and teach old friends to look at them afresh, but we must guard vigilantly the individuality and historic integrity of our parks and gardens – so that future generations may enjoy the green legacy of these haunts of ancient peace.

Case Study 1
Returned from Exile: the Restoration of the Chinese House at Stowe

The great party the National Trust held at Stowe in 1998 to celebrate
the completion of the restoration of the Chinese House was, in more
ways than one, an unforgettable occasion. It was cold and wet, and
somehow the caterer forgot to feed the assembled dignitaries who
huddled dejectedly in the VIP tent. Spirits were only raised by the
appearance of a full-size junk on the lake, blazing with fireworks, and
the extraordinary spectacle of the Chinese House itself, a fragile
painted structure, topped by monstrous gilded fish, back at Stowe after
an absence of 250 years. But despite this inauspicious debut, the
story of the discovery, repatriation and restoration of the Chinese
House is a remarkable one, and makes for an interesting, and not
entirely unproblematic, case study in conservation.

The exact origins of the Chinese House at Stowe are shrouded in
mystery, but it appears in the gardens in 1738 when it was described by
an anonymous visitor as a 'house built on piles, after the manner of the
Chinese'. It stood on a platform in a formal pond on one of the eastern bastions of Lord Cobham's garden, and a crude contemporary
woodcut shows it as a wooden teahouse with a wide oversailing roof,
on which reposed a pair of large fish finials. It was painted inside and
out with brightly coloured *chinoiseries*, and was clearly intended as a
whimsical fishing temple. Its designer is not known, but it was probably
the earliest Chinese-style garden building to be built in England.

The Chinese House was typical of the flimsy structures with which
Lord Cobham loved to populate his garden, but it did not enjoy the
favour of his successor, Earl Temple, who on inheriting Stowe in 1749

lost no time in ejecting it from the garden. It was gone by 1750, but reappears in the garden at Wotton, a nearby house belonging to a subsidiary branch of the family. It stood on an island on the lake at Wotton and was carefully maintained, its fragile painted exterior protected from the elements by canvas covers until 1957, when it was dismantled and taken to Ireland. Here it remained, forgotten and decaying, until it was rediscovered in the 1970s.

Time, and the Irish weather, had dealt unkindly with the Chinese House, but its great importance as an early monument of the *chinoiserie*-style was recognised. The Georgian Group campaigned for its repair and it was eventually purchased by the National Trust in 1992, so as to return it to Stowe. However, it remained in packing cases for many years, while funds were sought for its restoration. The money was finally raised in 1998 as a memorial to Gervase Jackson-Stops, formerly the Trust's Architectural Adviser.

The restoration of the Chinese House was carried out under the guidance of the Stowe Project Team, which directs the restoration of the gardens at Stowe. It was a complicated project for, although a simple structure, the Chinese House was covered inside and out with precariously preserved paintings. Only the four walls were old, and two of the external sides had been stripped almost bare of paint by the elements. However, the interior was remarkably well preserved and, beneath crude overpainting, so were the other, more protected, sides of the exterior. The woodwork was carefully conserved by Hugh Routh and John Hartley, who also made a new roof, closely modelled on the one shown in a *Country Life* photograph of 1949. The paintings were painstakingly consolidated by Alan Bush and Alan Berry, who also recreated the lost areas using enlargements of the *Country Life* photograph. One of the biggest surprises was how much of the old paint survived, and there was evidence of five separate decorative schemes, one on top of the other. It was decided to recreate the fourth and best preserved of these, although sections showing the earlier schemes were discreetly left exposed in the interior. The two fish finials were carved by Ben Bacon using the 1744 woodcut as a model.

While the restoration of the Chinese House is generally agreed to be a success, the Trust has been less fortunate in finding a location for its new acquisition. All agreed that it was impossible to return the pavilion to its original site at Stowe, as the pond and its bastion had long been swept away. It was first proposed to re-erect the restored Chinese House on a lake in the Lamport Garden, an early nineteenth-century pleasure ground behind the Palladian Bridge. This had the advantage of keeping the Chinese House separate from the rest of the landscape garden at Stowe, where it no longer had any historical place. However, we were advised that the damp atmosphere would imperil the carefully consolidated painted surfaces. Nor could we protect the garden from vandals – an ever-present menace at Stowe. Finally, after much debate, the Chinese House was re-erected in a nearby glade, fenced round with a high wire security fence which follows the line of the 1st Duke of Buckingham's Pheasantry. This is separate from the rest of the garden at Stowe, and is safe, but the absence of water makes it a not wholly sympathetic setting for a fishing temple. Moreover, the security fence is hideous, although the enclosure has been thickly planted up with trees and creepers in an effort to disguise it. But the new site does closely resemble the setting the Chinese House had during its last years at Wotton, when the photographs that guided its restoration were taken. While the Chinese House is undoubtedly important as a pioneering structure of English *chinoiserie*, and is interesting as the sole, and almost miraculous, survivor of Lord Cobham's flimsier follies, the return of this exotic exile to Stowe poses problems. Indeed, doubts have been raised as to whether we should have returned the Chinese House to Stowe at all.

Case Study 2
The Sculptures at Antony

Jeremy Pearson

Delightfully located in the south east of Cornwall on the banks of the rivers Tamar and Lynher, Antony has been the home of the Carew family since the fourteenth century. Following the marriage of a member of the family to an heiress in the early eighteenth century, a new house was built in Pentewan stone and the surrounding grounds reorganised. Clumps of trees were subsequently planted, and a large parterre later laid out before the north front of the house. However, this was swept away in the early twentieth century and the garden returned to more manageable proportions. In the 1930s Sir John Carew Pole and his American wife Cynthia concentrated on establishing a fine woodland garden on the fringes of the formal area; now owned by a charitable trust, this 24-hectare (60-acre) woodland site contains a wide variety of well-established magnolias and rhododendrons as well as the National Collection of *Camellia japonica*.

The house and immediately surrounding garden were given to the National Trust by Sir John in 1961. He continued to live there until 1983, when his son Richard moved into the house with his young family. Sir Richard, who succeeded his father in 1993, takes a keen interest in modern art; he was chairman of the committee responsible for creating the Tate Gallery, St Ives, and is also a trustee of the Tate Gallery in London. Many of the rooms in the house are hung with contemporary

Torpoint by William Pye, on the
West Lawn at Antony with the
eighteenth-century dovecote in
the background.
(NTPL/Derek Croucher)

works, helping to maintain a dynamic quality which Sir Richard values greatly: 'The house is our home, it is not a museum.'

He feels the same about the grounds: 'they are ever-changing, and although the essential framework of the garden is inviolate we feel at liberty to make alterations, either by planting or by placing sculpture'. The first joint venture between the National Trust and Sir Richard in this respect was a new piece of sculpture for the rectangular area of garden to the immediate west of the house. Earlier in the twentieth century this had been ornamented by six columns with Corinthian capitals and a fountain in the centre, but the 'Italian Garden' was removed in the 1950s, leaving an easily maintained lawn. The main exit from the house to the garden overlooks this area, from which there is a fine view down a wide twentieth-century yew walk with the nearby conical yew tennis court shelter. This striking topiary feature dates from the 1870s, and provided the inspiration for the water feature which now graces the West Lawn. It was felt that moving water should be an important element in the reworked area, but that large jets of water would be inappropriate given the windy Cornish weather. In 1996 William Pye was approached to design a work for this area. Inspired by the way in which heavy rainfall runs down tarmac roads in rippling waves, he created *Torpoint*, a fascinating bronze cone down which a steady flow of water cascades. The surface tension of the water creates subtle and ever-changing patterns, matched by a soothing variety of sounds.

The shock of the new was certainly apparent in the weeks that followed the installation of *Torpoint*. The initial response of many visitors was disapproving – they disliked the intrusion of something so patently modern into an historic setting. Yet as the weeks passed and the rawness of the bronze and surrounding York stone paving mellowed, so visitors became more enthusiastic. The cone is now much photographed, and considerable favourable comment is received about the intriguing nature of the water movement.

In the following year *Hypercone* was commissioned from Simon Thomas, a sculptor with Cornish connections but now living in Bristol. This 3-metre-high (10 foot) waxed iron work of 'rings within rings spiralling' was also inspired by water. As waste water circles and descends the plughole in a basin, so does the shadow and varying light move on these complex shapes. This sculpture was placed in the Summer Garden, a small and confined space in which it stands against a background of species hydrangea, surrounded by the delicate fronds of Angels Fishing Rods.

The success of these two new introductions encouraged further ventures in modern sculpture in the following years. A two-dimensional wall sculpture in Peperino volcanic stone by Steven Cox, entitled *Dono*, was placed under a small shelter on a wall outside the west door. This is a particularly successful relief and has proved to be a very satisfying and complete work. Inspired by the earlier ideas of the tondo, it turns a simple decorative motive into a continuous Gordian Knot, which catches the light to great effect.

Much further from the house, and set within the woodland garden, are two other pieces of sculpture. Peter Randle-Page created *Dartmoor Stone* in 1996. This takes the form of a large granite boulder, split asunder to reveal a complex Celtic-style carving within. It is a thought-provoking piece standing in a small quarry near the highest point of the garden at Jupiter Point. The latest sculpture in the grounds is secreted in the woods of Westdown. *Wrapt* by Eilis O'Connell arrived in September 1999. This striking 3-metre-high (10 foot) piece of greyish blue bronze is a dramatic funnel-shaped piece of contemporary sculpture, its title a play on words – 'rapture' or 'wrapped around'.

As well as these works of modern sculpture, a number of pieces of furniture and wooden plant pots have been commissioned from local cabinet-makers. A very fine black-painted wrought iron gate has been made recently by Minehead-based blacksmith James Horrobin. This handsome single gate with adjoining screens leads into the Summer Garden, its design inspired by many of the flowers found nearby, including the celebrated magnolias.

The grounds at Antony have long been admired for their beauty and high levels of maintenance. Now there is a new dimension to help enliven the scene. Many visitors come especially to see the modern works of art, which have become a much-complimented feature of the garden. Although the intention is not to create a sculpture garden, there are still one or two potential sites for new works of art. Much care (and lively discussion!) goes into the commissioning and placement of each piece, and the National Trust is grateful for the support of Sir Richard Carew Pole and a local charitable trust. This highly successful partnership shows that there can be a worthwhile and popular role for new works of art, and innovation generally, within the context of historic gardens.

7

Ecology and Nature Conservation in Gardens and Parks

Matthew Oates

Wildlife gets everywhere, to a greater or lesser extent. It is therefore inevitable that many of the 88,000 or so native and regular migrant species that occur in the UK find their way into National Trust gardens and parks. They occur as permanent garden residents, as regular incomers breeding in the adjoining countryside, or as occasional vagrants.

The fact that gardens and to a lesser extent parks are essentially artificial – or man-made – habitats does not lower their value to wildlife, particularly as most of the habitats in lowland Britain are the by-product of man's activities and so are termed 'semi-natural' by ecologists. Indeed, there are remarkably few genuinely natural, let alone pristine, habitats within the UK. Habitats in states of artificiality are commonplace, with formal gardens certainly ranking towards the more extreme end of the spectrum of habitats produced by man's actions. The truth is that since the Bronze Age man has been the primary influence on the British landscape, whether in conjunction with, or in opposition to, natural processes.

Our semi-natural habitats are dependent on man's activities insofar as they will change into other habitats – mostly woodland – if the practices and processes that brought them into existence are not continued. In effect, wildlife habitats that are the by-products of culturally redundant activities now require purposeful nature conservation management to ensure their perpetuity.

One of the major current problems for wildlife in the UK is that many of the cultural activities that benefited wildlife, such as coppicing

The Herb Garden at Hardwick Hall boasts a wide range of nectar plants, including lavender, and attracts a variety of visiting insects and other wildlife.
(NTPL/Stephen Robson)

and traditional hay meadow management, were discontinued during the twentieth century. Moreover, during radical agricultural and silvicultural revolutions they were largely replaced by activities that were highly damaging to wildlife. Massive losses in natural and semi-natural habitats occurred during the century. As examples, 99 per cent of traditional hay meadows, 80 per cent of chalk and limestone grassland and 50 per cent of ancient woodland were lost. During the century extinction occurred at a rate of one species per year and many 'common' species suffered enormous declines; the skylark, for example, declined by 52 per cent during the period 1970–98.

The significance of gardens and parks for wildlife has increased greatly because of the scale of habitat loss, coupled with the degree of fragmentation and isolation of surviving habitats in the modern landscape. Furthermore, there is evidence that people's perceptions of gardens and parks are taking this increasing significance into account. Decline and increasing rarity, perhaps in conjunction with the development of perceptions on animal welfare, are now driving nature conservation concern and action. However, the extent to which the UK nature conservation movement is helping this process is debatable, for the language of biodiversity may not be the best medium for conveying often complex ecological messages to a population that is becoming increasingly urbanised.

Why the National Trust?

Nature conservation is a primary function of the National Trust. A clear remit to conserve flora and fauna is enshrined within the National Trust Act of 1907, although it is in need of contemporary interpretation as the wording ('and as regards lands for the preservation … of their natural aspect features and animal and plant life') is somewhat archaic to say the least. The acquisition in 1899 of the Trust's sixth property, part of Wicken Fen, was in order to preserve its nature conservation interests, albeit largely so that people could continue to collect butterflies and moths there.

The Trust's nature conservation work is now developing rapidly, driven by a genuine desire for the organisation to establish itself as the UK's largest land-owning environmental and nature conservation organisation (28 per cent of Trust land is legally designated for its nature conservation interest). In this, it undoubtedly has the backing of its massive membership, now standing at over 2.8 million. The Estates Department offices at Cirencester contain a team of four in-house ecologists (the Trust's Advisers on Nature Conservation) and a

Biological Survey Team of four, plus some support staff. Out in the field, the Trust's countryside and gardens staff are becoming increasingly skilled in nature conservation matters.

One of the essential duties of the Trust's Nature Conservation section is to maintain an overview of the condition of habitats and scarce species on Trust land. It therefore needs to co-ordinate information from surveys, facilitate monitoring and maintain databases. In nature conservation situations where there is inadequate information there is a tendency for features of importance to be discovered only when it is too late to save them, and clearly we need to avoid this.

The Trust already holds adequate information on the wildlife in its parks, as the Biological Survey Team has prioritised the production of reports on all Trust parks on account of their indigenous wildlife importance. Conversely, when the Team was formed some 20 years ago a decision was taken not to survey gardens, largely because of the scale

The eighteenth-century landscape park at Blickling Hall is noted for its magnificent trees, mainly oak, beech and sweet chestnut. The wildlife value of the park has been assessed by the Trust's Biological Survey Team and is carefully monitored.
(NTPL/Mike Williams)

of the task of surveying the wider countryside and the non-natural status of most garden habitats. Consequently, no central information base exists on wildlife in Trust gardens; information is only available at a local level, generated by the interest of the gardens staff and visitors to gardens. In this respect the Trust is behind English Heritage, which has been conducting wildlife surveys in the few gardens in its care for a number of years. It is therefore difficult to reach an overview of the significance of the Trust's gardens for wildlife and determine priorities. This chapter is the first step in that process.

Gardens and Parks as Habitats

Many gardens were created out of old woodland or traditional, 'unimproved' grassland. It is therefore unsurprising that elements of the original wildlife have transferred into the garden. This is even more true of parks, many of which were sculpted out of ancient woodland or medieval deer parks, such as those at Calke and Clumber, and occupy sites which have had some continuous tree cover, including the presence of veteran trees, since the time of the original wildwood which covered the British Isles after the last Ice Age. Such on-site continuity of habitat supply is exceptionally unusual in lowland UK.

Curiously, species can survive at subsistence level in radically altered habitat-situations, despite adverse recent changes and current management. Consequently, species can linger, rather unrealistically, in parks and gardens as relics of bygone eras (as at Croome Park). Sometimes they are viable concerns, sometimes they are lost causes; more usually, though, our knowledge of scarce specialist species is inadequate for us to determine this viability, and conservation effort has to function speculatively.

The distinction between resident and vagrant species is particularly important within the context of gardens, for gardens attract a great diversity of vagrants from far and near, notably nectar-dependent insects for which the modern countryside is becoming increasingly hostile. True vagrants are accidents of nature and they are more likely to be noticed in situations, such as gardens and nature reserves, where people are in enhanced states of visual perception. The more conspicuous vagrants, such as birds like the hoopoe, will readily be noticed in a garden open to the public. Some of these spectacular wanderers may even breed occasionally; the golden oriole appears to have bred at Antony in 2000. Of course, the majority of vagrants are less dramatic, though nonetheless noteworthy species. They can still generate considerable excitement amongst specialists, as the author discovered in August 1996 when he spotted his first-ever long-tailed blue butterfly,

The exotic hoopoe is a scarce annual migrant to Britain. It occasionally appears in Trust gardens and has a penchant for feeding on manicured lawns, where it probes the turf for insects. (Robin Chittenden)

Rooted in History

Gardens and parks are important habitats for most species of British bat, including the long-eared (shown here). Bats use gardens and parks for feeding, roosting and breeding, and active measures are taken at many Trust properties to meet their particular requirements. (NTPL/Hans Christoph Kappel/BBC NHU)

an exceptionally scarce wanderer from the Mediterranean, in the White Garden at Barrington Court.

The richest wildlife habitats in gardens and parks are, in attempted priority order: pond and bog gardens, veteran trees (especially oak, ash and beech), and wildflower meadows and banks. There is also an interesting 'bits and pieces' category. These will be covered individually in the following paragraphs.

In terms of groups of species, gardens are important for a diversity of birds, mammals, amphibians, insects, lower plants (especially lichens and mosses) and fungi. Parks and gardens may well be important sites for spiders, though inadequate information exists, notably from gardens.

Gardens are rich habitats for songbirds, including resident species and summer and winter visitors. They are particularly important for species which breed in hedges and dense scrub or in holes in trees. Gardens are currently important strongholds for song thrush and spotted flycatcher, both of which have declined enormously in recent years and are now priority species targeted by the UK biodiversity initiative. The treecreeper, an insectivorous bird which often roosts communally in winter in soft-barked trees such as wellingtonia, is another bird that fares well in gardens and parks. Various bats, all of which are protected by law and have exacting requirements, feed, breed and roost in many Trust gardens and parks. Noctule bats, in particular, roost in holes in trees at numerous Trust properties, their presence often given away by piles of droppings. Stoats and weasels, which are rarely seen, occur in a surprising number of Trust gardens and parks. Gardens are especially important sites for reptiles and amphibians, particularly newts, for which ponds are important breeding sites.

In terms of insects, gardens are important for nectar-dependent species, such as butterflies, moths, hoverflies and wild bees. The shortage of suitable nectar in the modern countryside means that gardens are important refugia for such insects, which may be breeding outside the garden but visiting in search of nectar. However, most modern garden cultivars hold little nectar, as it has been bred out of them in order to produce longer flowering periods. This is a major nature conservation issue within the context of gardens. For example, the true ice plant *Sedum spectabile*, which is a major garden nectar source in September, has all but vanished from nurseries, having been replaced by nectar-less hybrids such as the more easily-cultivated *Sedum telephium*. Also, few, if any, modern annual cultivars hold much nectar.

Gardens are also rich habitats for insects such as various hoverflies and ladybirds whose larvae are predators of aphids; insects which feed on plants, bushes and trees; and of course all the predatory and parasitic insects associated with these. A few plant-associated insects actually

Butterflies, such as these small tortoiseshells, show a marked preference for the traditional ice plant (*Sedum spectabile*), here growing in the foreground. The modern hybrid 'Autumn Joy' behind is much less rich in nectar and distinctly less attractive to insects.
(Matthew Oates)

Rooted in History

have a stronger presence in gardens than in the countryside as their favoured foodplants are more widespread in cultivation, albeit often in the form of cultivars. A good example is the golden plusia moth, which breeds on monkshood, a plant frequently grown in gardens but very rare in the wild. The moth has recently taken to cultivated delphiniums and is increasing. Another example is the picture-wing fly *Phytomyza hellebori* whose larvae mine the leaves of stinking hellebore, a plant far commoner in gardens than in the wild.

Parks and gardens with old trees can be important for insects associated with decaying wood, for epiphytic lichens and mosses and for fungi. Indeed, many parks are of national or even European importance for these interests, as illustrated in the table below.

Top National Trust gardens and parks nationally important for invertebrates, fungi and/or lichens associated with veteran trees
(Based on information available 2000; not all properties surveyed for all interests.)

Invertebrates	Fungi	Lichens
Attingham Park (beetles)	Arlington Court	Arlington Court
Calke Park (beetles & hoverflies)	Calke Park	Crom Estate
Chirk Castle Park (beetles)	Chirk Castle Park	Dinefwr Park
Clumber Park (beetles)	Erddig Park	Dolmelynllyn Park
Croft Castle Park (beetles)	Gowbarrow Park	Dunsland Park
Croome Park (beetles)	Knole Park	Gowbarrow Park
Dinefwr Park (beetles)	Plas Newydd	Lanhydrock Park
Dunham Massey Park (beetles)	Stourhead	Whiddon Park
Erddig Park (beetles)	Tatton Park	
Hanbury Hall Park (beetles)		
Hardwick Hall Park (beetles)		
Ickworth Park (beetles)		
Kedleston Hall Park (beetles)		
Knole Park (beetles)		
Powis Castle (beetles)		
Walcot Park (beetles)		

Saturated in Wildlife: Ponds and Water Gardens

The value of ponds for wildlife is well appreciated within our culture. It is something learnt in childhood, through pond-dipping excursions. It is less widely understood that bog and marsh habits are equally rich, though with many different inhabitants. A good marsh may support a hundred species of daddy-long-legs!

Most National Trust gardens and many parks have lakes, ponds, water gardens, bog gardens and the like. Some of these water bodies are

Now rather uncommon in the wild, stinking hellebore is widely grown in gardens. This provides new opportunities for dependent species such as a scarce picture-wing fly, whose larvae feed on hellebore leaves.
(Robin Chittenden)

Right: Ornamental garden ponds, as here at Tintinhull, provide valuable habitat for newts and water-loving insects, which in turn attract birds.
(NTPL/Andrew Lawson)

The downy emerald is a scarce dragonfly occurring in certain Trust gardens. Its presence is evidence of the value of garden ponds to a wide range of wildlife, and not just those more typically associated with gardens.
(Robin Chittenden)

natural features which have been incorporated into the landscape design. A few are features of antiquity, such as medieval stew ponds and old brick pits. Most, though, are artificial constructions of recent origin. With the exception of severely-polluted water systems, the likes of which should not occur on National Trust land, all are of actual value to wildlife, even the smallest pool or pocket of 'squidge'. Much of the wildlife is associated with the submerged, floating and emergent vegetation, or with creatures dependent on that.

Many Trust garden ponds are of considerable importance to wildlife. For a start, at least a hundred gardens have ponds or pools which are used by the great crested newt, an amphibian that is fully protected by law. Many are regionally important sites for dragonflies and damselflies. Species of note include the brilliant emerald, which occurs at Sheffield Park and Scotney Castle, and the downy emerald, ruddy darter and white-legged damselfly which are local species that occur in several gardens. A host of other, smaller but often equally beautiful, insects occur around garden ponds, such as the brilliantly-coloured soldier flies, and various hoverflies and beetles whose larvae feed on aquatic plants. Many rare and curious species undoubtedly occur, but they await discovery. It is unlikely, though, that most Trust garden ponds and water gardens support more than the odd rarity, as the scarcer species tend to be specialists of long-established, more natural wetland habitats.

Several important issues affect Trust water gardens. Water quality is vital, as many plants and animals are intolerant of even mildly-polluted water, and algal blooms develop readily in stagnant, nutrient-enriched water during hot summers. Water pollution in Trust gardens most often emanates from agriculture, including organic and inorganic fertilisers, and often from Trust land itself. Pollution has also been caused by inadequate visitor toilet facilities, as for example occurred at Stourhead before new facilities were installed in the early 1990s. Leaf accumulation can cause serious problems as too many fallen leaves will de-oxygenate the water and produce stagnant, lifeless conditions.

Silt, which is often valuable topsoil that has been allowed to be washed off from nearby fields, is another important issue that particularly affects ponds and lakes through which streams flow. Such ponds function as highly efficient silt traps, especially where the surrounding land has friable soils which are used for arable farming. De-silting can be extremely expensive, and may need to occur every decade or so, which begs the question of whether such ponds are truly sustainable. The lake at Arlington Court, for example, was de-silted in 1979–80 at a cost of around £40,000, only for it to silt up again within fifteen years. The lake is in a narrow, steep-sided valley, which means that the cost of diverting the main water course to solve the siltation problem would be astronomical – around £500,000. The viability of a lake here is seriously open to question, but the donor's Memorandum of Wishes (the terms by which the property was conveyed to the Trust) requests that the lake should be perpetuated and, in any case, it is a designated Site of Special Scientific Interest. The Trust is committed to de-silting the lake again, at a cost of some £90,000, and to putting in soil conservation measures (silt traps, grass buffer zones on arable slopes, etc.) to reduce the rate of siltation. The alternative is the natural extension of the adjoining rich carr woodland.

The sustainability of mirror ponds in gardens and parks is of considerable concern to the Trust. These ponds, serpentine lakes, and the like, are sited to reflect aspects of the surrounding designed landscape, which means that they need to be largely or totally void of floating or emergent vegetation so that they can function properly as mirrors, depending on the scale and extent of vistas. Of course, vegetation development is inevitable, especially where siltation occurs. Unlike mirrors, ponds are dynamic things, full of life, and subject to massive natural changes, which mean that they are duty-bound not to stay unchanged. Ecologists would argue that mirror ponds are a denial of natural processes, and even of nature itself, and that they were created before, and have no sustainable place in, our age of ecological enlightenment.

The Moon Pond at Studley Royal exemplifies the dilemma that can arise in Trust gardens when different priorities come into conflict. The pond was designed to reflect a mirror image of the Temple of Piety, but this requires the regular clearance of vegetation, thereby reducing wildlife value. Somehow the Trust has to strike a balance between the integrity of the original design and the conservation of the wildlife that now lives there.
(NTPL/Geoff Morgan)

Escape to the Wildwood

Britain is of major importance within the European context for wildlife associated with ancient broad-leaved trees. Indeed, there are more large old trees in the British landscape than in any other European country outside the Mediterranean region. Oak supports by far the most associated species, though ash and beech are also rich. Conversely, non-native and naturalised species support relatively few associates. The two best habitats for these valuable veteran trees are ancient pasture-woodlands, of which the New Forest is the best-known example, and ancient deer parks such as Windsor Great Park. All told, the Trust owns about one-third of the best park and wood-pasture sites for wildlife associated with ancient trees in the UK. This list includes famous parks such as those at Arlington, Calke, Clumber, Dinefwr, Dunham Massey and Knole. There are also a number of Trust gardens that include old native trees of great wildlife value.

The National Trust cares for 69 landscape parks, the majority of which support at least some ancient native trees. To the naturalist, these parks are habitats rich in fungi and beetles, craneflies, fungus gnats and other esoteric invertebrates associated with different stages of wood decay, hoverflies which breed where sap oozes from lesions in the trunks and boughs, lichens and mosses growing on ancient hulks, bats and birds which utilise holes in trees, and moths and other leaf-feeding insects which breed on the foliage of large, old trees. To the aesthete, parks are designs in their own right, providing the setting for the mansion and the backdrop for the garden. To the historian they are artefacts of considerable importance. To the farmer, they are farmland. To many visitors parks are places where one can walk, relax and, in some cases, see deer at close hand. The Trust, of course, has to balance and integrate all these perspectives. The problem is that, as was the case at Croome Park (see case study on pp.142–5), the Trust often discovers the full wildlife significance of a parkland property long after acquisition, and when restoration plans which may adversely affect wildlife are already advanced. The wildlife importance at Croome is so great that the Trust has had to delay aspects of its plans for the faithful restoration of the Brownian landscape until the key species in question have transferred to newly-created alternative sites.

There are numerous issues affecting the condition and future of wildlife in National Trust parks and gardens, some of which are better understood than others. Before the wildlife importance of parks was generally appreciated, many Trust parks were let out under agricultural tenancies which allow and even encourage farmers to improve the land. It is only recently, however, that conservationists have begun to realise that many modern agricultural practices are highly detrimental to parkland wildlife and especially to the old trees that are central to the parkland experience. Thus, there is growing evidence indicating that the use of artificial fertilisers and even some organic fertilisers, such as slurry, adversely affect trees. Fungi and lichens are particularly vulnerable, but the main problem is that of the premature death of trees. In some parks even young trees are suffering die-back. Compaction of the ground beneath trees due to high stocking levels or heavy machinery, sometimes generated by visitor car parks, is causing additional stress to trees, and at a time when unusually acute fluctuations in climate are occurring. The National Trust is having to recognise that much of its parkland holding is in a state of considerable crisis.

In relation to these problems, internal disputes within the Trust over the desirability of dead hulks and fallen limbs in parkland vistas pale into insignificance, as does the issue of public safety beneath dead or dying limbs. Such matters are resolved, relatively easily, by agreeing a zoning strategy and carefully moving dead timber into designated areas.

Many necessary conservation measures have already been undertaken, such as moving car parks that are inappropriately sited under, or close to, veteran trees.

Rooted in History

A Bank Whereon the Wild Thyme Grows

Many Trust gardens have wildflower meadows or banks. Most of these are pockets of old grassland dominated by native species of grasses and herbs, often with plantings of spring bulbs or flowering shrubs. Many are floristically rich, harbouring plants which are indicative of ancient grasslands, such as adder's tongue fern and various species of orchid. Within the context of the modern agricultural landscape they are valuable refuges for plants and their associated insects.

Wildflower gardens, and indeed gardens in general, are now important sites for many nectar-dependent insects which have been largely ousted from the modern landscape. For example, gardens are significant habitats for many of the numerous British species of bee and wasp, all of which are utterly harmless creatures, which have suffered catastrophic declines in recent decades. These creatures nest inoffensively in dry banks, trampled path edges, hollow or pithy stems of trimmed shrubs, holes in old fence posts, tree trunks or logs, or in holes in the mortar of old walls. Many of them only visit the flowers of certain types of plant. For example, during the National Trust's

Opposite: Old tree stumps and fallen limbs are important habitats for invertebrates and other wildlife. Wherever possible they are left *in situ*, but health and safety concerns (as well as visual impact in certain cases) must be weighed against conservation value.
(NTPL/Roger Hickman)

Below: Wildflower meadows are a feature of many Trust gardens, serving to increase wildlife value and raise awareness of native flora. Here at Acorn Bank the orchard is left uncut so species such as the ox-eye daisy can thrive.
(NTPL/Stephen Robson)

centenary garden party in the grounds of Buckingham Palace in July 1995 the author discovered a colony of a rare mining bee, *Macropis europaea*, which nests in earthy banks and collects pollen only from the flowers of yellow loosestrife. Similar discoveries can be anticipated in National Trust gardens.

Wildflower meadows and banks are relatively dull if they are dominated by coarse grasses that permit few flowers to flourish. Much depends on soil fertility, the management regime, and the successional stage of the grassland. The problem here is that grazing, which is the most effective method of management for promoting grassland biodiversity, is impractical in most garden wildflower areas. In addition, inadequate knowledge exists on the nature conservation management of grasslands by cutting. However, it is clear that the cuttings must be removed or the sward becomes matted, to the detriment of the herb content, and that some form of mosaic-cutting is desirable in order to produce a varied structure and promote a flowering sequence. The Trust is well placed to develop knowledge on the practical management of wildlife-rich grassland through means other than grazing. Some exemplar sites already exist on Trust property, including at Rowallane where a cutting regime has been developed that is highly beneficial to the wildlife interest; the cutting is scheduled to allow key plants to set seed, and involves machinery that removes the cuttings carefully.

Hedges, Lawns, Walls and Compost Heaps

There are a number of other garden features that are of considerable value to wildlife, the most obvious of which are hedges and bushes. These are, of course, valuable nesting sites for songbirds, particularly as the severe hedge-trimming practised by most farmers has rendered much of the country's hedge system unsuitable. It is curious that the nation that can claim to have invented hedges does not know how, or is unwilling, to manage them sensitively, and even more strange that people accept the current condition of our farmland hedges. It is not surprising that the garden hedge system at Sissinghurst Castle, for example, is by orders of magnitude more suitable for nesting birds than any hedge in the surrounding countryside. Given this importance, Trust gardeners endeavour to ensure that their hedge-cutting is concentrated outside the nesting season. Thick, old hedges are also important for other forms of wildlife. Old box and yew hedges and bushes are especially good for a range of invertebrates, including many spiders, and are therefore valuable feeding-grounds for insectivorous birds and other predators. They can also be useful hibernation sites for animals such as the hedgehog.

Many of the older National Trust gardens have lawns of considerable antiquity. These too have their specialist plants and animals, although the Trust is only just beginning to discover them. Recently, an old lawn at Dinton House was found to support an unusual range of wax cap fungi, including some very scarce species. This discovery was only made when the lawn was threatened by plans – later abandoned – for the creation of a parterre. It is probable that many old lawns, on suitable soils, support interesting ranges of mining bees and digger wasps. Some scarce specialists can be anticipated and detailed survey work is required.

Sunny but sheltered walls with soft stone or crumbling mortar are utilised by a range of masonry bees and wasps, many of which are scarce, and the even rarer bees, wasps and flies which are parasatoids of these innocent hosts. The bullet holes in the soft limestone walls of Montacute House, for example, which appeared when troops were stationed there during the last war, could well harbour some scarce bees. Holes in old walls certainly accommodate more than just nesting tits and pied wagtails. The Trust now runs training courses for its building managers on wildlife in buildings as this is a major issue, particularly in view of the legal protection measures afforded to bats.

Even the humble compost heap is, or can be, a valuable habitat. For a start, compost heaps are major breeding grounds for the grass snake, a declining species and one which is a beneficial creature to have in gardens. Many Trust gardeners are careful to avoid disturbing compost heaps until the grass snake eggs have hatched.

Of Nuts and Sledgehammers

Wildlife species protection laws are deeply valued within our culture. They affect many National Trust gardens and parks, most notably those supporting great crested newt, bats or badger. The protection extends to the essential habitat features, which means that Trust gardeners need to apply for a licence to clean out or modify a pond utilised by the great crested newt. Increased protection measures for this species are anticipated under forthcoming European legislation. The implications for the Trust, and in particular its gardeners, could be enormous, for the newt can utilise small, highly artificial pools, even tiny concrete basins. Meanwhile, the Trust has vital roles to play in the conservation of both bats and buildings. The two can, and do, come into conflict, and solutions tend to be expensive. Equally, badgers are notorious for their ability to damage lawns, and organisations like the Trust have to be careful as to how they deal with these issues,

The presence of great crested newts in a pond or water feature creates particular issues which must be incorporated into the overall management plan for a garden. (Paul Sterry)

valuing both the lawn and the animals. Solutions are often reached through lateral thinking, such as providing better alternative feeding grounds in nearby fields.

Problematic and Dangerous Species

The Trust is becoming increasingly aware of its responsibilities as an environmental organisation and is developing and implementing policies to ensure that its activities are beneficial or benign. Many Trust gardens are now run on environmentally friendly lines and some are managed organically. In all gardens, the use of potentially harmful chemicals is tightly regulated and integrated pest management is practised. Further improvements can, and will, be made. These necessary concessions may limit the range of options available to Trust gardens staff in matters such as slug control.

Animal welfare perceptions also impact upon how the Trust deals with potentially problematic species, such as deer, rabbits, moles and grey squirrels. Such species can cause serious problems in gardens and parks, but control measures need to be fully justified, the options carefully examined and humane methods favoured and sensitively implemented.

In addition, creatures which are potentially dangerous to people often occur in Trust gardens and parks, most notably the adder and the hornet. Both are scarce species with normally placid temperaments. Trust garden staff need to know where they occur and deflect the public away from them, or at least advise of their presence and give instructions that eliminate undue risk.

The Way Forward

It would seem logical, particularly at a time when it is seeking to broaden the appeal of its properties, for the National Trust to adopt a policy of seeking to enhance wildlife in its gardens, so long as the key elements of each site's design are not compromised and that gardens remain fundamentally concerned with gardening. There is probably much that can be done to benefit wildlife in Trust gardens through the fine-tuning of current management practices. However, this is a complex matter, not least because the terms 'enhancement' and 'compromise', and even 'gardening', are open to varying interpretation and because beauty, rightly, tends to be in the eye of the beholder. For example, should nest boxes, bat boxes and artificial bee nest sites be standard features in Trust

The spectacular hornet is a local species in need of protection. It can, however, pose a potential threat to visitors if disturbed unduly, and so its presence in a garden must be carefully managed. (Robin Chittenden)

gardens, or would they constitute visual intrusions in some garden contexts or unjustly favour certain wildlife elements over others? Nonetheless, the premise that the Trust should shape aspects of its management techniques to encourage wildlife (rather than taking actions that could potentially compromise a garden's historic layout) is a useful starting point from which to determine a clear policy.

Another, apparently sound, principle is that the Trust should adopt practices in its gardens and parks that are as environmentally beneficial or benign as possible, and to accept the ecological benefits that this stance brings. It is, of course, a principle which the Trust should be – and indeed is – adopting as a matter of course. However, by itself this would probably not suffice, for wildlife losses could still occur and opportunities for wildlife enhancement be missed.

The most useful single measure that the Trust can adopt to further garden wildlife conservation is to facilitate proper surveys of the wildlife in its gardens, especially the fauna. The Trust's head gardeners and property managers need that information, and in a readily digestible format, so that they are aware of the wildlife significance of their gardens and can make decisions based on adequate advice. This would greatly reduce the risk of damaging actions taking place out of ignorance. It would also facilitate the implementation of simple, practical remedial measures that do not in any way compromise the garden design. In addition, Trust garden staff need access to training aimed at enabling them to develop a better understanding of ecological and nature conservation principles, and to make the best use of wildlife survey information, in terms of conservation measures, the avoidance of wildlife-related difficulties, and the production of interpretation material for visitors.

Certainly, the Trust knows that to ignore ecological principles in its gardens and parks is a recipe for natural disasters, such as algal blooms in lakes. The organisation is also becoming increasingly aware that even in established formal gardens change is inevitable, albeit at a gradual pace, and that wildlife is of both cultural and ecological significance. The precise relationship between nature and gardening needs further clarification, for although gardens cannot by definition be left to nature it is clear that nature, partly through wildlife, is an integral part of gardens and gardening. The National Trust is well placed to develop the concept of 'wildlife gardening' by integrating key aspects of its philosophy into the management of formal gardens and parks, without compromising the landscape design and history.

'*Oh what made
fatuous sunbeams
toil?'*

Wilfred Owen

Croome Park lies a few miles south of Worcester, and was 'Capability' Brown's first complete landscape. It covers over 600 hectares (1,480 acres) of woodland, parkland and agricultural land, at the heart of which lies Brown's mid-eighteenth-century masterpiece, complete with lake and several exquisite park buildings. However, the twentieth century lent hard on Croome, with severe intrusions occurring in the form of the M5 motorway (with the associated pollutions of noise, light and chemical run-off), a Second World War airfield, a radar tracking station, a sewage farm and the usual clutter of tarmac roads, telephone and electricity lines, and efficient drainage systems. Nor did the park escape the ravages of twentieth-century agriculture and forestry; rather the opposite. By the time the National Trust acquired the core of the designed landscape early in 1996, the park was not even a shadow of its former self, and was further threatened by a golf course proposal. What the Trust did not anticipate was that the park would prove to be a site of considerable importance for wildlife.

The Trust acquired the park to save it from further degradation and, over time, to carry out a faithful restoration of the landscape design implemented during the period 1747–1809. A hardened pragmatist might argue that, although the Trust exists to save features of significance from threat, by the mid-1990s Croome had rather passed through threat into the realms of total destruction, and the Trust should therefore have recognised a lost cause and placed its energies and resources

The historical development of Croome Park has created a range of wildlife habitats that make current management of the site especially complex. One particular issue surrounds the proposed return of the lake to its original 'open water' appearance. This will remove an important wetland habitat, which will be compensated for, hopefully, by the creation of new lagoons and reedbeds nearby.
(NTPL/David Noton)

elsewhere. Time alone will judge the wisdom of the decision to acquire the park, but it was certainly a brave and ambitious move and one which was soundly backed by the Heritage Lottery Fund (HLF) to the tune of £4.9 million.

For some inexplicable reason, south Worcestershire is a remarkable region for scarce beetles and other insects associated with ancient trees, especially oak. The majority of these are creatures that live in decaying timber or are associated with the fungi therein. A great many oak hulks were grubbed out at Croome during the 1960s, but the few that survive support a remarkable fauna, including two exceedingly rare beetles. Croome Park ranks amongst the top twelve UK park and pasture-woodland sites for insects associated with decaying timber (see table on page 131) and may even be of European importance for this fauna. Whether this interest would exist if Croome were not in the south Worcestershire beetle hot-spot is another matter, and how long it will survive given the paucity of the oak habitat there is also open to question. Indeed, most of the old oaks are dying and many of the scatter of younger oaks are suffering acute premature die-back. It is probable that arable cultivation has severely damaged tree roots, that the tree systems have been adversely affected by fertilisers, and that arable farming has greatly hindered the water and nutrient-foraging capacity of the trees. It may therefore be that the Trust has acquired degenerate trees supporting a doomed fauna. Nonetheless, the Trust is committed to endeavouring to keep the veteran oaks alive for as long as possible, and at least until new generations have been recruited to replace them. The beetles can consider themselves lucky that veteran open-grown oaks are an integral part of the designed landscape at Croome, for Brown incorporated pre-existing old trees into his grand design and planned for subsequent generations. Consequently, their future is certainly compatible with the landscape restoration plans.

The other major nature conservation interest at Croome is not so fortunately placed. The designed landscape includes a lake and contiguous artificial river over a mile long. These are designed to be void of dense vegetation and to merge with fields grazed by cattle. However, for the last five decades arable farming has been practised in the park. One of the impacts of this has been the rapid sedimentation of the lake and river, perhaps at a rate of up to one metre in thirteen years, and the subsequent colonisation by marshland vegetation and its associated birds and invertebrates. Currently, the serpentine river is heavily dominated by bulrush beds which form a regionally important breeding ground for reed bunting and grasshopper, sedge and reed warblers. A host of insects of marshland and reed-infested water occur, including a number of scarce dragonflies. In effect, Croome River is one of the best wetland wildlife sites in Worcestershire. However, as Croome is deemed to be the fountainhead of the greatest single English contribution to art – the English landscape style – and Croome River is cited as one of Europe's most important artificial lakes, the Trust is committed to re-establishing open water conditions throughout the length of the river and within the confines of the original banks. Of course, little of the current aquatic and marshland flora and fauna would survive such radical change, although it would not persist in its present state for much longer anyway, given current rates of siltation.

After much lateral thinking, the Trust has decided to resolve the conflict of interests by creating new lagoon, reed bed and marshland habitats along the edge of the park, at the north end and close to the motorway, and to complete the dredging of the lake and river once the nature conservation interest has transferred successfully to these new locations. These new features will also act as a natural filter and water purification system, helping to solve the problems posed by mildly polluted water running into the park's water bodies off the motorway and by silt and chemical run-off from agricultural land outside the Trust's boundaries.

The issue of agriculture in the park is more difficult. Currently, much of the park is under arable farming, whereas designed landscape parks are supposed to be pastoral landscapes, with extensive grasslands grazed by cattle and sheep and cut for hay. Moreover, Croome was designed partly as a centre for radical new methods of stock husbandry. When the Trust acquired Croome the park was in four separate secure agricultural tenancies, each of which allowed one further succession under agricultural law. In brief, the landowner has no right to force a tenant farmer to change his farming practices, and of course the National Trust would not wish to act in a draconian manner anyway. Nonetheless, arable farming has contributed heavily to the current poor condition of the park, and in particular to the demise of the ancient trees and to the problems of siltation and poor water quality in the lake and river. The Trust is committed towards restoring the park to grassland in the medium term, for grassland restoration was a condition of HLF funding. Initially, grassland buffer zones were established around the margins of fields bordering the lake and river, and positive working relationships were developed with the tenant farmers (and with the owners and managers of the adjoining land). The Trust is currently negotiating the future of farming in the park with its tenants. It has already been agreed that the most important part of the park will be returned to pasture, and the Trust is optimistic that suitable compensatory agreements will be reached over the future of the remainder. The current agricultural crisis presents a window of opportunity for such negotiations.

Other complex nature conservation issues exist in the park, notably the fact that it is an important feeding area for a sizeable population of the rare and protected lesser horseshoe bat. The Trust does not own the Croome Court buildings where the bats roost, but does own the land over which they roam to feed, and the bats are most particular as to where they fly and about what they eat. They, too, are likely to benefit from the envisaged changes in agricultural practices in the park.

Croome Park is currently a long way from being the realisation of Brown's vision of Ideal Nature. It is arguably a place where the past and future are of more significance than the present, although of course the present has a role in linking the two together. Croome may prove to be a good example of the National Trust's ability to integrate nature conservation with other, very precise, objectives.

8

Gardens Open to View

Susan Denyer

Probably no two people see a garden in the same way. Each of us brings our own expectations, knowledge and experience to a garden when we visit it. We gain pleasure from what we see, from the sounds, smells and ability to touch. Gardens offer an opportunity for us to connect with our environment on many different levels. Yet the way we view gardens is deeply personal, and may be very different from the manner in which they were perceived by their creators. As we cannot divorce ourselves from our own time, space and culture, we may see in gardens qualities unknown to those who planned them. Gardens that stand the test of time seem to be able to transcend social and cultural boundaries and speak a language that is as relevant now as it was when they were created.

Visiting gardens is a way of possessing them, albeit temporarily. Our possessive instincts can at times lead us to want to be the only people to experience all this. Small and intimate gardens, or gardens divided into 'rooms', reinforce this sense of possession and heighten our satisfaction at individual responses. At other times the pleasure of shared experience can be equally strong. Large landscape gardens with wide paths seem to invite a parade: too few people and they feel empty.

In opening its gardens to the public, the National Trust has to be sensitive to all these feelings and aspirations. Managing access means trying to allow each one of the millions of visitors to our gardens to have the feeling of space they desire, while at the same time welcoming as many people as possible to share in the enjoyment. It means trying to assess the significance of gardens not just in terms of the importance of the plant collections or the esteem of their designers and patrons, but also in terms of atmosphere, of a sense of place and of spiritually restorative powers. It also means respecting age, mellowness and, at times, benign neglect.

The bust of Sir Thomas Gresham in the Temple of British Worthies at Stowe. From the time of its creation, Stowe was open to visitors and was the subject of one of the earliest garden guidebooks, published in the 1740s. (NTPL/Rupert Truman)

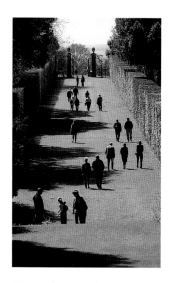

Most gardens were designed to be enjoyed by their owner and a few friends. Avenues and vistas, such as here at Hidcote, were therefore intended to be viewed in terms of their design and effect, without the 'clutter' of large numbers of people! Opening properties to public access has necessarily changed all this.
(NTPL/Ian Shaw)

The Trust's guidebooks invite visitors to see gardens dating from a certain decade or century, or gardens laid out by a particular designer or owner. But in fact this is only part of the story. Gardens cannot stand still – from the moment of their creation they begin to change as the processes of nature take over – and so what visitors come to enjoy is actually the result of a series of negotiations with the forces of change: a present-day evocation of the intentions of their creators, combined with the effects of time, all overlain by the perceptions of those who have nurtured them.

However, there is also a negotiation between visitors and the gardens they visit. Very few gardens were created for large numbers of people. Places like Stowe, Stourhead and Studley Royal are the exceptions: created for display on a magnificent scale, they were always intended to be visited by comparatively large numbers of people – and visitors in their colourful clothes combined with the garden to create dynamic tableaux. These gardens seem at home when full of visitors, and visitors in turn do not generally mind seeing many others share in their enjoyment.

Even in these expansive gardens there can come a moment when too many people crowd the spaces and begin to have a negative effect on the pleasure of others. Many landscape gardens were designed to control views – the paths through them build up a sense of anticipation as they wind through woodland or constructed tunnels and then open out to reveal the unexpected long view of a lake, temple or ruin, as in the case of Studley Royal. For many of these 'surprise' views, one could argue that people need to be looking at the view rather than seeing others within it, if the image is to have the intended effect. In suggesting walks round gardens, the Trust tries to ensure that the original intentions of the designer are respected and interpreted, whilst at the same time acknowledging the practical realities of contemporary public access.

At Stourhead, one of the lakeside paths was redirected slightly away from the water, so that people walking along it did not impact on the views of other visitors observing the lake from the opposite shore. Was this the right thing to do? Perhaps this is controlling people too far, but giving visitors a sense of surprise and excitement, in the spirit of the original concept, can be a way of explaining gardens and of connecting today's visitors with yesterday's landscape designers.

Gardens designed as private spaces for their owners and selected friends usually have to absorb many thousands more visitors now than they ever did before they came into Trust ownership. It is clear that if the Trust is to fulfil its promise to care for properties 'forever, for everyone', we must accept that these gardens are now public arenas, and that

The attractions of some larger gardens, such as Stourhead, were designed specifically to be shown off to groups of people. This 1775 view by Copplestone Warre Bampfylde shows various visitors enjoying the grounds and views. (NTPL/Angelo Hornak)

the relationship between people and spaces has changed accordingly. However, the Trust strives wherever possible to find a middle way, by which something of the feeling of a private garden, into which the fortunate few have been allowed, is retained, whilst simultaneously inviting in the many. All public access involves some intervention – people inevitably alter what they come to see – but this is particularly so in Trust gardens, where so many different factors must be take into account. The amount and type of access has to be balanced first against the impact people have on the 'spirit' or atmosphere of the garden, and secondly against the physical conservation needs of the design and contents.

The narrow paths and small spaces of gardens, such as Tintinhull (left), appeal strongly to visitors, but can pose problems at busy times. In particular, pathside plants risk being trampled, as here at Sissinghurst (above).
(NTPL/Andrew Lawson and Ian Shaw)

The confined spaces and small 'compartments' of gardens such as Hidcote quickly fill with visitors and careful management is required to avoid undue congestion. (NTPL/Ian Shaw)

Providing a satisfactory circular route is a necessary intervention in many gardens. When they were in private hands their owners knew exactly where to go and did not necessarily need to travel all the way round on each excursion. Nowadays, some visitors may only come once and so want to see as much of the garden as possible. They need help in identifying the best route to see the garden's main features, to enjoy the views from the most effective angles and on how to be secure in the knowledge that they will end up where they started. To achieve this sometimes means putting in new paths or formalising others so that the route is clear.

Access must also be tailored to meet the specific requirements of different groups of visitor. For example, the less mobile may wish to tour a garden by wheelchair or motorised buggy, so that they can see as much as possible. Providing such access can sometimes lead to the modification of routes in order to provide paths with acceptable gradients. The challenge is to provide access for all without excessive standardisation, which risks ironing out the very idiosyncrasies that contribute to the peculiar charm of some gardens.

Children are another special group of visitors requiring particular attention. Besides providing simple enjoyment, how can we provide happy memories of gardens for children in ways which might colour their adult years? The Trust aims to provide children (and their families!) with an experience that is both educational and fun, through the use of activity trails, children's guidebooks and quizzes, as well as hands-on activities such as 'bug-hunts', story-telling and planting workshops. Some gardens now have adventure playgrounds, often cleverly sited so as not to disturb the main views in the garden and, where possible,

Special events aimed at families are a popular and effective way of interpreting gardens and making them a more exciting place for younger visitors. Here Westbury Court's gardener Richard Bentley explains old varieties of English apples on Apple Day. (NTPL/Ian Shaw)

Rooted in History

sections of a garden are designated as children's areas. For example, part of the woodland garden at Knightshayes Court has been developed as a natural adventure area in which children can run around and explore. It also serves as a venue for special events, with artists sometimes working there with the children, encouraging them to touch and appreciate the trees.

Another way in which opening a garden to visitors has an impact on the very thing they come to see is the need to have the garden presentable and interesting throughout the months it is open. Some gardens were never intended to have year-round interest, or even full 'open season' attractions – they may have been created for their owners to view only at certain times of year. For instance, at Belton House the family visited only for the spring and so vast arrays of bulbs and bedding plants (including tulips, wallflowers and some 20,000 pansies) were set out in the 80 beds of the Dutch Garden to provide spectacular displays for a brief few weeks. In 1905 the head gardener planted no fewer than 16,000 daffodils along the Lime Avenue to provide a dramatic spring-time approach to the house. At other properties, such as Stackpole, the gardens needed to be at their best in early autumn to coincide with the shooting season, when the family would be entertaining.

Restricting the opening of such gardens to times conceived for the original family is not a realistic option today. Nor would empty flowerbeds be appreciated by our visitors! Some gardens are therefore adapted to reflect their new purpose by being planted up with species chosen to provide interest over a longer period of time. Are such compromises acceptable? Perhaps the purists would argue not, but if we think of gardens as a continual dialogue between people and their surroundings, then it is reasonable for the dialogue today to include the people who visit these places. A garden can still reflect what is special or significant to it, but an added overlay may allow it to interact with a wider audience. Much depends on the significance of the garden: some gardens, such as that at Upton House, where the earlier kitchen garden was largely planted up with ornamentals in the 1920s to designs by Kitty Lloyd Jones for Lord Bearsted, have had a history of change in response to varying circumstances over many centuries, and there one could argue that the continuation of change is acceptable (if not desirable?). Gardens such as Westbury Court, however, reflect a specific period or fashion, and so to add new features or dramatically alter what is there is much less appropriate.

In some parts of the country the Trust's gardens and parks are rightly enjoyed as accessible areas of countryside offering recreation possibilities. This is particularly true in parts of East Anglia, where the flat

The creation of the Winter Walk at Anglesey Abbey is an excellent example of how the attraction of a garden can be extended into what were always considered 'dead' months.
(NTPL/Stephen Robson)

Protecting lawns and other sensitive surfaces from the ravages of feet is a constant concern for gardeners. Path 'spread' can be a problem in places where large numbers of people gather, such as near an entrance or exit point, and it can be necessary to cordon off areas of turf so the grass can recover.
(NTPL/Ian Shaw)

farmland can make for a rather uniform walking experience. At Felbrigg, Sheringham and Blickling the Trust's parks provide year-round enjoyment, proving particularly popular in the winter months. Meanwhile, recent years have seen the introduction at Anglesey Abbey of a Winter Walk, planted with shrubs and perennials that look their best outside the summer months.

In Cornwall, for different reasons, visitors are wanting access outside the traditional six-month summer opening season. Climate change means that spring seems to arrive ever earlier, and so for the magnolias, camellias and spring bulbs to be seen at their best, some gardens are now opening in February and attracting thousands of visitors.

In metaphysical as well as in literal terms, perhaps the greatest impact visitors have on gardens is through their feet. In large numbers, feet can be very destructive. Gardens with grass paths are the most vulnerable, and this vulnerability is exacerbated in wet weather and during winter. To make gardens more robust, grass paths are sometimes relaid in gravel. This change is not undertaken lightly, as in small spaces the character of the garden can be altered greatly and, particularly in woodland gardens, grass paths are a key part of the overall design. More preferable is intensive management of the turf to try to mitigate the effect of intensive use. In a few gardens, ways are being explored to reinforce the carrying capacity of turf at certain 'pinch points'. For instance, rubber granules have been incorporated into grassed areas in some Devon gardens and at Nymans, thereby successfully increasing their resilience.

How do gardens speak to people? Can we fully appreciate a garden if we know nothing about what the owner or designer intended to convey? And how do we, or should we, gain the knowledge we feel we need – particularly when we might not know what exists? It is clear that people have varying requirements and learn in different ways, and that the Trust therefore needs to tailor its information accordingly. This involves using a variety of different techniques and media, such as live interpretation (costumed characters), audio guides, practical workshops, guided tours and exhibitions, as well as guidebooks. The key objective is to ensure that the story of a garden is told from a range of perspectives, so that it relates to the diverse groups of visitors that have come to see it.

As the years go by, so the gap between today and the time when Trust gardens were created grows; and as the gap increases, so knowledge of the 'language' used by past garden designers diminishes. Very few people now understand the classical allegories in gardens such as Stowe or West Wycombe, or appreciate the painterly connections with the picturesque landscape gardens of the Lake District, or sense the tensions between classic and romantic notions at Sissinghurst. Such references are not part of today's vocabulary or education. Nor can we expect visitors to have a detailed knowledge of garden history in order to know why Stourhead or Biddulph Grange represent defining moments in the development of gardens.

The traditional way to understand a garden is to read its history in a guidebook and then visit with the benefit of background knowledge. This appeals to some visitors but not to all. Perhaps the majority prefer to experience the garden first, to see what is there, and then to begin to ask for more information, perhaps on the plants, or on the origins and process of the garden's creation, its ownership, maintenance and use. And it is sometimes only on subsequent visits to a garden that the need for more knowledge is felt. How is this best delivered? The Trust is constantly looking at how its dialogue with visitors can be improved.

Biddulph Grange was one of the first gardens to have garden volunteers responsible for talking to visitors and helping to guide them. Some two hundred people now share this work throughout the opening season. Biddulph is laid out as a form of global journey from Egypt to China, and so the guides both explain the route and also tell the story of how the garden was rescued from dereliction. A similar system is in place at Hardwick Hall, where specially trained volunteers are on hand to talk to visitors in the herb garden.

Plantsman's gardens need suitably qualified guides to interpret them. Particularly popular and effective is for the gardener to talk direct to visitors, sharing his or her knowledge and giving an insight into the skill with which plants are chosen and blended. At only a few properties can gardeners talk to visitors on a daily basis – they would simply have too little time left for gardening. Special out-of-hours events, such as garden evenings, are one way of ensuring that visitors have the chance to meet the staff responsible for managing a garden. Meanwhile, guidebooks remain the main artery for information on the history and development of gardens. In recent years they have been subject to close attention in terms of their format, content and 'tone', and now present a different aspect from the worthy but rather staid publications of 20 years ago.

Debates on the most appropriate and effective ways of providing information are nothing new. Garden guides have a long history and have often aroused strong emotions. Three of the earliest guides were published in the 1740s for visitors to Stowe. These offered a description, a dialogue and illustrated views of the garden. They were said not to be for those who had never seen the garden, but rather to 'renew the Idea of it in those who have' – the first examples of souvenir guides. They were challenged in 1750, when a different publisher brought out a more populist version, written in conversational style with a more attractive layout. This led during the next few years to a 'battle of the guidebooks' with the more scholarly models eventually winning.

Guidebooks remain one of the most popular forms of interpretation. In recent years the format has been extensively revised and the number of full-colour guides increased.
(NT)

Rooted in History

As with house guidebooks, those for gardens are now much more extensively illustrated than in the past. Greater use is made of visual material from different periods – historical photographs, engravings, reproductions of watercolour views, and, of course, contemporary photographs, drawn from the ten photographic shoots that take place in Trust gardens in an average year. What the images actually show has also changed, with more emphasis now on the individuals that work in the garden, thereby helping to highlight for visitors the behind-the-scenes work that goes on throughout the year and to make the point that gardens are about people as much as plants! Guidebooks now attempt to do two things: first, to allow to let you to dip in and gain information whilst actually on a visit and secondly, to provide an attractive souvenir to look at afterwards.

As gardens are in a constant state of change and development, garden guidebooks are revised more frequently than their house equivalents. Some seasonal guides are now produced, to reflect differing aspects of the year in a garden. Meanwhile, the whole range of guidebooks and guiding literature has been greatly expanded in recent years. Guide leaflets – short guides, often illustrated with a bird's-eye view of the garden and colour pictures – provide easily accessible information on how to navigate the garden, where the main viewpoints and features are located, and what the thinking was behind its creation. There are also sensory guides for the blind and deaf, children's guides and audio guides (both in cassette form and as 'wands'). The Internet is also proving an effective means of helping to interpret gardens and keeping visitors informed. The Trust's Estates Office website holds a range of information on gardens, such as extracts from recent survey reports and news on Trust policies, such as going 'peat-free'.

Guidebooks cannot be neutral – the messenger always intervenes in the way facts are selected and pictures presented. Indeed, some of the earliest guides did not set out to present factual descriptions: one of the early Stowe guides presented, through an imaginary dialogue, a debate on the successes and failures of the garden. Value judgements are inevitable and contemporary Trust guidebooks try not to shy away from making them, whilst also ensuring that key facts and information are conveyed in an accessible and interesting style.

One area where visitors particularly welcome specific facts and detailed information is on what plants are in a garden. Where a garden is known primarily for its horticultural value, it seems to be a case of the more information the better! Interestingly, visitors to gardens often like to be given catalogue lists with scientific names, unlike house visitors, who do not seem to want lengthy tracts on chattels or architects. Perhaps this is because cataloguing nature has always seemed easier to accept than cataloguing what is man-made. However complex, gardens can be broken down into elements that are universally acknowledged.

Providing information on plants can be done in several ways. Many head gardeners provide plant lists locally at their properties; with the advent of desk-top publishing they can be responsive to annual or even seasonal changes in the information they provide. Some gardens have plant tags; others provide small displays in buildings within a garden, perhaps in a small potting shed; yet others have a chalk board high-lighting what is in bloom or particularly attractive each week.

Understanding can of course also be achieved by looking at gardens in a new light through someone else's eyes. *Arts in Trust* is an initiative enabling artists to work with groups of schoolchildren or visitors in gardens, helping them to express their feelings for the garden spontaneously and in a variety of ways. The work they produce may be wholly ephemeral or perhaps intended to last a season. The clay sculptures with raised arms which welcomed visitors to Castle Drogo during 2000 resulted from a collaboration between a Japanese ceramicist living in Devon and groups of students and other visitors. Artists can also help to prolong visits and encourage visitors to record their own impressions. *Paint the Garden*, a project in which artists provide a supply of art materials and encourage visitors to 'have a go', started at Calke Abbey and has been so successful that it has been now extended to other properties.

In some gardens, professional artists have been invited to mount exhibitions for a summer season. At Blickling, an 'In Memoriam' exhibition collected together examples in wood and stone to show how letter cutting could produce beautiful and evocative memorials. In 2000 this was followed by *Views across the Lake*, which invited artists and craftspeople to respond to the gardens at Blickling – part of the garden becoming an interactive gallery for the season.

Other art forms are also proving a popular way of enjoying Trust gardens. *Dance in Trust* has proved a highly successful initiative at a number of properties, including in the gardens at Osterley and Blickling. Wide-ranging community groups come together and, with the help of the Rambert Dance Company, produce a new dance inspired by the property. This dance is then performed to visitors.

A wide range of special events is held in Trust gardens, many of them on a grand scale attracting thousands of spectators. In an average year, over 400 different gardens events are organised, ranging from apple blossom day at Ardress House to the spectacular *fêtes champêtres* held at Stourhead and Cliveden. Gardens such as Claremont, with its huge stepped amphitheatre, were specifically devised for performances and pageants, so it is very appropriate that such events continue to take

National Trust gardens are now increasingly used as venues for art exhibitions and workshops. Castle Drogo provided a dramatic back-drop to the huge clay sculptures created by Japanese ceramicist Taja. (NT/Mark Rattenbury)

Rooted in History

place there. In spite of the fickle British weather, many landscape gardens host successful performances of music, dance or drama, their spaces providing informal backdrops to events which bring enormous shared enjoyment. Increasingly these offer visitors the chance to participate in dance or improvised drama, and such events can be an effective way of attracting people who might not otherwise be interested in visiting the gardens.

One powerful way in which people can interact with gardens is through sampling their abundance. Many gardens in which the plants were grown primarily for show had a secondary role producing cut flowers and plants for the house. Sometimes this involved bringing plants on in glasshouses; at other times flowers for cutting were grown in special beds. This link between house and garden is nurtured at many Trust properties, so that flower arrangements within the house can be sustained using plants traditional to the house. At Cragside, for example, particular efforts are made to grow varieties popular in the nineteenth century, for display in this quintessential Victorian house.

Greenhouses for bringing on plants were usually part of the working end of the garden, within or near the kitchen garden. The Trust owns over 100 kitchen gardens, from the vast and complex such as at Clumber Park to much more modest examples like the Apprentice House at Styal. Over the past few years interest has increased in how these gardens were organised and managed, and in the unusual and local varieties of produce. Concerted efforts are now in hand at several properties to bring kitchen gardens back into full working order, two of the biggest projects being at Tatton Park and Wimpole Hall. Meanwhile, many more kitchen gardens are worked on a smaller scale to produce high quality wholesome produce. At Barrington Court food from the garden is used in the restaurant: the same is true of Calke Abbey, where surplus produce is also sold to visitors. To see food growing in environmentally green kitchen gardens and then sample it in the nearby restaurant is proving to be a very satisfying and popular experience for visitors.

Many visitors derive inspiration for their own gardens from what they see at Trust properties. Sometimes it is the design and layout that inspires – gardens such as Hidcote and Sissinghurst with their series of rooms must have spawned thousands of smaller-scale copies. Just as important however is the desire to possess some of the rare and interesting plants that are found in Trust gardens. Satisfying that demand is not easy. Growing plants is time-consuming for gardeners, and the enterprise is often barely profitable if the full costs are charged. The Trust has tried to franchise plant sales at some properties, whilst at others, such as Osterley, very successful plant fairs have been held with plants grown by volunteers. But these solutions do not satisfy the demand for specific plants related to specific gardens. At present the Trust's first priority is to sustain, through its nurseries, some of the many endangered species in its gardens. In the future sharing that unique resource will be given higher priority.

Meeting visitor expectations must be achieved not just in terms of intellectual and spiritual rewards, but also through providing physical comforts. Out of a total of over 200 gardens open to the public, only a handful now have no dedicated car park; and only very few have no refreshment facilities. This is in distinct contrast to the picture even 25 years ago, when bringing thermos flasks and parking in fields was more the norm.

Around 11 million visitors arrived at Trust gardens by car in 2000. Making access by car easier has to be balanced against the environmental impact of these journeys. Freedom to travel and to visit is a wonderful thing, but do the benefits justify the cost? The Trust must evaluate not just the carrying capacity of its gardens in terms of conservation but also what the wider impact is of so many car journeys. At present the policy is not to enlarge car parks if alternative means of access can be offered. Of course, the Trust cannot coerce its visitors, but it can encourage alternatives. Over the past few years green links have grown apace, and ways of visiting our properties by public transport are now widely advertised and promoted. For new properties, an environmental audit is carried out to look at how visiting can be made more sustainable. There will always be some properties where public transport cannot be made to work: this is where the Trust can take an overview of all its gardens and try and meet green targets on a national basis, as well as at the local level.

Refreshments at gardens are seen by most visitors as an essential part of their visit. Indeed, they are widely recognised as being central to the enjoyment of the visit, particularly if they involve sampling local produce and sitting in atmospheric surroundings. How to deliver these refreshments without compromising the gardens is a constant but exciting challenge. Health, safety and hygiene standards now mean that informal tea-rooms in only lightly adapted buildings are hard to operate. Converting buildings to satisfy regulations and provide the necessary lighting and plumbing can sometimes mean that otherwise suitable buildings, such as stables or barns, require so much adaptation as to destroy their integrity.

Particularly in well-visited gardens, putting up a new building is often the only realistic solution. Whether these buildings should be a statement or should pretend to be invisible is debated long and hard. Should they look like a temporary tent – as at Nymans – or pretend to be a farm building, as at Stourhead? Or can they be good modern designs that take their vocabulary from the local surroundings? Two recent new tea-rooms have tried to achieve the latter. At Coleton Fishacre a small tea-room was finished partly in corrugated iron and partly with a canvas awning, whilst at Glendurgan the new building is more like a lean-to behind sculpted stone walls which link it to the rest of the garden. In both instances, neither structure tries to emulate existing buildings but both succeed in sitting well within their respective garden landscapes.

The annual budget for conserving and maintaining the 200 or so gardens and 69 landscape parks open to the public is around £11 million. Large schemes for developing gardens and major conservation projects are funded separately. To achieve all that it does, the Trust relies heavily on drawing in support from outside organisations and from individuals through fund-raising, sponsorship, legacies or donations.

Gardens are amongst the most popular places for visitors and this is perhaps reflected in the large amount of external support that is attracted

Sudbury Hall's annual *Day of Dance* is a celebration of dance, music and costume involving participants from many different cultures. (NTPL/Chris King)

each year. Perhaps it is also a reflection of the imaginative projects that can be offered. Over the past three years, Gordons Gin have sponsored work on juniper restoration schemes at Chartwell, at the Cheshire Cottage at Biddulph and at Knightshayes; Royal Sun Alliance helped to fund the restoration of Croome Park; and recently a substantial legacy from Mrs Denise Leffman has been offered to restore the Sunken Garden at Lyme Park.

Equally important are the smaller amounts of money given by individuals who respond to fund-raising. National Trust associations and centres, many of which have close links with their local gardens, have over the years made substantial impacts through their fund-raising activities on such aspects as new gates, new planting schemes or the restoration of garden ornaments and sculpture.

Perhaps because gardens give so much pleasure it is not surprising that the Trust receives very large numbers of requests each year for people to fund seats in memory of friends or relations. Unfortunately it is usually very difficult to satisfy this demand and so instead people are invited to help in other ways, such as by making donations to specific gardens or gardens-related projects.

Anyone who has created a garden knows the strong possessive instincts that the process engenders: only you understand both the grand plan and the minutiae of individual plants, when to be ruthless and when to nurture. In most Trust gardens the original designers, patrons or gardeners have long since vanished from the scene and their gardens been taken over by those who subsequently tend and look after them − gardeners, restorers, tenants, managers, or perhaps local committees. How can that spark, which ignited the garden in its early years, be kept alive by those who follow? Who should have a say in the way they develop and evolve? Whose garden have they become?

If visitors are to respond to gardens they need to sense that people are behind what is on view − and not just dead people. Gardens need a dynamism to take them forward to the next generation and only if they look as if they are understood and loved will they come alive for those of us who visit.

Opening gardens to view is so much more than a mechanical exercise for the Trust. Simply opening the gates and saying 'come in' neither satisfies the visitors nor makes the most of what the Trust can offer. A more complex and sensitive response is called for. We need to offer pleasure, understanding and involvement in creative, dynamic and sustainable ways, so that people are welcomed as constructive and essential parts of the life of gardens. At the same time, as custodians for the nation, we need to care for gardens in the long term so that they offer their benefits now and in the future.

So many people enjoy being in gardens that the demand to visit is potentially huge. The Trust is constantly looking at new ways to meet this enormous and exciting challenge with vigour and understanding in order that it can unlock the vast potential of its gardens − for everyone's benefit.

Case Study Sissinghurst Castle

Set deep in the Kent countryside, the celebrated garden at Sissinghurst has changed very little since it was created by Vita Sackville-West and Harold Nicolson in the 1930s. Comprising a delightful series of small compartments set around the surviving tower of an Elizabethan manor house, the garden is rich in romance and atmosphere, and has become something of a legend, attracting large numbers of visitors, including many from overseas.

Sissinghurst's fame and popularity present enormous problems for those who care for it. The small scale of the garden 'rooms' and narrow paths is such that both overcrowding and wear-and-tear – particularly the impact of feet on delicate surfaces – are ever-present potential problems. Here visitor management is not just a case of avoiding damage to the features and contents of the garden, but also one of maintaining the enjoyment levels of the visitors, by trying to retain a sense of the uninterrupted vistas and peace and quiet that Vita and Harold would have enjoyed, as well as ensuring that the garden looks its best at all times. But how can 175,000 people each year experience these pleasures without changing or damaging the very thing they value so highly?

Behind the calm façade, immaculate hedges and contained magic of the 'rumpus' of colours within the beds, lies a tightly controlled management regime. The fact that much of this remains invisible, and that visitors do not feel unduly 'controlled', is a measure of its success. But what are the issues this regime has to address?

At the time when Vita and Harold owned the garden they had perhaps a hundred visitors a year. Narrow grass paths were perfectly adequate and plants cascading over the paths did not present a problem. Nor did it matter if the garden did not come into its own until early May, or was somewhat untidy in late autumn. If in some years the half-hardy plants failed, or Vita and Harold could not keep up with the weeding, no one felt cheated. But now the garden must look in tip-top condition throughout the open season (April to October) and has to cope with many thousands of feet on its delicate pathways and through its narrow access points.

By the 1970s it was clear that visitor numbers had reached the point at which parts of the garden were beginning to suffer, and so at that time some of the grass paths were replaced by local stone, bricks and tiles, following a precedent established by the family, who had already replaced one path with York stone earlier. However, it was rightly felt that wholesale replacement of the grass paths with more durable alternatives would adversely affect the overall look and feel of the garden, and so now the remaining grass paths are maintained by an intensive programme of weekly fertilising, scarifying and spiking, and by mowing at seven-eighths of an inch in height.

The physical configuration of Sissinghurst creates particular difficulties for those responsible for the care of the garden and its visitors. That so many people come and enjoy their visits is testament to the success of the techniques employed to manage such large numbers.
(NTPL/Ian Shaw)

The grass on the paths is therefore prevented from giving way to sticky clay soil under the weight of feet, but this can never be the whole solution. The number of visitors and their frequency also need to be controlled, to keep them within sustainable levels. Similar parameters apply to the protection of the overflowing borders, which provide such a wonderful foil for the formal structure: too many people at any one time will encourage trampling along the edges of the paths.

Visitors to Sissinghurst are subtly managed in terms of where they go and, within reason, in which order they see the garden. Routes are carefully chosen to ensure that the number of 'pinch points' is minimised and that everyone gets to see what they want without feeling unduly hassled or crowded. (NTPL/Ian Shaw)

In order to try and establish the 'optimum' number of visitors, ie the number of people considered commensurate with the impact on the garden and on visitor enjoyment, a computerised counting system has been employed to monitor those visiting the garden and to make projections. 'Acceptable' levels of congestion have been calculated for each area of the garden, and the amount of time visitors spend in the garden overall assessed. In summer this amounts to about one and a half hours, more if it is hot (when visitors often sit in the shade) and much less on cold days. From this data, it is possible to develop an understanding of what constitutes an acceptable flow of visitors at different times of year. This is then translated into the number of people per hour that can be allowed though the gate if undue overcrowding or excessive wear-and-tear are to be avoided. To achieve this number, Sissinghurst operates a timed-ticket system, by which visitors are issued on arrival with a ticket advising them of the time they may enter the garden. Although visitors may not enter until the time indicated, there is no restriction on how long they may spend in the garden, and generally the waiting time is not very long (indeed, at certain times of day and year entry may be possible immediately).

But how might visitors be encouraged to visit in numbers that match those which can be allowed in through the gate? If too many turn up at the 'wrong' – or busiest – times of year, this can lead to longer waiting periods and understandable frustration. This is where positive information and targeted promotion plays a part. If the garden is promoted equally throughout the year, too many people may try and visit at the most popular times. Publicity and information are therefore aimed at 'spreading the load' and encouraging visits at times when demand might be less, or impact on the garden less of a concern. Clearly, some people may have no choice about when they can come, and so every effort is made to accommodate them, but equally it is perfectly possible to encourage others to visit when the garden is quieter. This is particularly so with local visitors. Like many Trust gardens, Sissinghurst is seen by local people as 'their' garden, and considerable effort has been put into suggesting that they come at quieter times, without the crowds of visitors that come from further afield at peak periods. In winter, when the garden is closed, visitors are encouraged to enjoy the woods and lakes of the wider landscape – Vita loved the fact that the garden was set amidst beautiful countryside and that the formal boundary of the garden was not a visual barrier.

Although the source of occasional grumbles, by and large timed tickets are appreciated by visitors. They generally welcome the reassurance that the system provides – knowing that they will be able to visit the garden even if it means waiting a while (important if they have travelled a long way) – and are usually supportive of the rationale, when this is explained to them. Absolutely key to the success of timed ticketing, however, is the provision of on-site facilities to help visitors pass the time whilst they are waiting to enter the garden. At Sissinghurst these include an exhibition on the history of the garden, a well-stocked shop and a restaurant, as well as the country walks that have been developed around the perimeter of the garden.

Spreading the visitor load throughout the open season does, however, put the onus on the garden staff to ensure the garden is looking its best at all times. To achieve this, the team of six gardeners works to a tight programme, with each season's work timetabled to within a few days. Over and above this daily work, the broader canvas of the garden's planting needs to be reviewed and maintained to provide interest throughout the year, especially in the early part of the open season.

Vita's and Harold's vision was of a dynamic garden – they tried out new plants, experimented with shapes and colours and added new areas, gradually evolving Vita's painterly vision within the strong archi-tectural framework created by Harold. As with most gardeners, the garden was always 'going to be better next year'. The Trust has continued with this vision, experimenting with new combinations of colours, textures and shapes, introducing new plants or reintroducing old types, and occasionally abandoning some plants for a few years. This is done in a way which respects the original atmosphere and palette of colours for each area of the garden, and does not alter the thinking that under-pinned Vita and Harold's planting. Whilst ensuring that the garden looks in excellent shape at all times, no attempt is made to even out the show, for instance, by using modern varieties of roses to extend the flowering season; nor is too much colour introduced in August, a time when Vita and Harold were often away and the garden 'rested'. Instead, visitors are encouraged to understand the garden, to appreciate how different areas reach their peak at different times of year and to see that even when a part of the garden is not a haze of flowers, there is much to appreciate in terms of form and texture.

Although this regime is in some respects different from how the garden was managed when it was taken on by the Trust in 1967 – for a start there are far more gardeners now – the changes are in essence practical rather than philosophical. They help to keep the garden dynamic, to allow it to remain relevant and, above all, to enable it to fulfil its new role in providing enjoyment as one of the most inspiring and popular gardens the Trust owns.

9

Putting on the Show

Katie Fretwell
with help from John McKennall, Jim Marshall and Julie Schofield

'For the last forty years of my life I have broken my back, my finger-nails, and sometimes my heart, in the practical pursuit of my favourite occupation …'.
Vita Sackville-West, 1958

National Trust gardens are fundamentally dependent on the skills, vision and dedication of each gardener and, whilst gardening has its roots in antiquity, the role of the gardener has changed over time. If we look at how that role has developed, and at the huge demands now made on garden staff, it is perhaps not unreasonable to regard our gardeners as positively heroic, coping with tremendous pressures while remaining (on the whole!) patient and cheerful. They are both the Trust's front-line troops and its best ambassadors, and undoubtedly deserving of far greater reward than the Trust can ever afford to pay them in terms of salary.

Gardeners in History

From at least Jacobean times onwards, gardening was a highly respected and valued profession. Eminent botanists and garden designers vied fiercely for the title of Royal Gardener, a well-rewarded and prominent sinecure – for example, it was the Gardener himself who was deemed worthy of handing the first British-grown pineapple to King Charles II in *c.*1675. In Georgian Britain Lancelot 'Capability' Brown set a prominent example of one who rose from lowly origins and a start as a garden boy to a position of high national regard. Through hard work,

Brilliant late summer colours on the formal terraces at Coleton Fishacre.
(NTPL/Neil Campbell-Sharp)

determination, skill and a gift for communication he rose swiftly through the ranks, becoming Head Gardener and Clerk of Works at Stowe before establishing himself as a freelance landscape designer. By the end of his career he was highly respected, accepted as a gentleman and equal by the nobility, and with a national public profile and his own small mansion. Only weeder women seem to have toiled without any hope of higher things!

By the Victorian era the gardening system had become highly regulated, with two distinct levels of garden staff; trained gardeners and labourers. Labourers carried out the unskilled digging and hoeing, moving as required to the farm for the harvest, to forestry in the winter and back to garden work in the spring and summer. Trained gardeners, on the other hand, made a progression through four stages; from garden boy to apprentice, to journeyman and finally master gardener. The journeyman's lot was a tough one. He was expected to move frequently, staying perhaps from two months to two years in each situation, learning assiduously from each head gardener. He would have been young, and unmarried, with gardeners usually only taking wives when they made head gardener (a grade that came with a separate house). Indeed, advertisements in *The Gardeners' Chronicle* often carried the admonition 'no incumbents', and Joseph Addison, Head Gardener at Lyme Park from 1907 to 1922, was lucky that no mention was made of his five children at his interview.

Pay was poor, considering the huge effort journeymen put into training. In his *Encyclopaedia of Gardening* (1824) John Claudius Loudon advised 'every young man who has entered on the profession of gardening, to be most assiduous in his endeavours to add to his stock of knowledge, from books, from observation, and from personal intercourse with eminent gardeners'. Furthermore, 'a gardener must not only be a good practical botanist but possess some knowledge of chemistry, mechanics, and even of the principles of taste … Drawing, at least of ground-plans, is indispensable, and for a first-rate situation, sketching landscape, and some knowledge of French, equally so.' As if that were not enough, he should also 'understand the principles of English Composition' and be capable of writing 'a paper on his art, fit to be in the Gardeners' Magazine'. One gardener who appears to have taken Loudon's advice to heart was Eugene Fitzalan (1830–1911). After an apprenticeship at Florence Court and two years travelling as an improver (or journeyman), with a spell in Veitch's famous Devon nursery, he emigrated to Australia, becoming a poet, as well as a botanist and pioneer.

The hard regime of the gardeners' training system was physically embodied in the bothy, the accommodation provided for trainees.

Bothies were generally part of the range of lean-to support buildings against the back of the kitchen garden, and were pretty basic. *Gardening World* in 1884 described a typically bad example: 'It faces north and is near the stoke-hole, and so shaded by high walls that a gleam of sunshine seldom reaches it. Its roof is leaky and its walls damp, and it is altogether a disgrace to the garden.' By contrast, the bothy at Ascott was 'a model of what such erections should be, being well appointed inside, and having a picturesque exterior also'. It accommodated five men, and comprised 'five rooms, viz, living-room or mess-room, two bed-rooms, a large kitchen and a bath-room fitted well enough for any gentleman's house'. Few bothies survive unaltered today; the one at Llanerchaeron is possibly the best surviving example in the Trust.

View across the vegetable garden towards the bothy at Llanerchaeron. (NTPL/Chris King)

As the kitchen garden reached its peak, huge quantities of fruit, vegetables and flowers were produced, often painstakingly packed for transport to a London mansion, as well as supplying the country house and its large retinue of servants. The advent of the railways made such long-distance transportation increasingly feasible. For example, at the end of the nineteenth century the head gardener at Cragside, the Armstrong home in Northumberland, was despatching fresh flowers and plants almost daily to the family house in London, sending them on the night train so that the flowers could be in vases before the family arose the next morning. Meanwhile, in gardens across the country whole armies of gardeners were required to maintain the almost industrial system that underpinned such production, typified by the smoking chimneys of the heated garden walls which secured the earliest crops. The top head gardeners were the celebrities of their day.

The Head Gardener at Petworth surrounded by his staff and their equipment, in a photograph from the 1880s. (NT)

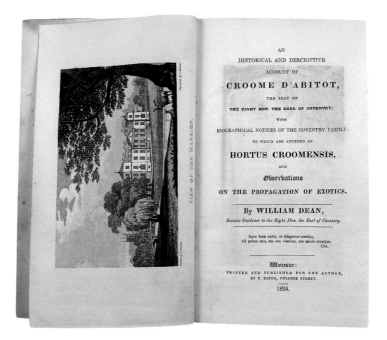

The frontispiece of *Hortus Croomensis*, published in 1824 by the Head Gardener at Croome Park, William Dean. (Trustees of the Croome Estate/Robert Anderson)

In 1824 William Dean, the highly respected Head Gardener of Croome Park, produced the definitive monograph on the estate, eloquently describing the garden and its history and furnishing an impressive plant list running to over 700 different types. John Fleming (d.1883), Head Gardener of Cliveden, was famed as a pioneer of bedding-out, exemplified in the huge parterre he designed and planted up each year with some 22,000 bulbs and annuals.

The British training system was highly esteemed, and throughout the nineteenth century British gardeners attained top positions all over Europe, including at the Russian court. Gardening was often a family career, with several generations successively entering the profession. Gradually colleges sprang up to take on aspects of the training, and around 1900 even women were deemed capable of professional gardening. However, two World Wars eventually broke the system: many gardeners never made it back from the trenches to restore lawns ploughed for potatoes; the great houses themselves were sold off or demolished as estates incurred huge death duties and struggled to remain financially viable; and cheap food imports and oil crises put an end to the kitchen garden. Gardens became smaller, and manageable by their owners. Gardening ceased to be a clever career option; and college courses shifted towards the less practical, more financially rewarding aspects of horticulture, such as garden centre management.

As Jane Brown perceptively pointed out in *The Pursuit of Paradise* (1999): 'If the legacy of the old head gardeners lingered anywhere it was in the backrooms of the National Trust's gardens. The National Trust retained a loftily autocratic attitude to its gardeners for many years, which Graham Stuart Thomas as Gardens Adviser had to work hard to mollify. In 1979 he dedicated *The Gardens of the National Trust* to the head gardeners. His successor as Chief Gardens Adviser, John Sales, … brought about a revolution, in that through the improved status, and visibility, of the head gardeners, the whole professional structure has been boosted and revived.'

The Unspoken Value of Gardeners

Speak it ever so softly, because it might appear cranky, but it does seem that the very activity of gardening brings a garden to life. We can perhaps best appreciate this by looking at the plight of many of our public parks in recent years. The adoption by local authorities of compulsory competitive tendering in the 1980s decreed that all gardening work be contracted out to the cheapest bidder, often with unskilled staff. Without the benign touch of a caring gardener, many parks became soulless places. When no one cares whether a plant flourishes once planted, so long as it is according to the specification, whether the grass is dead or alive, so long as it is the correct height, whether the 'keep off the grass' notices are actually more prominent than the flowers, a garden gradually dies in spirit. Gardening by contract is as likely to produce great gardens as painting by numbers will produce great works of art – ie never, because both render essentially creative arts wooden and lifeless. But the situation is even worse in gardening, where much of the art lies in being responsive. Great gardens are created over time by closely observing and responding to plant growth and weather conditions, by taking advantage of opportunities like chance seedlings or the loss of a tree. No contract could ever be written to cover all the eventualities of truly skilled gardening.

Ultimately the short-term paring of costs in public gardens led to the loss of a whole generation of skills, and most parks became somewhat desolate places. In time even the financial savings proved to be illusory. With no gardener to keep an eye on things, to care about the place, to bring in volunteers and to provide the interest that attracts visitors, many parks became lonely and unsafe, which deterred would-be visitors even further. In such cases security becomes an issue, making costly CCTV or policing necessary.

Finally, after years of low levels of maintenance work carried out with no regard to future development, a park will need at best a thorough, unsightly overhaul, or, at worst, a massively expensive restoration programme. Restoration in this case should be seen as an admission of failure — the failure to maintain a garden.

Hopefully, the tide is now turning for public parks, following public campaigns, and the management of many is now being reconsidered. In the meantime, the degradation of local authority parks has placed even greater pressure on the National Trust. Our urban and semi-urban parks and gardens — Speke, Saltram, Beningbrough, Osterley — have become the alternative new public parks, as people have sought safer, more attractive sites in which their dogs or children can let off steam.

The Vital Role of Trust Gardeners

Thankfully, the Trust never went down the contract route. John Sales as Head of Gardens championed gardening as a performance art, pointing out that head gardeners have a role equivalent to that of great conductors in bringing alive an art form. In fact, Trust gardeners have been encouraged to take on more, not less, responsibility for their gardens. So that Steve Biggins, Head Gardener at Calke Abbey, for instance, can declare 'this is my place … Calke is where I am and Calke is what I do'. The result is that the 450 Trust gardeners, including 80 head gardeners, take great care over and pride in the overall presentation, standards and development of their place.

A programme of in-house training enables Trust gardeners to take on more responsibility for making thoughtful day-to-day decisions about their gardens. This in turn helps to fulfil the organisation's remit to realise the full individuality of each property — gardeners who engage fully with their property and its conservation are better able to bring it vibrantly alive and to foster the spirit of the place. Even Christopher Lloyd, gardening guru of Great Dixter in Sussex, whilst extolling the joys of private ownership and his freedom to develop his garden in his own fresh way, admits that conservation has its place, and that where the National Trust 'recognises [a] gardener's ability and offers support, the situation need not be too bad at all'.

Today, despite new machinery and advanced technology, the nature of gardening is essentially the same as in earlier centuries — even the tools are remarkably similar to those wielded by previous generations. The National Trust remains resolute that the core of gardening work is, and should always be, largely hands-on. However, there are now many more pressures on head gardeners. For a start, there are far fewer hands to carry out the same work, and many more visitors to satisfy. Besides which, the job has come up to date, in that head gardeners are now effectively garden managers, with responsibility for budgets, staff and even fund-raising. And as the Trust's remit has broadened, so gardeners have taken on many additional aspects, such as interpretation and the management of volunteers. Today's head gardeners have ever more plates to keep spinning. They are required to be both skilled hands-on craftsmen and modern managers, with a high degree of autonomy and visibility, just like the top chefs in Michelin-starred restaurants, but without the fame!

Trust Gardeners Go Further

A major element of the head gardener's role is the recruitment and supervision of garden staff. With work nowadays based on teamwork, rather than the strict autocracy of the past, head gardeners must ensure that their staff are motivated, as well as organised and appropriately trained. Although the number of gardeners has fallen dramatically – for example, from over 30 at Petworth in 1878 to just three today – this has brought other responsibilities, including the selection and mainte-nance of expensive specialist machinery, and the recruitment and organising of troupes of volunteers.

Philip Whaites at Wimpole organises his volunteers simply and effectively. A blackboard lists all the day's tasks, so that on arrival each volunteer simply heads off to tool up and get stuck in. The 25 or so regular garden volunteers are the mainstay of the restored kitchen garden and parterre, and Phil puts on social events as a way of saying 'thank you'. The help and enthusiasm of the 3,000 or so volunteers who assist in Trust gardens is invaluable, and they also represent an important way for the Trust to reach out and become involved in the wider community. In a similarly mutually beneficial way, the Trust is

At Osterley Park, volunteers have set up cutting beds in the walled garden to grow appropriate flowers for the eighteenth-century-style arrangements in the house. (NT/Barry Williams)

The Palladian Bridge at Stowe provides a backdrop for the garden restoration team and their Head Gardener and Property Manager, Frank Thomson.
(NTPL/Jerry Harpur)

keen to accommodate long-term volunteers and students in garden placements. Those from overseas seem especially to value our gardens and reputation for training. To this end we have pushed for the creation of more bothy-type housing (basic, but not as basic as the Victorian original!) attached to gardens. So there are always one or two European horticultural students in the garden flat at Knightshayes, for instance, and an international mix in the Corinthian Arch at Stowe, all helping with a wide range of planning and practical tasks under the guidance of each head gardener.

Head gardeners must organise all the routine work of a garden, as well as plan and implement any agreed project work. Both aspects may also involve supervising contract work, such as grass mowing or the creation of new car-parking areas. Each head gardener is responsible for managing a garden budget; some becoming consummate wheeler-dealers and stretching minuscule budgets by exchanging produce for plants, and so on. Health and Safety regulations are becoming increasingly onerous, and gardeners must be well versed in the safe use of chemicals, including appropriate use, storage and disposal. Gardeners are also key members of the property team, liasing closely with their property managers (unless the gardener is actually the property manager as well, as is the case at garden-led properties such as Stowe). They may also call upon and work alongside a range of other experts, both from within the Trust and outside, including archaeologists, conservators, pest specialists, soil analysts and so on. In turn, they are also asked to help with many of the varied activities the Trust is involved in.

The Trust tries to hand over just as much autonomy as each head gardener is capable of handling, judging when they have the right degree of experience, for instance, to take over the selection of plants. Although, with staff spread thinly, this may amount to more than they might get in other situations, as Steve Biggins cheerfully says 'I've got so much rope, I could hang myself three times over'.

Today's head gardeners need to be well versed in conservation, with more and more compiling their own garden conservation plans, besides keeping planting records and perhaps producing plant surveys and planting plans, or even undertaking historical research. After all, they are the ones on site, they put in the plants, and meet the visitor who mentions that their father used to work there. And with all this goes computer literacy, as a tool for keeping records. Many also take a strong lead in public relations and garden-related events, such as Meet-the-Gardener walks, gardening masterclasses, Apple Day displays and plant fairs. Several gardeners produce interpretation literature, like the quirky monthly leaflets put together by Mick Little and his team at Castle Drogo. Who could fail to be both charmed and educated by their enthusiastic descriptions of the star plant performers and behind-the-scenes techniques ('we cut the hedges with professional electric cutters, mobile generator and tower scaffolding, a good eye, and loads of Earl Grey Tea')?

That visitors nowadays are keen to learn about garden craft skills is demonstrated by the success of kitchen garden restorations at Clumber, Calke and Wimpole. They are also interested in the evolution of gardens, and these days the Trust aims to make restoration projects that would previously have been carried out behind closed doors, accessible to visitors, as at Croome. (Although we must try not to raise expectations too much – visitors can be very disappointed to discover only newly-planted shrubs where they expect a mature garden.) With spring seemingly earlier each year, there is also pressure to open earlier, and Anglesey Abbey's new Winter Walk has proved very popular (see p.152). However, this time of year is a valuable opportunity to undertake more destructive tasks, such as sterilising borders and tree-felling, which must be carried out without visitors around, so winter opening – although increasing – is not likely to become the norm.

The head gardener's power-house is the garden work area, where modern glasshouses, tool store, compost heap and office with computer are all screened from the casual visitor's gaze. The glasshouse may have mist propagation facilities, but will still require careful attendance by staff, for instance, to monitor the newer techniques of Integrated Pest Management (IPM), which rely on close observation and the careful use of interacting predatory bugs and chemicals to control, rather than completely wipe out, pests (see p.204). Many of our gardeners carry out informal trials and research into these and other new techniques and innovative materials, such as peat alternatives and the chopped tyres now being used to alleviate wear on grass paths. Where individual gardeners are keen, they are encouraged to develop more wildlife- and environment-friendly techniques, or even to go completely organic, as at Snowshill or Plas-yn-Rhiw. Several Trust gardeners bring a keen interest in wildlife to their work – Malcolm Hutcheson originally chose his situation at Sizergh Castle for its ornithological potential, and works closely with the warden to improve the wildlife habitats in the garden.

Bird's-eye view of the gardeners at Anglesey Abbey, showing the wide array of tools and machinery: a long way from the Petworth equipment (see page 169). (NTPL/David Levenson)

Above all, gardeners are required to develop a suite of skills involving observation, anticipation, judgement and timeliness – a sort of seventh sense or 'gardener's eye'. As they develop, applying this foresight to their garden, understanding its history and style and adding to it appropriately in a creative way becomes the essence of the job. As Nick Brooks at Hinton Ampner says, 'I see the role of the gardener not as a maintenance operative, but as an artist. Furthermore, I see us as creative artists in our own right. Despite the fact that we are painting on Ralph

Dutton's [the last owner, who gave the garden to the Trust] canvas, we go beyond merely 'cleaning pictures', because a garden is a living, growing, developing and also dying thing … The gardener is doing more than just painting pictures; he or she is an architect and a sculptor, working in three dimensions with materials which fight back constantly.'

Similarly, at Sissinghurst, Sarah Cook is maintaining the traditional creative way of working. 'Sissinghurst has always been actively gardened', she says, 'rather than merely maintained – by a partnership of two minds since the days of Vita Sackville-West and Harold Nicolson.' Today she and Alexis Datta, Assistant Head Gardener, together fulfil the two roles. Each head gardener is primarily responsible for that creative thrust forward in their own garden, with particularly gifted ones encouraged to go further, where appropriate. For instance, Jimmy Hancock at Powis developed the garden's reputation for spectacular and inventive pot planting schemes, since safely entrusted to Peter Hall (see case study on pp.184–6).

Gardeners need to be strong plantsmen. They are responsible for maintaining and propagating their historic plant collections, while growing any plant really well means building profound knowledge of the way it develops, so as to prune it correctly, or transplant it or even to know when to give up on it. Gardeners are also increasingly responsible for recording plants and plant collections. Valerie Anderson at Antony has set up her own database on the hemerocallis and camellia collections, with photographs and details of each cultivar. Michael Hickson at Knightshayes has overall responsibility for the Plant Conservation Programme, propagating the rarest plants in the Trust (see case study on pp.98–9).

The selection of plants is an important part of the creative process. Trust gardeners need to be able to resist their own favourites and choose those right for the style of their garden. At Coleton Fishacre David Mason steels himself against completely filling the place with the spiky exotics that he loves, and which do well in the mild Devon climate. Instead, he takes pains to bear in mind the ethos of the D'Oyly Cartes who created the garden, successfully representing both Lady Dorothy's feminine taste for pinks and pastels and her husband's preference for bold foliage. He replicates some of their outmoded 1930s plantings, like flowering cherries, while at the same time trying to move the garden forward in a way that they would be happy with. 'Coleton is not a museum, but an evolving ecology', he says.

The combination of the manual and the mental can give great job satisfaction, but we should also acknowledge that there are huge pressures on gardeners. Because they identify so closely with their garden, the temptation is always to be better, to restore more, to expand and create new features. We, and they, must be realistic about the limitations of time and staffing, and exercise restraint. However, we are all impotent in the face of nature and climate, which affect gardens to such a degree – the bouts of drought, rain, disease or extreme frosts which at best make it difficult to keep on top of work, or at worst can practically destroy a garden. Archie Skinner at Sheffield Park, for one, was nearly heartbroken at the devastation of his work of 21 years in the 1987 storm. The very fact that the state of the garden is so readily apparent to so many visitors is a stress. As Steve Biggins at Calke explains, 'I know that 90,000 people are coming this year to see it … say I get two days behind, everybody and everybody's granny is going to come and say, "Look at that, look at that, look at that." So the pressure we're under to get it right is immense.'

Visitors can assume that gardeners are paid to do their hobby, but being a professional is a very different matter; for one thing, it is no longer a relaxing alternative to the day job. Again, Steve Biggins points out the distinction: 'When I leave this place – particularly in the summer when the hours are long – I'm absolutely drained, and the mere thought of going home and tinkering about with other plants is anathema to me.' The sheer scale that Trust gardeners work on – 130,000 plants bedded out annually at Waddesdon, 1,000 miles of lawn to mow at Anglesey, 4 miles of hedge to trim at Hidcote – highlights the difference. And to some extent, the very success of their management mitigates against their work being recognised; when a garden looks perfect, it is hard to appreciate just how much hard work has gone into achieving that look.

The ever-increasing pressures on gardeners were recently scrutinised by the Trust, resulting in a reaffirmation of the importance of hands-on gardening work. Eighty per cent of garden work should be ongoing labour, which is very precious and must not be swallowed up by paperwork, security duties or helping to put on events, all of which are growing responsibilities.

Gardeners' Training

The National Trust provides two distinct types of training for gardeners – managerial and technical, which together aim to nurture gardeners' organisational, creative and practical skills; to spin those plates faster, better. Managerial training is general to all disciplines and includes, for instance, supervisory skills and time management. Technical training courses, on the other hand, are specifically tailored to the requirements of gardeners at different levels.

Developing gardeners attend thoroughly down-to-earth courses on new techniques in lawn care, pest management, garden machinery maintenance and other practical aspects. Aspiring head gardeners have workshop-style courses with stimulating exercises, discussion and tours of private gardens to broaden their vision and deepen their understanding of conservation planning and garden artistry. The suite of courses aims to ensure that each gardener attends at least one course every three years. Finally, a three-yearly conference brings together all head gardeners to share experience, set new policy directions and inspire through garden visits and lectures. Here the 'buzz' of gardeners exchanging ideas and experience is at least as important as the more formal stuff.

Gardening is a never-ending journey. There is always something new to learn, and Trust gardeners are all encouraged to continue their own training in an informal version of life-long learning – by taking part in job-swaps, study tours or outside courses and conferences. When the orangery at Hanbury was about to be restored, Head Gardener Neil Cook went to Florence to learn from the experts the niceties of citrus culture. The twinning of Hidcote with its sister garden on the French Riviera, Serre de la Madonne (also created by Lawrence Johnston), launched in September 2000, should similarly promote, via exchanges of staff, ideas, skills and understanding, the type of cross-cultural fertilisation that will ultimately enrich each garden.

Home-grown Gardeners – the Careership Scheme

Some ten years ago, perceiving a developing crisis in the lack of skilled entrants into horticulture, the Trust took the bold step of introducing a national gardener apprenticeship called Careership. Today this scheme is highly regarded for the quality of its training and is proving very successful. The three-year apprenticeship is firmly founded on practical, garden-based, on-the-job training, complemented by short residential blocks of college learning. Emphasis is also placed on detailed and extensive plant and garden history knowledge.

Twelve gardens are selected each year for an apprenticeship, with only one apprentice at each garden over the three years. The head gardeners involved are required to qualify as National Vocational Qualification (NVQ) Assessors, and are selected for their commitment to training and willingness to devote time to mentoring. Each apprentice is monitored on a monthly basis as they work towards achieving a range of awards, including NVQs at Levels 2 and 3, the Royal Horticultural Society (RHS) General Certificate in Horticulture and a

Gardens History certificate. At the end they also receive a National Trust Apprenticeship Diploma.

Over the life of the scheme some 56 apprentices have graduated and have gone on to work for the Trust and in private, botanical and RHS gardens. In 2000 two former apprentices were promoted to head gardener posts, with several more now in assistant head gardener posts at prestigious gardens. The system is really proving its worth.

Careership, as the name implies, is a career start and is open to both school leavers and mature applicants. For many apprentices, gardening is a second career, with backgrounds ranging from tax officer to graphic artist, while others have completed degrees in non-horticultural subjects. Applicants, whatever their age, need to demonstrate a clear commitment to practical training and have a strong interest in gardening.

Steven Porter, who graduated from the National Trust's Careership programme and is now Head Gardener at Glendurgan. (Sam Morgan-Moore)

Rooted in History

English Heritage, the Royal Parks Agency and the Historic Royal Palaces have since become aware of the Trust's apprenticeship and have become Careership partners, with their apprentices attending the college training alongside National Trust representatives. In 1998 the National Gardens Scheme (NGS) endorsed Careership by generously supporting, year on year, the funding of five additional apprentices for the lifetime of their apprenticeship.

Trust Gardeners Last Longer

Trust gardeners are passionate about their work and are hugely committed to it. Once they have found their true sphere, they tend to be in it for the long distance. David Masters, Head Gardener at Nymans, reckons 'you need to be in a garden at least five years before you get the feel of it' and has now been there for twenty. However, this is no record, and he is beaten by one of his staff, Philip Holmes, who has worked at Nymans for over 30 years. Meanwhile, Hughie Trefor was one of our longest-serving gardeners, working at Powis for 44 years.

The long service of gardening staff is a great boon to the Trust; such continuity helps ensure that long-term aims are achieved. In addition, long-serving gardeners are vital links back to the donors or even the original creators of the garden. Michael Hickson was made Head Gardener of Knightshayes Court in 1963 at the tender age of 21, and jointly helped to create the garden with Sir John and Lady Heathcoat-Amory. He is still there today, although both his original employers have passed on. In effect, he carries a living torch for the garden. 'I came first as a student to the painters', he says 'and was finally allowed to paint myself. They were very good gardeners and our relationship was great fun.'

Similarly, at Sissinghurst, Pam Schwerdt and Sybille Kreutzberger had already worked for Vita Sackville-West for some eight years before the garden came to the Trust in 1967. When 'the girls', as she called them, retired in 1991, they handed over the baton to Sarah Cook, who had been working alongside them to inherit the living mantle of Vita's style. At some places whole dynasties of gardeners are linked to the property – Richard Ayres was Head Gardener at Anglesey Abbey like his father before him, and Martin Puddle's father and grandfather were both Head Gardeners at Bodnant.

Younger gardeners are encouraged to move around within the Trust to broaden their knowledge and experience. Mike Snowden, who became so much a part of Rowallane that it was difficult to imagine the place without him, was actually responsible for the huge restoration

Two specimens from the old rose collection at Mottisfont Abbey: 'Mabel Morrison', hybrid perpetual 1878 (top); 'Alain Blanchard', gallica 1839 (above). (NTPL/John Vere Brown)

effort at derelict Erddig in the 1970s, after having started his National Trust career at Bodnant. Surprisingly, many gardeners 'inherited' with a property adapt well to the very different ethos of the Trust. Frank Thomson had worked at Stowe School for some ten years before being taken over with the garden by the Trust, but took to the restoration effort like a duck to water. He responded wholeheartedly to the huge responsibility this placed on him, and has been a mainstay of the place, and the process, ever since.

Many come to gardening as a second career – David Mason at Coleton Fishacre trained first as a geologist and travelled extensively, while rumour has it that Philip Whaites at Wimpole was once a night-club singer. This broad experience is valued, as is the input from incomers like Peter Clarke from English Heritage's Audley End, now at Ham, and Neil Porteous at Clumber, who developed specialist knowledge of kitchen gardens at Normanby Hall, near Scunthorpe. Of course, the Trust does sometimes lose gardeners – Gary Lavis of Trelissick left to work at Probus Garden and Jan Michalak of Ickworth to take an MA in building conservation, but then we hope they become good outside contacts, perhaps even returning later with widened experience – Michael Walker left Beningbrough Hall to go to privately owned Harewood, but has since been enticed back to Waddesdon.

Not all gardens have the same requirements, and it is important to match the qualities and skills needed at each place with the right gardener. Energy and determination may be the prime qualities required where a restoration scheme is just getting underway, whereas tact and plant knowledge may be more valuable assets at an established garden where tenants or donors also have input; volunteer management and vision are essential at Croome, while topiary and hedge-cutting are paramount respectively at Mount Stewart and Hidcote. But perhaps the most important quality required is for the gardener to be in sympathy with their garden.

Because each gardener ultimately becomes the best expert on their own place, they develop intimate knowledge of the site – which is the warmest bank, where the soil is deepest, where the frost lingers longest. At Acorn Bank Chris Braithwaite, besides studying and testing the traditional uses of each of the herbs he grows, also knows their detailed cultural requirements and the part of the garden most likely to suit them. David Stone at Mottisfont Abbey has become a specialist on old roses and Malcolm Hutcheson at Sizergh is an expert on ferns.

The best gardeners somehow allow their properties to mould them, to become experts in their own sphere. For instance, Mike Snowden at Rowallane has become an authority on wildflower meadow management, mowing and composting (he is especially satisfied by composting

Rooted in History

memos from the regional office!). Philip Cotton at Cliveden is skilled in pond management, rebuilding the pool in the Water Garden in separate sections so that draining no longer has disastrous consequences. If you want to know about bedding, Michael Walker at Waddesdon is your man, as he does it *par excellence* on a huge scale, using computerised planting plans. David Mason at Coleton Fishacre has a huge network of plant experts around the world, exchanging rarities. Richard Ayres, the recently retired Head Gardener at Anglesey Abbey, admits to being a galanthophile, and the snowdrop collection there continues to grow accordingly. Sissinghurst gardeners are especially skilled at pruning and training plants, restraining (or retraining) rampant old roses into neat spheres every winter. These then are the gardens which in turn become especially renowned for training, and many Trust gardeners have spent a formative few years at Cliveden, Anglesey or Sissinghurst.

There are now more women working in National Trust gardens, although we only have as yet some nine female head gardeners. As Valerie Anderson, Head Gardener at Antony, points out, modern technology has made things slightly easier for women, by reducing 'the need for brute force … When we're spraying I don't have to lug five gallons of water about on my back, just a 5lb container.'

All Trust gardeners are stars, worthy of much greater tribute than is ever paid to them. However, most are quietly modest, and only a few get wider acclaim. Fred Stoker at Petworth became a radio regular; Nigel Davis appeared in a TV series on the restoration of Biddulph Grange, while Gary Rainford at Lyme, like many Trust head gardeners, has become something of a local celebrity, judging flower shows and responding to gardening matters on local radio. Richard Ayres, recently made an MBE, was *Country Life's* Gardener of the Year in 1999 and 2001, and, along with Barry Champion (Trelissick) and Michael Hickson, has been awarded the RHS Associate of Honour.

In conclusion, with all the skills required of our gardeners, and all their years of training, it really is no longer appropriate to call them just gardeners. Perhaps they should be retitled Professional Heritage Gardeners? This would also help to dispel the lingering image of the old-fashioned jobbing gardener, which still clings to the profession. After all, why should master chefs have a monopoly of attention? Our gardeners are just as skilful and articulate (though perhaps not so flamboyant) as those TV chefs. The Trust still needs to do more to highlight the importance of our gardeners, both individually and as a whole. We need more profiles of gardeners on Trust websites, more head gardeners on TV and radio. They should re-assume the celebrity status of their Victorian counterparts. And how about recreating the post of Royal Gardener, as a figurehead for the whole profession?

Case Study 1
A Life in the Day of a Head Gardener

*Peter Hall,
Head Gardener,
Powis Castle*

My first true association with plants began as a toddler staying with my grandparents, where my job was to pick off the yellowing Brussels sprout leaves and offer them up to the cattle in the neighbouring field. Sometimes I picked green leaves too if 'Gramps' wasn't watching, just in order to smell the warm grassy breath and watch the long pink tongue draw down the special treat. I loved his vegetable plot with its neat and immaculate clean-hoed rows, and as he laboured in his retirement he reflected on his past escapades in 'the War'. He even had a sword, which he used to hack down nettles in the wilder corners; this was definitely the job for me!

It was he who read, in one of his many gardening papers, that the Crown Estate was seeking trainees for a two-year course in the Royal Gardens at Windsor. I was studying A-level English at the time, and on informing my teacher that I was to finish his course for gardening I encountered my first taste of the prejudice which seems to come from certain quarters.

'So, you are going to dig roses are you, Hall? '

'No sir,' I replied, 'I am going to dig soil', and with that I left to begin my chosen career.

Those early days draw images of raking autumn leaves around Virginia Water, dibbing leeks into rock hard soil in the walled garden of Home Park, misty dawn collections of manure from the stables at Sunningdale, or huddled in the brew shed of the Valley Garden toasting sandwiches on a boiler which spewed out smoke which seemed to make only the eyes of us novices stream. This was the life; an excellent grounding which certainly sorted the wheat from the chaff.

A National Diploma at Pershore followed, and a few years managing a commercial nursery convinced me that my passion truly lay in seeing the whole growing process through, from sowing to planting, cultivating, training; the lot. Who could I work for that had that permanency of planting and care? The choice lay between private gardens, the Royal Horticultural Society, botanic gardens or the National Trust. That's it. I loved Hidcote, I even did my courting there. The National Trust preserves forever. What could be better. I have a National Diploma. It's 1978. I am 26. I'll be a head gardener for the National Trust.

So it was, in the autumn of that year that I began as an 'assistant' gardener at Wimpole Hall. Yes, I had learned that one needed at least a hundred years' experience before one could aspire to become a head gardener at that time. Still, I worked hard, I did as I was told, I learned and I listened, and rose after eighteen months to the position of 'gardener'.

After another year or so I accepted the position of 'single-handed gardener' in the restoration of Canons Ashby. There I was, alone in the garden, with 36 builders restoring the mansion; a good grounding for patience and the need for clearly defined barriers. I was running a garden though, and all the actions and results therein were down to me. I had budgets and plans to work to, I had a garden to uncover, and each day was a joy with no one to bother me, no one to distract me from the pleasure of restoring, not even the public, until it opened three years later.

So it was in 1985 that the offer of head gardener appeared in the renovation of Dunham Massey garden near Manchester, following on from the great head gardener of his day, the renowned Harry Burrows, formerly of Hidcote. I worked with Harry for six months before he retired, and I learned more in that short time than in all the years prior. His plant knowledge was vast, his experience expansive, and his humour as dry as his passion for gardening was deep. I was by then a fit 33-year-old, and one of the youngest head gardeners in the Trust, but I remember digging with him one day on the north parterre, levelling the site after removing an old lime tree. He talked and worked in an apparently effortless, methodical way and yet he covered the ground at alarming speed; I was grateful for every short breather during his occasional pauses to relight his pipe.

Peter Hall, now Head Gardener at Powis Castle, digging in the lime nursery at Dunham Massey. (NT)

Harry was the 'old school' that I had heard of, and aspired to; a breed apart from the modern gardener. I spoke with him much in his retirement, where he kept a close and watchful eye upon my progress, often approving but sometimes bemused by the perplexity of 'new thinking' and 'modern legislation'. When I left ten years later to take up the position of head gardener at Stourhead, he said rather worriedly 'There's no garden there you know, only trees'. Of course, this is one of the most beautiful gardens anywhere, but for very different reasons from those that inspired Harry's passion for plants and his roots in the intimate garden at Hidcote. Working within this outstanding example of British garden landscape design satisfied an itch I had to scratch for the bones of garden history. There was a timelessness too which is hard to describe, but the people involved in the garden exuded peace and tranquillity, none more so than my predecessor, Fred Hunt, the most kind and contented man I have had the pleasure to work with, and someone whom I continue to consider a friend. He combined those magical qualities of passion for his work, determination, patience and, above all, willingness to share his knowledge with others.

The attraction of my present position at Powis Castle is for the care of a garden combining all the major periods of design, with plantsmanship and garden variety rolled into an evolution of over 300 years of glorious successes and mistakes, with strokes of inspired genius for good measure.

So, the question arises, is there a difference between the lot of the 'old school' head gardener, and that of the modern counterpart? The subject is complex enough without generalising greatly on the work of so many individuals, with so many varied gardens and so many factors influencing garden-making, that I won't try. A passion for the work however remains paramount, an acceptance of a frugal lifestyle sensible, an ability to adapt your *modus operandi* essential and a sympathetic partner in life a distinct advantage. It would be imprudent to think that conservation plans, planting records, visitor services, staff development, personal development reviews or even risk assessments would all be unfamiliar to our distant head gardener forebears whereas property managers, litigation and welcome host training certainly would. At this point the multiple ownership of gardens starts to separate from that of individuals who own gardens, with the former having to succumb to a uniformity arising from even-handedness to its staff, the desire to centralise its administrative organisation and purpose, and the necessity to respond to external pressures.

The time lag between the vision of those head gardeners I aspired to, and the period it took me to reach their position, resulted in the fact that by the time I got there, their lifestyle had gone. Fortunately time and adaptability enabled the process to be gentle, almost unnoticed unless reflected upon.

My day is spent advising or urging people to garden rather than as I used to, by doing it myself, or explaining to others why we do what we are doing, or how much it will cost, or recording what could be so we can either make it happen, or prevent it. I feel as comfortable with spreadsheets, databases, word processing and computer-aided design software as I do with a pair of secateurs, and with an eye to the past am always open to new ideas and ways of working. Sometimes I get into the garden and actually do what I was trained to do, or just look at plants, compare them, adjust them, play with ideas, but if this is not written high on my list of objectives then I inevitably have to get back to more 'important' work.

Perhaps I have now become the new 'old school'. Who knows, in years to come modern gardeners will say 'Those old head gardeners, spending all there time fussing in offices, bothering with plans and records, carrying out workplace inspections, developing training plans and co-ordinating with the visitor services people. Why can't they be forward thinking like us, and concentrate all their effort on those rare and specialised skills of pure gardening, and leave that uncreative work to the robots?' Now, that would be progress!

Fred Hunt, Head Gardener at Stourhead for 27 years and now a close neighbour of mine, has been a great source of help during my first four years at Stourhead. His careful guidance and measured advice has helped me make difficult decisions, without him ever trying to make them for me. When we started to discuss how the role of head gardener has changed over the years, I was quite sure of the differences, but as we delved deeper, I was surprised to realise that most of the changes are superficial, and that essentially the role has not altered greatly.

Fred started at Stourhead in 1969 as Head Gardener 'designate', working alongside the Head Gardener for his last year before retirement. This does not happen today, and we are lucky if there is any hand-over period at all. In some ways the passing on of knowledge is not quite so important now, as we record more, and incoming head gardeners can quickly get to grips with the garden's direction through conservation plans and advisers' notes. However, a good deal of personal knowledge is lost this way, and the old system had its benefits.

Perhaps surprisingly, the staffing at Stourhead is almost exactly the same now as in 1969. Today we have a Careership trainee and volunteers, where in the past the garden staff was supplemented with government employment schemes. The head gardener's role of managing and motivating the gardening team has not changed, and nor has the motivation of those who work for the Trust: Fred's staff always wanted to work for the organisation. The main change, I feel, has come with the aspirations of the staff. It was not uncommon in Fred's day for gardeners to work almost their whole lives at one garden: two gardeners had over 60 years' experience between them when I started at Stourhead. Today gardeners come into horticulture for a career, and modern thinking means they expect rapid promotion. Head gardeners have to try to fulfil these aspirations by providing good training and encouraging the development of their staff.

Fred was always cautious about employing over-qualified people, but we do now employ far better qualified gardeners. Today gardening careers usually start with a college course in horticulture, instead of entry from school as a garden boy. With my well-qualified team, I am able to pass down far more responsibility, especially to my assistant, than would have happened in the past. This is just as well, as there are so many more demands on my time that the team needs to be able to think for itself. However, the downside is that good, aspiring, dynamic gardeners develop and soon move on to new roles elsewhere.

The demands on head gardeners today come from many quarters and reflect the changes that have taken place within the Trust. When Fred started, the half-dozen staff of the Trust's local regional office

Case Study 2
The Changing
Role of the
Head Gardener

Richard Higgs,
Head Gardener,
Stourhead

occupied the estate office at Stourhead. This office is long outgrown, and the regional office is in a separate building in Warminster, with ten times the number of staff. Everything about the organisation is now far more professional, and the head gardener is a cog in a much larger wheel. Whereas in the past Fred and his team may have patched up a garden building (to a high standard, nonetheless), we would now have several meetings with colleagues from other Trust departments, and then with contractors, to achieve the same result. Meanwhile, the Trust's public affairs team is always looking for stories to promote our gardens, an essential part of our work in today's media age, but one which can take up a lot of a head gardener's time. Fred observed these changes towards the end of his years at Stourhead, and wisely recognises that there is no going back. Overall the changes are for the good, but for the head gardener they mean different working practices and the need to cope with a myriad of new demands.

Head gardeners have always had a high profile, but today, particularly with the great public interest in gardening matters, they really do risk being propelled into the public eye. Events and filming, promoting both the garden specifically and the Trust and its work in general, often rely on input from the head gardener. This can of course be enjoyable, but such activities (including tapping the keys to write this!) do mean more time away from the garden. Realistically of course, we must recognise that the job of head gardener now covers many tasks which, although important for the condition and future of the garden in its wider context, are not directly related to gardening *per se.*

Fred argued very strongly that 'everything in the garden must come through the head gardener'. This still holds true today, nowhere more so than in the field of garden management. Conservation has become a more precise science, and head gardeners must be aware of the rationale behind decisions. Today we must make decisions in the light of garden and property conservation and management plans, as well as recording everything more closely. The head gardener has a key role to play in the production of many of these plans. The danger comes when we spend so much time planning that we cannot do the 'doing'. At Stourhead I have a relatively large team and help from volunteers, so I can divide my time fairly well, but I know from less fortunate colleagues that increased responsibilities in the areas of management and administration are taking them away from practical gardening.

Health and Safety legislation and its impact have become a large part of my job. The days of literally riding shotgun around the garden potting squirrels are long gone, and we now have to pay much time and attention to health and safety issues. Using chemicals involves so much paperwork that some gardeners think it good enough reason to go

Richard Higgs, Head Gardener at Stourhead, with his team. (NT/Steve Day)

organic! Fred laughs at the leaky watering can that in his day was used to transport herbicide.

Much of my time is spent juggling budgets to ensure that the best use is made of resources. I am pleased to be part of the budgeting process, and the days when Fred would have to apply personally to the financial controller to buy a new rake are thankfully over. It is also very satisfying to be part of the decision-making process. The introduction at many properties in recent years of the new post of Property Manager (an overall management position that combines responsibility for all aspects of a property) has been a good thing with regard to the standing of the head gardener as a professional in their field. In my experience it has highlighted the head gardener's role as head of his or her department, and has ensured that everything in that department is channelled through them.

In conclusion, I would say that head gardeners today still command the same respect as in the past. It is essential that they are seen as professionals, and the only way to do this, I believe, is to be professional, something for which Trust gardeners are rightly renowned. In some respects, I expect that I have become the 'paper gardener' that Fred hoped he would never be (or even an 'E-gardener', to bring it right up to date!), gardening for some of my time from behind a desk. But whilst the role of the head gardener has had to change to meet the demands of changing times, the outcome must still be the same; a garden must be maintained, conserved, and renewed to the same high standards as it has always been, so that visitors are able to experience it at its glorious best. If I am not the one making this happen, I will not be fulfilling the role that befits the title of head gardener.

10

Rooted in History – Growing Forever?

Mike Calnan

Conservation philosophy is in a constant state of flux. Views and values change, and the theories and practices described in this book reflect the ways in which conservation has developed over the last century or so. They are certainly not exclusive to the National Trust, and the proliferation in recent decades of other preservation-minded organisations and the evolution of a more defined concept of 'heritage conservation' have both helped the Trust develop its own approach and understand more clearly the wider context in which it now operates.

Conservation is often defined today as the negotiation of the transfer of significance from the present to the future, for the benefit of both current and future generations. The dilemma lies in identifying what is or is not significant and in how best to effect its smooth transmission from one particular moment in time to an undefined point in the future, without prejudging the taste and values of those who follow us. Central to this is the concept of the 'spirit of place', the qualities that make a particular garden unique and important.

In the rapidly changing cultural, social, political and environmental conditions of the early twenty-first century, there is a growing awareness of the need to rethink and redefine what we understand heritage to be, what it encompasses and what it has tended to exclude. According to English Heritage[1], 'Horizons have broadened, as have aspirations for the heritage and the role it plays in modern life.' We need to consider what our definition of that environment should encompass, and whilst acknowledging that there will always be limits to what should and can be protected for the future, we need also to ensure that 'heritage' becomes a more inclusive concept than has

The garden at Ham House is a recreation of the formal layout of the seventeenth century. There are few such examples in Britain, and so the garden's value lies in its rarity as an example of a particular type. In this case, therefore, innovation and change to the garden's content and design would not be appropriate.
(NTPL/Stephen Robson)

hitherto been the case. This is not just an egalitarian argument, it is also a matter of harsh practicality. Conservation is an expensive business and without the endorsement and financial support of a broader section of the community its scope for continued success will be greatly reduced.

It is certainly fair to say that the preservation movement was, from the beginning, led by the views of an elite – Ruskin, Morris, Octavia Hill and others – a small and self-appointed group which assumed responsibility for deciding what the public at large should value and wish to see preserved. Its success in the intervening period has rested heavily on our insatiable appetite for nostalgia, born out of our passion for the past. The late nineteenth-century origins of the National Trust were firmly rooted in associated notions of largesse and philanthropy, although as the twentieth century gathered pace the emphasis was allowed to move away from the original concept of securing areas of landscape as 'open air living-rooms for the urban poor' to one much more closely associated with the stately home. There is of course no doubt that the English country house, its garden and landscape park are one of our most significant contributions to world art, and that the Trust's role in saving so many of the finest examples is among the organisation's greatest achievements. Such places, often complete with classic herbaceous borders, have contributed to the development of the Trust's gardening image and helped demonstrate the standards the Trust is able to achieve. Yet the origins and very nature of the country house have traditionally inspired awe and curiosity among visitors, rather then self-identification. There has been little sense of interaction between the two, which in turn has been perceived by some as perpetuating a sense of elitism and of confining the Trust unduly to just one element of its broad portfolio.

Now there are real signs that the pendulum is swinging back again, and that gardens can play a full and constructive role in broadening the appeal of the National Trust and its properties to people who previously may have thought there was little on offer to them. Market research consistently reveals that the social and economic background of visitors to Trust gardens is generally much more diverse – and thereby more representative of the population at large – than of those to our historic houses. In a recent national survey, 37 per cent of visitors said they were attracted to Trust properties because of the gardens; in Devon alone, the figure is 50 per cent; put bluntly, gardens refresh the parts other properties cannot reach.

Despite gardens being the Trust's most popular destination, we constantly have to think of new ways of attracting visitors. In recent years there has been a slight decrease in the number of visitors to the traditional stately home, and certainly the number of people prepared to walk around an historic house looking at precious objects in glass cabinets is falling. Part of this development may be due to changed expectations and to a desire for a more interactive and personal experience, one that can be fulfilled more readily in the sensual and tactile surroundings of a garden. However, at the same time we are witnessing a growing appreciation of our common heritage, and it may be that the decline in historic house visitors is a reflection of a mostly urban-based public's growing lack of identity with such places. Heritage now needs to encompass all that we cherish, rather than simply what the 'experts' value, with local features increasingly recognised for their contribution to the richness of daily life. Essential components of neighbourhood distinctiveness, such as village greens, allotments, local gardening traditions, parks, vernacular building styles and materials or places associated with local history and traditions, whilst often unimportant in national terms, are an increasingly valued part of the historic environment.

As remnants of our common past, aspects of our everyday heritage are as significant to individuals as great monuments might be to a nation. A recent MORI poll[2] revealed that '98 per cent of the population believe that the historic environment is a vital educational asset, a means for the understanding of history and their origins and identity', but also indicated that many people feel excluded from the process of defining what heritage is. The Trust clearly has a key role to play in providing opportunities for involvement and empowerment on the part of local communities, not only on its traditional estates with their landscape parks, farms and gardens, but also in more urban situations, increasingly a focus area for Trust initiatives.

In recent years visitors to historic sites have shown growing interest in the ordinary and everyday social aspects of such places, and particularly in the lives of those who worked to maintain the country houses and huge estates – the servants, gardeners, woodsmen and craftsmen. The Trust has responded accordingly by opening up more and more 'below stairs' areas to visitors, and by expanding the social history aspect of interpretation, both on-site and through our publications. As we find out more about the properties we care for and the people who created and maintained them, so increasing opportunities present themselves, particularly from the point of extending this part of our work more tangibly into the realm of gardens, where a whole wealth of social history remains substantially untold.

So how might changes in notions of the heritage and historic environment affect the way we care for our gardens? On a practical level, any attempt to protect historic gardens now or in the future will be thwarted if we do not maintain the highest standards of research, survey, recording and analysis, and of conservation planning. Over the last few decades the Trust has worked towards establishing such standards, both through the formulation of its own policies and in parallel with developments beyond the organisation's immediate remit. Indeed, today we are as much influenced in our work by external standards as we are by our own experience in contributing towards them. Now more than ever, there is a need for clear guidelines and procedures in both recording and conservation planning if the future of a particular garden's significant historic elements is to be secured. Change in gardens can be rapid, and whilst new sources of funding may enable long hoped-for restoration work to proceed, grants may impose restrictive deadlines which can result in short-cuts and, potentially, the loss of important historic evidence. In the years ahead, the Trust must ensure that standards are upheld and an appropriate level of resources is applied to the vital work of planning, if we are to meet the responsibilities vested in us in looking after some of the nation's most valued garden assets.

Likewise, we must ensure the continuation of traditional garden craft skills on which the success of conservation depends. The role of the master gardener is as relevant today as it was two centuries ago, and as much an integral part of conservation as the retention of traditional building skills are to the preservation of historic buildings. Happily, the Trust has invested in its own training scheme for new recruit gardeners – Careership – with the invaluable support of the National Gardens Scheme (see Chapter Nine). The Trust also trains gardeners from English Heritage, Historic Royal Palaces and the Royal Parks Agency.

Combined with mid-career training courses, Careership has begun to supply the Trust with its own home-grown gardeners. Both Steven Porter at Glendurgan and Marcus Chilton-Jones at The Vyne have worked their way up through the ranks to become among the first in a new breed of conservation head gardeners, schooled just as much in conservation theory and practice as in traditional garden craft skills. For, unlike their counterparts in contemporary gardens, their responsibilities are not limited solely to caring for the present, but also for ensuring the transition of their garden from the present generation to the next. In the years ahead, we hope to do more to ensure we have the right skills in the right places, by developing and improving our training programmes.

British gardens rely heavily on plants for effect, so conservation is equally about looking after plants and planting traditions as it is about the care of fabric, layout and built features. We need to do more to reveal the full wealth of our plant collections, as Melissa Simpson explained in Chapter Five. The work of the Plant Conservation Programme at Knightshayes is central to the process of understanding our plant resource more completely. Without the Programme and the

Alison Pringle, a graduate of the Trust's Careership programme, is shown here when training as an apprentice with Andrew Sawyer, Head Gardener at Cragside. She now works with Andrew as his Assistant Head Gardener. (NT/John McKennall)

input of the Horticultural Taxonomist, the Trust would be unable to meet either the plant conservation objectives it has set itself or provide the leadership expected of us by botanical institutions worldwide. We must safeguard the historic plants in our care, whilst simultaneously working to ensure that our plant collections do not become moribund and that we continue to provide an injection of as wide and interesting a variety of plants as is appropriate, and a degree of experimentation, which all gardeners enjoy.

But whilst the Trust has achieved great success in the rescue and conservation of important gardens and their plant collections, and has made good progress towards the development of a cadre of skilled professional gardeners, the road ahead is not an easy one. Clearly it will not be enough simply to mark time and carry on doing more of the same, and there is a growing sense that the agenda must now encompass wider considerations, issues that lie beyond the garden gate, which our policy for gardens will need to accommodate. There are those, for example, who feel that we focus too much on the past at the expense of the present and future, and that it is about time that the Trust started giving some of its less historically significant gardens a makeover, thereby contributing to contemporary garden design and practice. Perhaps not surprisingly, it is often garden designers and journalists who cling most passionately to this view. In April 1998 Stephen Anderton, writing in *The Times*, asked 'Why shouldn't the Trust give some of its lesser historic gardens a suitable, vigorous, large-scale contemporary development to keep them alive?' Herein lies our dilemma. We operate in a world currently governed by a notion of conservation which generally guards against major change (other than restoration).

A futuristic garden, designed by Marshall's, and exhibited as one of the show gardens at the RHS Flower Show at Tatton Park in 2000. Increased public attention has spawned not just a plethora of makeover programmes on television, but also genuine interest in contemporary garden design. (Adrian Field)

But perhaps in adopting this view we are ignoring some of the more fundamental traditions of garden ownership and the reality of what conservation actually is?

On a small scale, 'development' goes on all the time in gardens. Plants are constantly being planted or replanted; they grow and are removed when they decline or die. In some plant collections, plants are changed when better ones become available. On a daily basis this is what conservation entails. To avoid loss of historic significance, the process must be guided by a plan setting out which features or components of the garden are sacrosanct. But even here, the job of the archaeologist and garden historian in determining what is important is an interpretative one. With gardens, where change takes place all the time, 'facts' die out, thus it is hard even in the best of circumstances to determine what the 'truth' is. So, we reach a conclusion that we will only ever know a certain amount about any garden, leaving everything else we think about it or plan for it open to further interpretation. Decision-making becomes a very subjective process and no two people will reach the same conclusions. Historic gardens are a canvas on which we paint our notion of the past. Generally, that notion is a historically governed one. So should this notion be allowed to include a contemporary interpretation, in a modern style, rather than a pseudo-historic one?

There will always be gardens such as those at Westbury Court and at Ham House, both landmarks in the history of garden design, that should be retained in as 'historically-pure' a state of preservation as possible. Like the Privy Garden at Hampton Court, the value of these gardens is as precious museum pieces rather than as continually evolving and developing gardens. However, in reality Westbury is not the garden it was in 1695, or at any other time since then; it has been altered and replanted many times over, and only one plant, the massive ilex oak at the end of the canal, dates from the period of the garden's creation (it is, in fact, even older; see p.96). The layout of the garden is more or less original, but the components are either rebuilt or reused. It cannot therefore be thought of as 'authentic' and to pass it off as such would be a deceit. This does not, however, diminish its value as a very fine evocation of the original.

In a garden such as Mount Stewart, where the influence of Lady Londonderry has been a major force and places limits on any significant structural changes, the 'spirit of place' nevertheless allows for a certain degree of latitude in the choice of plants. At Plas Newydd, where Lord Anglesey remains the guiding influence, there has been greater change and development, including the creation of 'Australasia', a new garden planted mostly with southern hemisphere trees and shrubs and with a pronounced 'Australian bush' feel. New beds and borders, water features, a trellis pavilion, and new gates and seating have given a 'Welsh-1930s-Italianate' flavour to a former terrace garden. This is a significant development, partly funded by the National

The reworked terrace garden at Plas Newydd is a good example of how the continued involvement of the donor family can help ensure the perpetuation of a dynamic quality.
(NTPL/Nick Meers)

Rooted in History – Growing Forever?

Gardens Scheme, and has made a dramatic feature of a part of the garden that was previously a backwater. Meanwhile, in each of the gardens at Dunham Massey, Hardwick Hall and Mottisfont Abbey, the Trust has injected whole new layers of planting, very much in the style of the late twentieth century and a move that has embellished rather than altered the gardens' historic layouts. But what might a greater degree of innovation bring to the Trust? Should our model for the future be English Heritage's 'Contemporary Heritage Gardens' initiative, through which the aim is to complement a site's historic layout by the introduction of new designs or layouts (on the scale a present day private owner might do), or the developments in European historic public parks, especially in Germany, Holland, France and Spain?

As a means of maintaining (or even establishing) relevance, allowing a contemporary interpretation of a garden's history has much to commend it. It certainly could be an increasingly valuable component in the process of garden stewardship, and offers real opportunities to extend the appeal of gardens as places both of recreation and of historic and contemporary interest, whether horticultural or in terms of design. Given that conservation is largely a matter of interpreting the artistic intent of a garden's creators, future verdicts on the success of conservation projects may depend on how well we interpret the past and which strategies – contemporary or historical – we adopt.

New ways of expressing our relationship with the past may contribute to relevance, which itself can be reinforced through interpretation. This is an issue for all owners of gardens open to the public, but especially so for the National Trust. In its role as the guardian of historic gardens on behalf of the nation, the Trust carries a duty to explain and present these sites effectively and in an appropriate manner.

Through interpretation we attempt to explain what a particular garden says about the way people thought in the past, what their values and motivations were, and why that garden is of value now. Making a garden understood and relevant to a contemporary audience is the greatest challenge, and this is increasingly so as people's perceptions change. Furthermore, individuals vary hugely in terms of what they expect from their visits to gardens, and yet the Trust has to try to cater for all. Interpretation will always include traditional guidebooks, exhibitions and guided tours; but modern technology and more interactive ways of explaining the past are now available to us and in the future will play an increasing part in our presentation of both our properties and our work. Interpretation may meet people's intellectual interests in gardens, but we must not forget the fact that most visitors come to enjoy the garden as a place of beauty, to refresh their spirits and to get away from it all.

Volunteer gardeners working in the walled garden at Llanerchaeron, which has been restored entirely by teams of volunteers. So successful has the project been that it is now regarded as a blueprint for similar initiatives at other Trust properties. (NT)

Striking an appropriate balance between the various – often conflicting – requirements of our growing number of members and visitors will continue to be a major challenge for the Trust. Generally speaking, it is fair to say that visitors are more demanding now than in the past. They expect better on-site facilities, more access and more information, and if something is not right, they will tell us. This attitude reflects well on the work and success of the Trust, in the sense that access to our gardens is increasingly regarded by our visitors not as a privilege, but as a right. Such a high level of perceived 'ownership' can only be a source of future strength, but it does bring with it a whole host of new responsibilities and challenges, and the Trust will need to understand these and respond accordingly. As we move from conservation on behalf of people, to be experienced by them passively, towards conservation with people, in which their active involvement is positively encouraged, so the need grows to identify the means through which this can happen. Volunteering is the traditional area in which people can get involved, and here there has been a 100 per cent increase in numbers since 1991. Currently some 3,000 people work in our gardens on a voluntary basis each year.

Community-based projects are another vehicle for public involvement, finding an appropriate focus in the restoration of kitchen gardens, for example, hitherto a rather neglected aspect of garden conservation but now very much in vogue. This is already happening at Llanerchaeron, where a farmers' market also takes place, providing the local community with fresh produce, and where the walled garden has been restored to working order by volunteers alone. Local groups, particularly children, could be encouraged to become involved in the on-site production of their own fruit and vegetables. The Trust does not yet have such a scheme, but interesting models do exist elsewhere (in Paris for example, where Air France has promoted a similar idea to schools) and merit examination and possible application to our own situation.

Such forms of involvement will hopefully lead to a new concept of 'ownership', one which engages local pride, identification, protection and support. Trust gardens can increasingly serve as a focus for the neighbouring community, both on an informal basis, as a place for recreation and socialising, as well as within a more organised structure – as venues for training courses in gardening, design and history, for example. In this way the historic environment can contribute directly to communities, and confer social and economic benefits. It is also a way of incorporating the historic garden environment into people's lives, adapting it to modern uses, in much the same way as many historic buildings have found new roles in our urban lives.

Such benefits are not always quantifiable and may not generate large levels of income, but they may be a way through which gardens can provide greater 'value'. Community benefit must surely be the bottom line in such cases. Individuals move from being observers to partici-pants, from being takers to contributors to their local economy and community. In future the Trust might apply this principle to urban areas, where traditionally it has not ventured too far. There are increas-ing opportunities, either through acquisition or partnership, to participate in the revival of town parks and urban green space. Gardens could become the glue that helps bond people and place together.

At no single Trust property are all these elements in place together yet, but the seeds of much greater community involvement have been sown widely in recent years and are already bearing fruit. The Trust is increasingly working in partnership with others to establish greater public involvement in its work. A good example of this trend is Tatton

The restoration of the vast walled garden at Tatton Park. Scheduled to take several years, the work is being carefully recorded and will be published in due course as an example of Trust practice. (NTPL/Stephen Robson)

Rooted in History

Park, where the Trust (as owner) and Cheshire County Council (as tenant) are working together on a lottery-funded restoration of the walled garden. At Wimpole Hall volunteers are playing a major part in the restoration of the walled garden. Another interesting local initiative, beyond the Trust, is that at Flaxland Farm near Canterbury, which has run a subscription system since 1996. Here local people take out a subscription for the supply of vegetables from the farm and, if they wish, participate in production and harvesting. The project offers ready access to organically produced food, as well as an opportunity to become part of a social activity and maintain contact with the land and nature. Flaxland may serve as a useful model for similar schemes in Trust-owned walled gardens and farmland, and perhaps constitutes one small solution to the current farming crisis.

In the years ahead conservation may well be measured – as ever – by social and economic criteria, but there are other challenges. During the last century man's activities had a serious impact on the earth's fundamental balances, the repercussions of which are becoming apparent from global warming and climate change. Global temperatures are projected to rise more rapidly in the next hundred years than in the last 10,000 years![3] Recent research[4] suggests we may witness not the predicted 2-3 °C rise in average temperatures by the end of this century, but something more like a 6 °C rise, with the climate moving north by more than 100 miles per decade, causing wildlife to migrate with it. Extreme weather events, such as storms, may become commonplace, with mild winters and a decline in frost-free days potentially bringing an increase in pests and diseases. Rising temperatures may lead to melting ice caps, triggering a possible reversal of the Gulf Stream away from British shores, which would have incalculable implications for our climate and vegetation. Rising sea levels could also result in seawater flooding of low-lying gardens, such as Westbury Court, within the next few decades. Trust staff are already considering this issue at Westbury, and how best to respond; should the garden be protected at all costs, regardless of the impact flood defences would have on surrounding land? Should it be abandoned or even moved? Any strategy will depend on an assessment of the garden's significance in the context of wider environmental issues and the cost and sustainability of protection.

Although it is important not to overreact to some of the more extravagant predictions, clearly we must take climate change seriously. This is why the National Trust, together with the Royal Horticultural Society and UK Climate Impacts Programme, is looking at what the consequences of global warming might be for gardeners and garden owners in Britain. Whilst we must recognise that gardeners have had to adapt to changing weather patterns and environmental conditions throughout history – including the 'mini ice age' of the seventeenth century, the industrial pollution and smogs of the nineteenth and mid-twentieth centuries, the great storms of 1987 and 1990, and the devastating floods of the 2000/2001 winter – it is the speed and scale of predicted climate change that now gives rise to greater concern than ever before.

Certainly we will need to be alert to change and more flexible in our approach to garden maintenance and conservation. For example, we may see changes in the range of plant species we are able to grow in Britain, which could in turn spell a partial end to the business-as-usual approach to garden conservation. If the climate alters enough, it may simply become impossible to replace like with like. The loss of elms in the 1970s due to Dutch elm disease completely altered the appearance of many landscapes, particularly in Oxfordshire and Warwickshire, as well as in gardens such as Wimpole, Hanbury and Anglesey Abbey, but has not lessened their significance. However, a wider impact, on many species at once, could have more serious consequences. Equally, gardens and landscape parks may become more important as sanctuaries for displaced wildlife as marginal habitats elsewhere become degraded or disappear altogether.

Nationally, new species are likely to take the place of those displaced, and the decades ahead could see further invasive and alien plants, insects and birds migrating north from continental Europe. Partnerships in which wildlife corridors and refuges are planned and provided may be a new area of activity, and could help to prevent the loss of further vulnerable native species. With one third of the world's habitats deemed under threat and many species faced with extinction by the end of this century,[5] the Trust's parkland and gardens – covering a wide range of growing conditions – may take on an increasingly important role in the

The garden at Bateman's was inundated by flood water in 2001. Such events are likely to be increasingly frequent as the effects of global warming become more apparent and severe. (NT)

conservation of endangered species. Indeed, the Trust is already involved in an effort to secure the future of the native lady's slipper orchid (*Cypripedium calceolus*).

Trust gardens can also provide appropriate homes for plants collected from the wild abroad, where their habitats may be threatened. The Conifer Conservation Project run by the Royal Botanic Gardens in Edinburgh specialises in species facing extinction in Chile, such as the conifer *Fitzroya cupressiodes* and the crimson flowering climber *Berberidopsis corallina*. Both species were first collected in the wild in the nineteenth century and introduced by their collectors to gardens that are now in Trust ownership. This unique genetic material survives today, and should help to ensure the protection of the species.

All is not bleak. Climatic and other changes are likely to present opportunities as well as threats. Longer growing seasons and milder weather may, for example, enable a greater range of plants to be grown and gardeners, as they always have, will no doubt rise to the challenge and revel in experimenting with new subjects. Equally, gardens could have a fundamental role to play in helping to change people's attitudes and behaviour towards the environment, through their ability to demonstrate the interdependency of life systems and the nature of our own relationship with the natural world around us.

What is clear is that innovation in gardens management will become not only desirable but unavoidable in the next few decades, and that flexibility will be the key to success and continuing relevance. Because of the uncertainty, the need to plan is even more critical, not least to avoid piecemeal management and short-termism. The protection of a garden's significant qualities will remain the paramount objective, but clearly any plan must allow a degree of flexibility to accommodate new thinking and the ability to respond to unpredictable events. To this end the conservation plan will be as valid a tool in the decades to come as it is in guiding the work we do today. It is vital therefore that we record what exists now as accurately and rigorously as possible, before it is lost, to ensure that management decisions are based on as full a knowledge of a garden as can be achieved.

The National Trust is committed to a more sustainable approach to garden conservation in the light of growing climate change and environmental concerns, particularly with regard to the use of chemicals, its consumption of resources and the generation of waste. Considerable efforts have already been made in the area of 'green gardening'. For example, Alfriston Clergy House, Snowshill and Plas yn Rhiw are already run on organic lines. Many other gardens, including the walled garden at Beningborough Hall are part-organic, and elsewhere the Trust has voluntarily reduced its dependence on chemicals to a minimum.

A project is underway to establish the criticially endangered lady's slipper orchid in certain National Trust gardens, which may in turn play a role in initiatives to reintroduce the orchid to other locations in the wild.
(Harry Smith Collection)

Biological forms of pest control are used increasingly in Trust gardens. At Belton tiny whitefly predators, *Encarsia formosa*, will hatch from suspended cards containing the black parasitised scales. (NTPL/Stephen Robson)

Many gardens, including Glendurgan, Rowallane and Belton, manage wildflower meadows on a chemically-free basis. At Clumber Park, trials are taking place to determine whether heritage vegetable crops or modern varieties grow, crop and taste better. From blind tests, early indications are that visitors prefer the taste of historic varieties almost every time. Organically-grown produce from the walled garden at Beningbrough and at Snowshill is already used in the on-site catering, and hopefully other properties will be able to do likewise in the near future. In many gardens, including those at Barrington Court and Wimpole Hall, the Trust is starting to employ an integrated pest management approach, whereby physical and biological control methods are put into practice and supplemented by chemical controls only when strictly necessary. By this method, chemicals are only used where they will not upset the balance. Biological controls include the tiny predatory wasp *Encarsia formosa*, used against whitefly in greenhouses, and the bacteria *Baccilus thuringiensis*, effective in controlling caterpillars on crops and ornamentals.

In a bid to minimise the impact of its operations on fragile and threatened habitats, the Trust has also ceased the use of peat in its gardens in all but a few very exceptional circumstances. Working with the agricultural and horticultural research organisation ADAS, it has trialled alternatives and is now marketing its own brand of peat-free potting compost for the production of the 350,000 plants raised in Trust gardens each year, and for those planted in gardens and sold in Trust plant outlets. Water conservation measures are already in place in many gardens, such as Waddesdon, Clumber and Tintinhull; many other properties are working to resolve the problems associated with the collection and storage of waste or 'grey' water. Recycling and waste composting, including ericaceous potting compost developed from harvested bracken, and based on experience gained at Rowallane, are also on the increase.

The Trust's advisory committees and senior management have already looked at the implications of the growing environmental issues and paved the way for future policy development. A sustainable garden conservation policy paper is planned; meanwhile all Trust gardeners are encouraged to minimise waste and adopt energy-saving, sustainable methods. Stourhead even has its own environmental group, established to look at recycling and to develop green initiatives throughout the estate. We may never return to the low-tech but highly skilled methods of the past, such as scything, but we will be encouraging industry to develop low environmental impact equipment and materials. With over 34,000 gallons (154,564 litres) being consumed in mowing 30 square miles of lawn a year (and costing some £136,000), the Trust is aware of the need to reduce its consumption of greenhouse gas-emitting fuels.

We are also looking closely at the question of 'green transport', especially as the vast majority of the 11 million annual visitors to our properties arrive in their own vehicles, thereby contributing further harmful emissions. Whilst acknowledging that for the majority there may be no alternative, we are actively promoting other forms of transport, such as cycling (with more on-site facilities), as well as working to improve public transport access (including special bus services, such as to Dyrham Park and Hidcote) and reduced tickets for those arriving by bus or train. We hope that more visitors will be encouraged to use public transport as a result. At Prior Park, access is only by public transport, by bike or on foot – there is no car park.

What future can we expect for all that we have achieved so far? It would be arrogant and naive in the extreme to imagine that the gardens we value today will be thought of in precisely the same way in future. We cannot assume our descendants will share our values or feel committed to what we believe in, or will carry on the work we have started, no matter what it says in the conservation plan! Flexibility must therefore be a key component of conservation, as it will allow future generations to decide for themselves how they conserve gardens whilst also ensuring that the 'spirit of place' passes on successfully from one generation to the next.

The quest for a new understanding of what garden conservation means at the start of the twenty-first century led the National Trust to convene its first ever Gardens Conference, held in the Assembly Rooms at Bath in May 2001. Attended by over 300 delegates and speakers from Britain, Europe and the United States, the conference focused on a range of issues related to the management of historic gardens generally, and to Trust properties in particular. It was a fascinating and long overdue forum, and saw the emergence of several key themes which, quite rightly, are likely to preoccupy our time and energy over the next few years. Many of these are areas in which the Trust is already active, and so it was reassuring to learn that we are already moving well along the right track!

Many speakers stressed the need for the Trust to overcome its exclusive image, which can act as a barrier to ethnic and socially excluded groups. The wide appeal of gardening was promoted as a catalyst to help to unite people and places, and the Trust was encouraged to broaden its definition of 'heritage' to include not just grand houses and their gardens but also vernacular gardens, urban gardens, parks and allotments.

The potential of the Trust in urban areas was also highlighted, and particularly through making its expertise available to help reverse the physical decline in urban parks. The Thames Landscape Strategy was held up as a model of how the Trust could help to develop sustainable solutions beyond its immediate boundaries, working in partnership with others to unite cultural, economic, social and environmental

The 2001 Chelsea Flower Show saw the launch of the National Trust's own brand of peat-free compost, trialled successfully in gardens such as here at Sissinghurst. (NTPL/Ian Shaw)

interests. The green movement and the environment were recognised as the major issues of the twenty-first century and the Trust was applauded for its commitment to leading by example in relation to best environmental practices in gardens.

There was an expectation that the Trust could play a greater national role in the training of gardeners, building on the success of its Careership scheme and working with other organisations to ensure national standards. The Trust was also encouraged to take the lead in promoting greater recognition of professional gardening skills, which are in rapid decline nationally. The need to invest in gardens to help to ensure a quality experience for visitors was linked to the fact that gardening generates £302 million for the UK economy, with much of this figure related to garden tourism.

Elsewhere, much greater 'hands on' involvement in schools, and an expansion of the volunteer base, were other areas in which the Trust was encouraged to push ahead with real vigour. Certainly enough came out of the conference to keep us busy for many years to come.

However, it is not just the long-term challenges of conservation strategy that confront the Trust. In the short term we face problems such as the over- and under-visiting of our gardens. Stowe, covering over 400 hectares (980 acres), only attracts 50,000 visitors a year, whilst Studley Royal has to cope with 300,000. Hidcote, designed to be enjoyed by one man and his friends, is unable to cope with more than its present 120,000 visitors, especially following wet weather, when grass paths are at their most vulnerable. Garden visiting may have to be rationed more widely in future, with the extended use of timed tickets and advance booking, as have been adopted at times at Sissinghurst and at Hill Top, Beatrix Potter's former home. However, there is often the scope for 'spreading the visitor load', by encouraging people to come at different times of year or even at different times of day. For example, evening opening has been successful at some properties, whilst more and more Trust gardens are opening during the winter, arguably the best time of year for appreciating a garden's shape and form. However, much essential garden work takes place 'out of hours' and any exten-sion in public access to a garden needs to be balanced against opera-tional necessities and practicalities. Even now, gardeners at Sissinghurst start their day at 6.30am, finishing by early afternoon so the garden can be left free for visitors. We shall undoubtedly see even more flexibility and experimentation in the future, both with opening arrangements and operational routines.

Both over- and under-visiting have financial repercussions, and it is an irony that Trust gardens are now competing amongst themselves for a share of the same visitor market. Perhaps in the end there are limits to the future growth of a garden-owning organisation like the National Trust, the boundaries dictated by the law of supply and demand. After all, the competition is tough, even if not as immediately obvious as one might think. There is evidence to suggest that, in some cases, Sunday superstore opening has had an adverse effect on visitor figures at nearby Trust properties. Certainly the Trust is seeking to attract people 'on a day out' and so any other potential venue for their leisure time represents competition.

With over 200 gardens 'in the bag' it may be time for the Trust to think carefully about the viability of further acquisitions. That said, there will always be those 'golden apples' we should save. Different types of ownership and protection, other than straightforward acquisition, might be contemplated in future. These may include partnerships and collaboration. Equally, with the cost of property-based garden conservation now reaching £11 million a year, the Trust must explore new ways of attracting income. Again, partnerships have a role to play.

This book opened by stressing how important gardens are to us; a gift and benefit unlike any other. Gardens have held us in their thrall for millennia and doubtless will continue to do so, possibly taking on even greater significance as spiritual retreats and antidotes to a life that is becoming ever more urbanised, pressurised and technologically driven. By virtue of the fact they are so well spread geographically, the Trust's gardens are particularly well placed to play such a role to many millions of people. In the short term, meanwhile, change for our historic gardens is inevitable and the Trust's role in managing this change will be absolutely crucial. We are constantly challenged by the need to know more about the properties we care for. Knowledge brings greater certainty, informs the decision-making process and thereby helps to ensure that a garden's significance is identified and maintained for future generations. It will also help us meet environmental challenges. At the end of the day, however, to conserve gardens effectively we must conserve the skills and expertise of our gardeners. Whatever happens in the more uncertain long term, the gardener within us will surely live on to create new gardens, thereby adding both to the roll-call of gardens potentially worthy of future protection, and to the opportunities that gardens provide to nourish and refresh the human spirit.

Notes
[1] Historic Environment Review, commissioned by Department of Education, Transport & The Regions, 2000.
[2] Undertaken as part of 'Power of Place: the Future of the Historic Environment', English Heritage, 2000.
[3] Climate Change Impacts on the United States: Overview', by the National Assessment Synthesis Team of the US Global Change Research Programme.
[4] GEO 2000: United Nations Environment Programme report (The *Independent*, 16 Sept 1999).
[5] World Wide Fund For Nature, 30 August 2000.

Case Study
Dyrham Park Garden Conservation and Redesign Project

When the National Trust acquired Dyrham Park near Bath in 1956, there was only a donkey paddock where there had previously been garden. Limited by minimal staffing and finance, the Trust sent the donkey away, tidied the paddock, removed eyesores like a tennis court, added a few hints at an old formal design shown in a Johannes Kip bird's-eye view (see p.70), and created one low-maintenance border to give colour for visitors.

More recently, much research has been carried out on the lost formal garden, which is well documented – besides Kip's drawing, Stephen Switzer published a long, enthusiastic description in 1718. Archaeological survey has also been fruitful; both earthwork and resistivity surveys indicate that Kip was pretty accurate, and suggest that the foundations of the formal garden still lie just beneath the present ground level.

The formal garden was the creation of one individual – William Blathwayt – an extremely successful official in King William III's government. The house itself closely represents Blathwayt's ambitions and promotion, with a fairly modest west front built c.1691, and a grandiose east front, with an orangery styled on that at Versailles, of 1698. The suitably impressive garden around was laid out to a design by George London, the Royal Gardener. Blathwayt worked for the King in Holland – one of his strengths was his command of languages – and was conversant with the trend-setting Dutch gardens of the time; his lodgings even overlooked the garden at the royal palace of Het Loo (see p.70). Blathwayt's Dutch-style garden, with a long canal flanked by

Rooted in History

parterres, fountains, terraces and a wilderness, was shoe-horned into the limited flat ground at Dyrham, and crowned by a stupendous cascade which utilised the steep slopes and ample rainfall.

Today, despite Victorian alterations, Blathwayt would still recognise his house, where many of his Dutch furnishings survive intact. However, his formal garden was short-lived, replaced by Repton with a swathe of informal landscape park c.1800. Victorian generations added some decorative elements to the west garden which were subsequently removed, and so we arrived at the rather featureless donkey paddock of 1956. In more recent years the Trust has restored both the top terrace and the orangery to their c.1700 layout. To the casual visitor, the garden is a beautifully managed place, with a relaxed and timeless feel to it. But deeper consideration suggests that we have arrived at a fork in the road for the present garden, and that a new direction is required.

While the garden has stayed more or less the same for the last 44 years, other things have moved on. As the conservation of objects has become a more scientific discipline, so it has been recognised that the delicate and aged furnishings of the house are some of the most important and vulnerable in the Trust, and that the house's very popularity with visitors poses a threat to the long-term conservation of the objects and surfaces within. However, the property has always been inadequately financed, and desperately needs to maintain income from visitors. One partial and imperfect answer to this quandary is to increase use of, and interest in, the park and garden, so that a separate ticket can be sold for these features, so reducing pressure on the house, but crucially maintaining income.

Another change is that, for conservation reasons, visitors to the house now enter via the west garden and west front, rather than the east front, as previously. Although this might appear to make the garden more prominent, it actually has the opposite effect, reducing it to just an entrance way. And with the entire garden visible at the entrance, there is little incentive to attract visitors to explore further. Further analysis of the garden's design reveals that it falls down in several other respects. It is in fact rather shapeless, with no coherent style or design, while its asymmetry, compounded by the lack of a visual division between house and stables, does not set off the splendidly formal architecture of the west front. Additionally, the recent loss of several large trees, in particular a champion copper beech, has left the garden quite threadbare. At this point, we should remember that the current layout is in effect only a holding operation, created by the Trust when resources were very tight; it is not historically significant, and so should not be considered sacrosanct. And so we began to think that the new direction might involve a redesign, and started mulling over possible options.

It is tempting, of course, to consider putting back the seventeenth-century formal garden. But in practice, there is very little to justify what would be an enormously expensive project. All the significant elements of the formal garden were on the east front, but this area now works very well as park, and any restoration here would destroy this historically important, and aesthetically pleasing, later layer. Far better, surely, to tell visitors more about the archaeology, so that they can discover and read for themselves the clues to the lost garden? In some ways, restoration could actually be a limiting exercise, reducing reliance on visitors' understanding and imagination. As the original garden was fairly fully removed, any attempt to put it back would therefore be a 're-creation' rather than a 'restoration', and so inherently of less value. Furthermore, archive information on the west garden is rather sparse, although more research and archaeology would probably fill some of the gaps. Finally, for visitors wishing to see a seventeenth-century garden 'in the flesh', there already exists the meticulously-restored, and almost exactly contemporary, example of the Privy Garden at Hampton Court, as well as Trust examples at Westbury Court, Ham House and Hanbury Hall.

But contemplating the formal scheme provoked the thought that, as a design, it worked very well, setting off the architecture of the house and providing an interesting sequence of spaces. What if we chose to evoke or reinterpret the historic layout, rather than attempt to replicate it? Reproducing those boundaries in hedges instead of the original stone walls would give the garden structure and suspense, but with a soft-edged, mellow feel more in tune with the simplicity and patina of the present-day house.

Thinking further along these lines, we realised that the 'evocation' approach could give us the freedom to do something far more interesting, to create a contemporary garden, not a pastiche, but something bold and of its time, whilst remaining sympathetic to the place. In this we would actually be following historic precedent, because the garden seems to have been redesigned every hundred years or so. The Trust would just be continuing this pattern. We could even emulate Blathwayt's choice of an eminent designer, and build on his links with Holland by employing a Dutch designer, someone like Piet Oudolf, whose prize-winning designs of massed, textural, soft-coloured, modern perennials set around clipped yews, seem very much in sympathy with our understanding of Dyrham garden.

This is the point we have reached to date. The garden management team has made a bold decision to go forward with a contemporary redesign, based on the bones of the formal scheme, aiming both to increase visitor interest and to provide an alternative focus to the property, whilst also setting off the architecture and creating a satisfying

Rooted in History

entrance to the house. However, the idea of a wholesale contemporary redesign is something of a new policy area for the Trust, and there are still many people to convince that this concept is right for Dyrham, both in general terms and with regard to specific details.

The Trust, therefore, is keen that the whole redesign process is made open to public scrutiny, and that the discussion and debate is carried out to others with an interest, from the residents of the house, to the 'Friends of Dyrham', local parishioners, schools that carry out arts projects in the grounds, and to all other visitors. To do this effectively we need a well-defined project plan, backed by a water-tight rationale. But we also need to continue to point out that good gardens are not made by committee. It is quite a dilemma that the original, private owners of these places had both the funds and power to carry out their own bold and idiosyncratic schemes, but that the Trust, working through team-work and consultation, runs the risk of trying to appeal to everyone and upset no one, so producing schemes that are unobjectionable, but ultimately rather bland and boring. We have therefore tried to build in flexibility to the Dyrham brief, and now look forward to working with a strong designer who will be allowed sufficient scope to come up with a really exciting detailed scheme. We hope that this will prove a liberating model for the Trust, thereby paving the way for a more nnovative approach in the future in gardens that lack strong historical antecedents.

Neptune looking down on Dyrham Park. Any new garden must respect the context and history of the property. (NTPL/Rupert Truman)

Index

(County locations of National Trust properties are given in parentheses)